TO SET THE CAPTIVES FREE

TO SET THE CAPTIVES FREE

LIBERATION THEOLOGY
IN CANADA

OSCAR COLE-ARNAL

BETWEEN THE LINES

TORONTO, CANADA

© Oscar Cole-Arnal, 1998
Published by:
      Between The Lines
      720 Bathurst Street, #404
      Toronto, Ontario M5S 2R4
      Canada

Interior design by Steve Izma
Cover design by Gordon Robertson

Printed in Canada

Between The Lines acknowledges the financial support of
the Ontario Arts Council,
the Canada Council for the Arts,
and the Government of Canada through the Book Publishing Industry
Development Program for our publishing activities.

The publisher and the author wish to acknowledge the generosity
and support of the Ursuline Generalate, Chatham, Ontario; the
Evangelical Lutheran Church in Canada, Winnipeg and Kitchener;
and anonymous donors through the Global Community Centre,
Kitchener.

Canadian Cataloguing in Publication Data

Arnal, Oscar L., 1941-
   To set the captives free: liberation theology in Canada

Includes index.
ISBN 1-896357-15-6

1. Liberation theology — Social aspects — Canada. I. Title.

BT38.A75 1998   261.8′0971   C98-930548-1

Contents

For my beloved Bonnie, companion, friend, lover, wife

and

In Memoriam

Dr. Carol J. Schlueter
(1948-1997)

and

Rev. Dr. John H. C. Neeb
(1949-1997)

colleagues and dear friends

Acknowledgements

FOR MANY OF US, LIBERATION THEOLOGY DESCRIBES A WAY OF LIVING that undergirds and shapes our way of thinking. Even before I heard the term I was two years into the American civil rights and anti-Vietnam War movements as a young parish pastor in a suburban Lutheran Church. Only after attempts to remove me from that charge and threats upon my life did I come across the term "liberation theology" in graduate school. The notion attracted me as a way of embodying my faith, and for the last thirty years I have attempted to live and articulate its principles. This book reflects that experience and my gratitude to those who have shaped my commitments and my life from the Scriptures to the present.

However, others deserve special mention, for they have touched me directly in ways that give life and breath to this Canadian theology of liberation. After all, the kind of theology portrayed in this book is communal. To leave these people unacknowledged would violate the realities of both solidarity and community that this book is meant to underscore so strongly. Constraints of space demand that I highlight just a few of these fine sisters and brothers, and there remain others, so many others.

I grew up in a western Pennsylvania steel town during the Eisenhower years, at the height of the Cold War. Although I was a rather typical anticommunist kid, I received a glorious blend of nurturing and challenge from my immediate family. Sarah Branthoover, my maternal grandmother, encouraged all my efforts and provided a steadfast love and religious faith that have sustained me for over fifty years. My dad, George Arnal, came from a classical Marxist family of French immigrant coal-miners, and only as an adult did I come to appreciate the legacy he tried to pass on to me years earlier. Naomi Branthoover Arnal bequeathed to me hunger for the truth, compassion for marginalized people, and the "chutzpa" to challenge authority. Thanks to all of you. I miss you and love you. Judy Arnal Zeman, a sister incomparable, remains one of my three best friends. All my life she has encouraged and supported me. We have marched together and held picket signs together, and she assisted me with social gospel research for this book. Her husband Frank and I were both activist ministers during the late 1960s, and I delight that he is now family.

For over thirty years Ed Madura has remained my dearest and closest male friend. As a moderate left-of-centre Democrat and agnostic he does not share many of my convictions, yet I could not wish for a better friend. He challenges my ideas, edits my material (including this manuscript), and supports me in the personal struggles of my life. Thank you, my friend.

In my first parish as an ordained minister I was tutored into radicalism by a marvellous couple, George and Julie McLeod, and they were assisted mightily by Dorothy and Bob Preston. The youth from that parish, local leaders of the NAACP (Jim White and Judy and Guy Fielder in particular), Joseph Hornick, and Father Donald McIlvane of Pittsburgh shaped and taught me in the struggles ahead. For the handful of about thirty to forty parish members who stood by me in the heat of battle during those glorious years I owe an abiding debt of gratitude. Similar feelings extend to the members of my second parish in Manor, Pennsylvania. During my graduate work (1970-74) I was trained by a number of professors in the field of Modern European History who challenged, prodded, and supported me. Special thanks go to Dr. Richard Hunt, Dr. Robert Colodny (an ex-American Lincoln Brigader), and my mentor and friend Dr. Seymour Drescher. Throughout those years I chaired a Lutheran Direct Action Committee and benefited immensely from the solidarity of the sisters and brothers therein.

In Canada I found networks of solidarity that have sustained me over the last two decades. Of course, my faculty and staff colleagues at the Waterloo Lutheran Seminary, a college of Wilfrid Laurier University, stand out in this regard. In their own ways each of them has contributed to my growth in liberation, and some have marched and carried signs with me. The students—so many of them over the years—-have taught and continued to teach me what liberation is all about. Even when I was an unwilling student they prodded, pleaded, and insisted that I challenge my own worn-out notions. A special thanks goes to the members of my Canadian Liberation course, where the students added their wisdom and insights to this manuscript and my life.

My house church, described in chapter 5, has sustained me, not only in my militancy but also in my sense of prayer and the transcendent. Sisters and brothers at the Global Community Centre, my home parish Faith Evangelical Lutheran in Fergus, Ontario, Ten Days for World Development (Justice), and the Holocaust Education Committee have their cherished place in my journey. And I owe a special thanks to trade union friends locally and elsewhere who inspire me with their convictions and courage. Wayne Samuelson, Paul Forder, and Jim Turk are three of them. My NDP colleague and friend Brent Boyer deserves special mention as well, and certainly my jailmates from two protests have a special place in my heart. Most recently I thank my sisters and brothers of the Waterloo Region Interfaith Movement for Social Justice who uphold me in a phalanx of solidarity.

Certainly I am absolutely delighted that my favourite progressive press, Between the Lines, is publishing this book. I render its people hearty thanks, especially to Marg Anne Morrison, the editor, to Paul Eprile, the marketing and sales coordinator, to Robert Clarke, who toiled over the detailed correcting of the manuscript, and to Ken Epps and Steve Izma, who gave freely with their time to help refine the narrative at an earlier stage. Gregory and Shirley Baum have encouraged my work over the years, and I have benefited immensely from Gregory's critique of the first draft of this manuscript. To Tony Clarke I express my deepest respect and gratitude. Beyond the personal inspiration he provides through his courage and prophetic voice, he encouraged this project and commented on the first draft in most encouraging ways.

Finally I am deeply grateful to my family for their unfailing support. To Liz, Barb, and Sarah (daughters of choice, as I call them), thank you for your love and special gifts. And to Bill and Brad, my two sons, words cannot convey the love and respect I have for you. You have marched with me, argued with me, and challenged me tenaciously. Your radicalism prods me onward. You are truly sons of my heart as well as my flesh. And Bonnie, your love and your friendship are the food and drink of my life. Christian companion, dear friend, wife, and lover, I cherish our life together. It is for these reasons that I have dedicated this book to you.

1 Setting the Stage

LIKE A RELENTLESS JUGGERNAUT THE ECONOMIC GIANTS MARCH ACROSS the globe, cutting a swath of human and environmental destruction in their wake. The current phase of capitalism, whether it is called globalization, the corporate agenda, neo-conservatism, or neo-liberalism, represents an aggression and expansion hitherto impossible. The vast economic expansion of the transnational corporations and the increasingly global structures of financial capitalism produce a corresponding assault not only on the poorer nations of the South but also major sectors of the population in the wealthier countries of the North. Not just the poorer segments of society but also the so-called middle classes of the Western democracies have fallen victim to this broad sweep.

Previous injustices pale by comparison. The gap between the rich and the poor has risen astronomically in both Western industrialized and developing countries. Economic and political elites ignore environmental factors in the mad rush for quick profits. Unemployment and underemployment have reached the proportions of a global epidemic. National boundaries and the capacity of governments to regulate capitalist expansion decay in the face of regional trade deals and the infinite interactions of international financial institutions. Technology, especially in its computerized and robotic forms, has enabled the transnational economic elites both to dispense with great numbers of workers and to shift capital and investment to any point on the globe with stunning rapidity. Massive profit gains, the so-called "bottom line," have taken the form of a "global casino" in which investment for instantaneous profits is connected with financial speculation rather than long-term investment in productive capacity that would provide jobs and vital services. Capitalism's goal of profit above all else has not changed, but its current phase of high-tech global control and frenzied greed places Canadians and their neighbours at a critical juncture in history as the millennium approaches.[1]

In the face of such wealth, power, and aggression, resistance might seem impossible, if not suicidal. Yet people are fighting back. Resistance movements in the impoverished countries of the South have struggled for decades against the ruthless alliances of Western financial capital, the transnational corporations, and the domestic tyrants who repress their own people to make the world safe for capital expansion. The overthrow of the Marcos regime in the Philippines and the Sandinistas in Nicaragua and the successful dismantling of apartheid in South Africa stand out as examples. More recently, the Chiapas rebellion in Mexico demonstrates active regional resistance to globalization policies in general and the North American Free Trade Agreement in particular.

In our own land resistance rises as well. Grass-roots movements have emerged and are gaining strength. The Council of Canadians, led by Maude Barlow, has emerged to challenge capital concentration both domestically and abroad. The last few years have witnessed a handful of protests that have been historic in both their size and their diversity. The anti-NAFTA "On to Ottawa" Trek, the Alberta nurses protests, the National Action Committee on the Status of Women (NAC) marches against poverty in Quebec and English Canada, the increasing militancy of the public-sector unions, the successful strikes of the Canadian Auto Workers (CAW), the massive Community Days of Action against the Ontario Harris government, and the mass protest of Ontario's teachers: all of these occurrences testify to the healthy resistance against the corporate agenda in Canada. To be sure, one dare not underestimate the power, control, wealth, and danger of the global corporate assault. Nonetheless, despite the relentless mantra of the "big-business"-owned media, globalization is not inevitable, and these movements of resistance, hope, and new visioning are proof positive of that.

Where do Christians fit into this larger picture? Certainly, whether in the developing world or in the more prosperous West, practising Christians are found among the proponents of globalization; but far more often they can be counted among its victims. As well, numerous followers of Christian teaching rank themselves among the resisters of the corporate agenda. Samuel Ruiz Garcia, the bishop of San Cristóbal in southern Mexico, demonstrates his solidarity with the peasant populace under his care, partly by his overt sympathies with the Zapatista resistance to the local effects of the NAFTA deal. Earlier on, Catholic priests participated actively in Nicaragua's popular Sandinista government. On the home front Christians joined trade unionists and other grass-roots movements in the Ontario Community Days of Action. In this respect they are replicating a long tradition both in Canada and throughout a two-millennia history.

This book proposes to identify the enduring validity of this radical-justice tradition, to set it within the Canadian context, and to provide very specific entry points for Christians and their friends to join the wider struggle against the corporate agenda and for a renovated society in which justice, compassion, and equality prevail. It is my hope that the book will provide both grist for reflection and a tool for action. And one recent development in a long history of Christian radicalism, especially useful for this process, is liberation theology.

To be sure, what we call liberation theology emerged at a specific time and place and cannot be simply replicated elsewhere. It reflects settings in the impoverished world of the South, where repression and wealth differentiation are extreme. The world of its incarnation involves torture, military regimes, neo-colonialism, active resistance, often armed, and masses of impoverished peasants thrown off the land and forced into huge slums that circle urban cores. A developed prosperous nation with a large middle class such as Canada stands as a world apart from the Latin American countries out of which liberation theology emerged, largely as a Catholic phenomenon. Canadians live in a parliamentary democracy, with a charter of rights, where the free expression of opinions and street demonstrations rarely lead to violent police action, let alone torture, repression, or death.

Surely, then, liberation theology seems to offer little for the Canadian scene — or does it? At one level, the answer is an obvious "yes." Liberation theology has already impinged on the Canadian scene. Ever since the Peruvian priest Gustavo Gutiérrez's pioneer work *A Theology of Liberation* (1969) was translated into English and French, this particular theological expression has found a large audience in Christian circles, both academic and otherwise. For over two decades numerous "liberationist writings" have filled shelves in left-wing and mainline Christian bookstores. In addition to works by leading liberation theologians, these writings also include Scriptural studies, histories, catechisms, journals, personal testimonies, conference proceedings, and the like. Much of this material has emerged from the publishing firm Orbis Books, operated by the Catholic Maryknoll Fathers. Academic institutions, such as universities and seminaries, have included such works in their curricula, and the language of liberation theology has become part of the standard discourse in theological disciplines.

However, the attraction of liberation theology for many Canadians and Americans runs deeper than academic discourse. It has inspired progressive Christians to deeper reflections and militant commitments. Included among Third World liberationist publications are an increasing number of related works from North American theologians, church leaders, and Christian activists who feel a magnetic attraction to liberation theology and seek to apply it to the different settings of the United States or Canada.[2] Such an attempt cannot and does not seek to create a carbon copy of this theology in a setting that is in sharp contrast to the raw oppression found in Latin America and elsewhere in the developing world. Yet more and more Christians in Canada and the United States recognize that many of the insights articulated by Gutiérrez and others provide ready tools that can be used both to articulate and live out the Christian gospel in a First World context. *To Set the Captives Free* endeavours to serve that wider purpose for a Canadian audience.

Towards that end I borrow five very specific insights from three liberation theologians, the Brazilian brothers Leonardo and Clodovis Boff and the American Robert McAfee Brown. I contend that these five perceptions can function as effective tools for Christian militants in their organization, resistance, reflection, and visioning vis-à-vis the corporate agenda.

1 In liberation theology the faith is viewed from "below," from the perspective of the poor and the oppressed.

The use of terminology such as the "poor and oppressed" has become such common stock in theological discourse that we can quite easily forget exactly about whom we speak: that shunned, disempowered, and brutalized sector of the human family that comprises the vast majority of the Earth's population. This huge group includes children and women, racial minorities, Aboriginal peoples, gays and lesbians, the economically marginalized, the elderly, the physically and emotionally scarred and maimed, much of the working class, and the underemployed and unemployed. Roughly one-half billion of these people are starving; one and one-half billion will never reach sixty years of age; one billion live in absolute poverty; one and one-half billion have no access to basic medical care; five hundred million earn less than $150 a year; over eight hundred million cannot read or write; and two billion have no safe water supply. The list, like a litany of horrors, could go on and on, but the point is starkly clear. Not just a few but most of our sisters and brothers on this planet are crushed, shoved aside, and brutally oppressed. It is these people who reside at the centre of liberation theology's concerns and who shape its discourse.[3]

2 Liberation theology requires a conscious social activism, and that is the soil out of which theological reflection must emerge.

Liberation theology's identification with the poor and oppressed does not arise from charity or pity. Rather it declares solidarity "with." The notion of *praxis* is central to this understanding. Praxis cannot be translated simply as "practice." It is more akin to the word *engagement* as employed by the young French middle-class radicals who aligned themselves with militant organized workers during the 1930s. Engagement called for a reflection and analysis that would grow out of concrete efforts of solidarity with those groups dedicated to transforming the society along just lines. The more recent term praxis parallels the notion of *partage* (a total sharing) employed by the French worker-priests to describe their total identity and solidarity with the oppressed working class. In short, liberation theology has a reflective component, but at the same time it creates its theological discourse out of the milieu of militant solidarity with the oppressed and marginalized sectors of society.[4]

3 This involvement of such a partisan nature puts liberation theology in a context of conflict, a context that the practitioners accept rather than deny.

One of the church's greatest temptations is to see itself as a disinterested arbiter of life's conflicts. It heralds its catholicity by pointing to the nature of its membership, which includes rich and poor and every gradation in between. Liberationists hasten to point out the illusion in this perspective. They view poverty and oppression as no accident, but rather as the result of human decisions that put power and profit above people. Hence the entire society, including the church, reflects the social structure of domination by the oppressor over the oppressed. Liberationists not only recognize the reality of class divisions but also repudiate the resulting inequities of these cleavages as intolerable in light of the Christian message. For them, solidarity with the poor and marginalized means an inevitable struggle against the powerful interests that are to blame for a brutal and unjust world.[5]

4 This context of militancy and conflict from the perspective of the marginalized has a profound impact on the tools liberationists use in their analysis. Among those tools are the social sciences.

Liberationists refuse to place disciplines such as political science, history, and sociology on the margins. For them the word and work of God can be discerned — indeed, must be discerned — in political, economic, and class relationships. A large number of liberationists draw insights unashamedly from Karl Marx, even in the face of the rabid anti-Red mentality of Western society in general and of the established Christian church in particular. They see the anticommunism of the West as being created and sustained by a vast ideological campaign of half-truths and out-and-out falsehoods.

This is not to say that Communist regimes, past and present, have not earned a high degree of criticism. However, the anticommunist ideologues and powerbrokers have always used "Red-baiting" tactics to divert attention from their own excesses and to undermine any and all popular movements for justice and democratic social change. Those liberation theologians open to the insights of Karl Marx are also critical of him and the movements that bear his name. For instance, the Boff brothers write, "Therefore, liberation theology uses Marxism purely as an *instrument*. It does not venerate it as it venerates the gospel. . . . Liberation theology, therefore, maintains a decidedly critical stance in relation to Marxism." Despite this critical stance, as Robert McAfee Brown points out, throughout its history Christianity has always employed the language and culture of its environment, frequently using non-Christian language and concepts through which to proclaim the gospel. As well, Karl Marx deserves recognition as one of the greatest social thinkers and critics of modern times. His understanding of oppression and class injustice has resonated globally with popular social movements. Finally, those Christians in solidarity with the oppressed and the poor have found frequently that Marxist militants have been involved in a similar solidarity for an even longer time than most Christians. Quite often Marxists and communists of the developing world have proven to be the most dedicated and self-sacrificing sisters and brothers of the marginalized sectors of their societies. Indeed, this has been the case quite often in the United States and Canada.[6]

5 Christian liberationists of the developed world, especially middle-class white men, must be deeply self-critical of their most fundamental values.

Robert McAfee Brown states that a basic self-criticism means "recognizing our ideological captivity." We need both a radically critical and self-critical spirit as well as the support and solidarity of others for such a task. I have already mentioned one ready example of this "ideological captivity": the virtually unchallenged assumption that "Marxist" and "communist" are *ipso facto* bad, a notion joined habitually to the conviction that "democracy" and "free enterprise" are not only good by definition but also synonymous categories. These and other phrases, profoundly value-laden, have become virtually creedal assumptions in our society.[7]

Brown employs the term "hermeneutical suspicion" as an antidote to this "ideological captivity." A frequently employed buzz word in theological and academic circles, "hermeneutics" or its adjective "hermeneutical" refers to the methods or principles we use to determine meaning and interpret reality. Quite specifically, Brown draws us to the notion of Biblical authority within the Christian tradition and asks us through what kind of optics we view the Scriptures. Virtually all theologians acknowledge that believers approach the Bible through their own perspectives and experiences. Brown would have us develop a suspicious attitude to our learned and utilized hermeneutics. In short, he is saying we need to critically examine our ideological captivity with respect to how we use the Scriptures.[8] One example of such ideological bondage emerges in our use of exclusive gender language, and today's Christian liberationists strive mightily to transform the language of worship and Christian writing to render it more inclusive. The dominance of patriarchal values in both our sacred texts and our two millennia of history makes this task necessary. A question that has come up for me in producing this book is: how does one address this issue when quoting historical material? One approach is to allow the quotes to stand as testimony to patriarchy's tragic and tenacious legacy, which haunts Christian liberationists to this very day. By doing this we remain true to historical accuracy while revealing, at the same time, how much work remains to be accomplished within a tradition that bears the guilt of continuing gender oppression. The other approach is to deliberately modify the quoted texts in the direction of inclusivity with appropriate indicators that this is happening. In this way sexism is both exposed and transformed at the same time. For the most part, I chose the first option.

Following are three examples of ideological captivity as found in Biblical interpretations habitual to North American middle-class Christians.

~ ~ ~

THE STORY OF THE CANAANITE WOMAN AND JESUS' CASTING OUT OF HER daughter's demon (Matthew 15:21-28) has been a troubling one for most Christians over the years. As long as I can remember there has been a visceral shock in response to how Jesus treated this suffering woman. She comes to him for healing — not for herself but for her daughter. Instead of responding to her with compassion, Jesus answers with the blunt cruelty of an insider to an outsider. "It is not fair to take the children's bread and throw it to the dogs." Anyone else but Jesus acting that way would have been condemned out of hand. However, because it was Jesus there had to be a higher, purer, more divine motive behind his words. Thus his response has been almost uniformly interpreted as a means of testing the woman's faith, teaching his disciples a lesson, and highlighting the profundity of the outsider's faith in his Messianic powers. At this point, liberationists employ Brown's "hermeneutical suspicion." Feminist Bible scholars and preachers have pointed out an interpretation that is probably closer to the mark. It goes something like this: here comes this outsider (a Gentile and a woman) to make a desperate request of an insider (this Jewish miracle worker who happens to be a man). At the very least he has some of the narrowmindedness and prejudices characteristic of all "insiders." Perhaps he is also tired and cranky and wants to be alone. So, instead of being sensitive and compassionate, he snaps at the desperate woman with a cutting and cruel quip of the tongue. But she is clever as well as desperate. Picking up on Jesus' sharp remark she turns the tables on him with the retort, "Yes, Lord, yet even the dogs eat the crumbs that fall from their owner's table." This is the sole time in the Gospels when Jesus stood on the losing end of a verbal confrontation. It was a teaching moment, but in this instance the foreign woman was the teacher and the man Jesus was the student. God used the Canaanite woman to teach Jesus a fundamentally important message of the breadth and depth of the gospel.[9]

~ ~ ~

YET ANOTHER EXAMPLE OF THE USE OF "HERMENEUTICAL SUSPICION" IN challenging a more traditional interpretation of a Biblical story revolves around the account of the "rich young ruler" (Mark 10:17-22). In the narrative a man approaches Jesus with the question, "Good teacher, what must I do to inherit eternal life?" After a brief comment Jesus responds by saying, "You know the commandments. . . ." Again the man speaks. "Teacher, all these I have observed from my youth." Jesus feels drawn to the man, apparently struck by the genuineness of his conversation, and concludes his advice with this statement: "You lack one thing; go, sell what you have, and give to the poor, and you will have treasure in heaven; and come, follow me." After this injunction the story ends on a rather sad note. After hearing Jesus' words, the man's "countenance fell, and he went away sorrowful; for he had great possessions."

Over a period of almost forty years I have listened to more than thirty sermons preached on this text. Save for three exceptions I have heard the same interpretation of this poignant story. This common understanding is summarized most effectively from the exposition portion of the well-known *Interpreter's Bible*, which deals with this passage.

> This was a prescription for a particular person with a specific need. Jesus was not laying down poverty as either a requirement or an ideal for everyone. He was a Good Physician, and did not prescribe the same pill for every patient. . . . Here he says, "If your wealth causes you to sin, cut it off." . . . Jesus was not giving a universal prescription in his injunction to sell all and give to the poor. But there is a universal principle in his words which is quite capable of universal application. Every disciple has need to get beyond the careful caution of negative avoidance into the unmeasured giving of self in positive devotion. Every disciple has need to get beyond the seeking of personal good, until his life overflows into the lives of others.[10]

"Hermeneutical suspicion" cautions us not to soften Jesus' blunt and radical injunction in this way. But this exposition broadens his clear call to his questioner into a safe generalized appeal to selfless discipleship, and the issue of wealth goes by the boards.

~ ~ ~

THE LAST EXAMPLE IS THE WELL-KNOWN SCRIPTURAL PASSAGE THAT concludes with Jesus' words "Render to Caesar the things that are Caesar's, and to God the things that are God's" (Mark 12:13-17). This brief account is almost always interpreted as Jesus' fundamental statement of his doctrine on church-state relations. Invariably people cite it as a proof-text to demonstrate that the church and pulpit should stay out of politics. The more common interpretation, especially among clergy and church leaders, suggests that the text reminds us that we have divinely ordained duties both with respect to the church and with respect to the state. Beyond that, so the teaching goes, Christians must be ever on the alert never to confuse these distinct obligations or to allow the political to take precedence over the spiritual. In short, the Jesus of this passage comes across as a cautious, middle-of-the-road, small "c" conservative.

Once again, liberationist "hermeneutical suspicion" calls for scepticism with respect to this interpretation. First of all, the context of the account remains one of conflict, not dialogue. The passage opens, "Then they sent to him [Jesus] some Pharisees and some Herodians to trap him." They attempt this by a combination of flattery and an extremely dangerous question: "Is it lawful to pay taxes to the emperor or not?" Jesus' impact and influence are dependent on the populace. He is a charismatic wandering preacher who is welcomed by the marginalized and not part of the religio-political establishment, and he does his preaching among a freedom-loving people who have fallen under the military and political might of the almost universally despised Roman Empire. Hence, if he says "yes, we should pay taxes to Caesar," he will offend his oppressed constituency. At the same time, Rome is for good reason fearful about revolution in Palestine. The land reverberates with rebellious freedom fighters committed to throwing off the Roman yoke. Indeed, because of this very threat Jerusalem is garrisoned by Roman troops under the ruthless, hardened military veteran Pontius Pilate. As a result, if Jesus were to counsel the non-payment of taxes he would most likely be reported to the authorities and arrested. Jesus' foes have caught him in a bind. The story ends and has its climax in Jesus' response, "Render to Caesar the things that are Caesar's, and to God the things that are God's."

Given this context, Jesus' statement does not fit with the more traditional interpretations about church-state separation. At the very least, his response to his enemies cleverly dodges their trap. He avoids the question by throwing it back in the laps of his foes. He outwits his challengers by answering them equivocally. However, his particular response also gives out a subtle message that would be clear to the nearby crowds but hidden from any onlooking police spies. He asks for his foes to bring him a coin, the Roman denarius, and demands of them, "Whose head is this, and whose title?" They respond, "the emperor's" or "Caesar's." At that point Jesus gives his famous "render to Caesar" retort. On the denarius was Caesar's face and a written reference to his deity and power. For the captive Jewish population the tax coin represented both oppression and, even worse, idolatry, and by drawing attention to these issues, Jesus was engaging in anti-Roman activity. His final injunction embodied a call for his people not to traffic in the politico-economic structures of the idolatrous oppressor. In short, he advocated a brand of tax resistance. As the Catholic Worker rebel Dorothy Day pointed out, "If we render to God what belongs to God, then there is nothing left for Caesar."

~ ~ ~

TRADITIONAL INTERPRETATIONS OF THESE THREE NEW TESTAMENT passages have served to soften radicalism and uphold the status quo.

"Hermeneutical suspicion" helps Christians challenge and move beyond such conservative safety.

The traditional Christian notions of sin and grace translate via liberation theologians into the categories of oppression and liberation. An examination of Biblical materials and subsequent church history demonstrates that these categories, of oppression and liberation, reflect the very heart and language of sacred Scripture and two millennia of Christian history. The goal of liberation stands at the very core of Christian teaching and practice. Sin, in such a framework, means the breakdown of God's intention, characterized by the shattering of relationships into a state of war—a war of self against self, of human beings against other human beings, of humanity against the Earth, and hence of humanity against God. War, domination, and oppression underscore what Christians call sin. In this scenario, salvation involves liberation from this bondage and breakdown wherever God's intentions of justice, peace, love, and harmony roll back the forces of destruction. Christians see this activity as centring on the person and work of Jesus of Nazareth. Thus this unceasing conflict between sin and grace, between oppression and liberation, re-enacts itself on the concrete stage of human history, and not simply in the hearts and souls of individuals. For these reasons Canadian Christians are called upon to discover, name, and act upon those forces in our society that augment oppression and those that enhance liberation.

The insights gleaned from liberation theology serve to inform and shape the following chapters of this book. Using the tool of "hermeneutical suspicion" I will examine briefly both the Biblical and historical traditions of Christianity in order to demonstrate that the liberationist solidarity with the oppressed primarily represents the continuation of a fundamental tradition rather than a radically novel option. After establishing, in chapter 2, the historical and theological roots to liberationist values I will turn, in the next two chapters, to the Canadian scene. My intention there is to set the reader in a historical context rich in both continuity and discontinuity, describing and highlighting where oppression sits enthroned in our land. Chapter 5 highlights the sources of militant opposition, both reformist and radical, to Canadian oppression throughout this century within the Christian tradition and outside of it. It is my hope that this study will help break the sense of isolation experienced by many Christian radicals and reformers, as well as their friends, and serve to guide them towards a more committed solidarity and reflection with the militant oppressed.

2 The Liberation-Oppression Struggle in the Christian Tradition

T HE COINING OF THE TERM "LIBERATION THEOLOGY" IS RECENT, BARELY one generation old. Nonetheless, its roots are as ancient as the Hebrew and Greek Scriptures and its sources of nourishment come from throughout the Christian church's entire history. Traditionally we have understood the faith mostly within the context of the conflict between sin and salvation or the confrontation between good and evil, especially as this relates to the individual believer. Yet, given the diversity and pluralism of language in Biblical and theological rhetoric, both Scripture and Christian historical writing describe this struggle between the purposes of God and the programs of organized evil in numerous other ways; and the notions of oppression and liberation especially remain as intrinsic to Christianity's tradition as certain others enshrined by overuse.

Liberationist Roots in the Hebrew Scriptures: The Foundation Traditions

At the very heart of ancient Israel's faith stand three promises that God gave to the people chosen for a covenant relationship. First, God pledged land and progeny to Abraham and Sarah, Isaac and Rebeccah, and Jacob and Leah and Rachael. Following this came the liberation of Israel from the bondage of slavery in Egypt, commonly called the Exodus. Finally, God gave the "promised land" to this freed people. These three concrete gifts constitute the core of Israel's "salvation" tradition. The ancient covenant recitations of God's people, especially in the example recited in Deuteronomy 26:5b-9, clearly display this foundation of belief:

> A wandering Aramean was my ancestor; he went down into Egypt and lived there as an alien, few in number, and there he became a great nation, mighty and populous. When the Egyptians treated us

harshly and afflicted us, by imposing hard labor on us, we cried to the LORD, the God of our ancestors; the LORD heard our voice and saw our affliction, our toil and our oppression. The LORD brought us out of Egypt with a mighty hand and an outstretched arm, with a terrifying display of power, and with signs and wonders; and [He] brought us into this place and gave us this land, a land flowing with milk and honey.

This text is hardly unique. Such covenant recital passages invoking these three fundamental traditions of ancient Israel appear throughout the Hebrew text. See, for example, the ceremony led by Joshua at Schechem (Joshua 24:1-13), the call of Moses by God (Exodus 3:6-17) and the liturgical recitation of these three liberation events in the Psalms (for example, Ps. 105:8-44). In all of this, the issue is never the high quality, wealth, power, or fundamental worth of God's people. Rather, the liberating God acted on the basis of radical love and solidarity: "It was not because you were more numerous than any other people that the LORD set [the divine] heart upon you and chose you—for you were the fewest of all peoples. It was because the LORD loved you and kept the oath that [was sworn] to your ancestors, that the LORD has brought you out with a mighty hand, and redeemed you from the house of slavery" (Deuteronomy 7:7-8). This binding to God of a mob of ex-slaves shapes and defines the covenant obligations of God's adopted people. With respect to the stranger who dwells among God's faithful, the Torah stated, "For the LORD your God is God of gods and Lord of lords, the great God, mighty and awesome, who is not partial and takes no bribe, who executes justice for the orphan and the widow, and who loves the strangers, providing them food and clothing. You shall also love the stranger, for you were strangers in the land of Egypt" (Deuteronomy 10:17-19).

This pattern repeats itself frequently throughout what Christians call the Old Testament. Ethical injunctions against injustice and oppression are linked to one or more of these fundamental traditions in which God acted as a promise-keeping liberator. One example from the prophetic literature comes when, after pronouncing God's wrath on Israel for trampling "the head of the poor into the dust of the earth" (Amos 2:6b-7a), the prophet Amos thunders: "Hear this word that the LORD has spoken against you, O people of Israel, against the whole family that I brought up out of the land of Egypt: You only have I known of all the families of the earth; therefore I will punish you for all your iniquities" (Amos 3:1-2). In the southern kingdom of Judah the prophet Micah railed against both the political and religious elite who governed the land. Note how his judgment is framed: "O my people, what have I done to you? In what have I wearied you? Answer me! For I brought you up from the land of Egypt, and redeemed you from the house of slavery." Because the nation's powerful have used injustice against the oppressed sectors of society (Micah 2:8-9; 3:1-3) in their mad scramble for wealth (Micah 3:9-11) God promises to punish the beloved covenant people. At the same time God proclaims the very content of what it means to respond loyally to that same covenant—not in profligate acts of public worship, demonstrations of religious piety, or in giving impressive gifts to the Temple, but rather to "do justice," to show covenant solidarity and to walk the way of God (Micah 6:6-8).

These particular citations are hardly unprecedented. They illuminate the very core of Israel's faith, a faith based on a covenant characterized by divine acts of liberation. God's fury at injustice and the holy call to a lifestyle of radical justice are built upon God's promises to the ancestors, God's freeing of slaves from Egypt, and God's gift of "a good and broad land" to this liberated mob. This faith goes far beyond the notions of salvation and liberation as some spiritualized, individualistic oneness with God in some great beyond. Instead, it is physical in its essence, with a fundamentally communal character. Land, progeny, shared prosperity, peace, liberation from oppression, justice—these are tangible concerns. They tersely summarize Israel's faith.[1]

The Content of God's Judgement

The contrast between God's condemnations of the chosen people when they violate justice and God's promises to them for a new and better age also highlights liberationist themes. In every instance the language and images of the Scriptural writers parallel the concerns of today's liberation theologians. Through the prophets God rails out against injustice. The prophets utter sharp proclamations against military alliances and the power of armaments. "You have trusted in your power and in the multitude of your warriors," announced Hosea. "Therefore the tumult of war shall rise against your people, and all your fortresses shall be destroyed" (Hosea 10:13-14a; note also Hosea 5:13; 7:11; 8:9-10, 14; 12:1; Amos 2:14-16; Jeremiah 17:5; 21:3-7; Isaiah 30:1-3).

Even more strident are the prophetic utterances against the nation's plutocrats and their corresponding oppression of the poor. Israel's great prophets inveigh against excessive wealth and link this richness to the misery of the poor. Hosea scorns the nation's arrogant rich (Hosea 12:8), and Micah is appalled that the powerful use high office to receive the fruits of bribery (Micah 7:3). Amos echoes similar sentiments with the accusation that the rich and mighty "trample on the poor and take from them levies of grain" (Amos 5:11a; see also Amos 5:12; 6:4-7a). In Judah the prophet Isaiah makes parallel judgements against the rich oppressors of the people who use their wealth against the poor through a twofold power embodied by their control of the courts and monopoly of the economy (Isaiah 5:7b-8, 21, 23).

This condemnation of the linkage of money and might emerges with great force from the prophet Jeremiah. "For scoundrels are found among my people," he exclaimed. "They take over the goods of others. . . . they have become great and rich, they have grown fat and sleek. They know no limits in deeds of wickedness; they do not judge with justice the cause of the orphan, to make it prosper, and they do not defend the rights of the needy. Shall I not punish them for these things? says the LORD" (Jeremiah 5:26-29). At one point God commands Jeremiah to confront the king with the divine command to do justice and set the oppressed free. The following words are at the heart of the prophet's announcement to the reigning monarch (Jeremiah 22:13-16):

> Woe to him who builds his house by unrighteousness, and his upper rooms by injustice; who makes his neighbors work for nothing, and does not give them their wages; who says, 'I will build myself a spacious house with large upper rooms,' and who cuts out windows for it, paneling it with cedar, and painting it with vermilion. Are you a king because you compete in cedar? Did not your father eat and drink and do justice and righteousness? Then it was well with him. He judged the cause of the poor and the needy; then it was well. Is this not to know me? says the LORD.

God's condemnation has fallen upon the king because of the monarch's pursuit of wealth with its corresponding crushing of the poor. Most significantly, Jeremiah asserts that solidarity with the poor and oppressed is the very equivalent of knowing God. It is especially striking that Jeremiah intrinsically links this powerful God-human bonding to the liberation of the poor.

The Content of God's Restoration

Correspondingly, the prophets utter words of hope. The divine judgement that falls upon the land because the wealthy and powerful have violated the covenant is not the end of the story. Through the prophets God offers the chosen people a new and better day, in very specific terms—justice, plenty, peace (*shalôm*). For example, the prophet called Second Isaiah offers a down-to-earth hope in which the vulnerable of God's people are offered a full and abundant table without cost (Isaiah 55:1-3b). Of course, covenant with God also means a new heart and spirit (Ezekiel 36:26a; Jeremiah 31:33), but it embodies equally food on the table for all. Hosea (2:18-23) expresses this holistic perception of the new age promised by God through the prophets:

> I will make for you a covenant on that day with the wild animals, the birds of the air, and the creeping things of the ground; and I will abolish the bow, the sword, and war from the land; and I will make you lie down in safety. And I will take you for my wife forever; I will take you for my wife in righteousness and in justice, in steadfast love, and in mercy. I will take you for my wife in faithfulness; and you shall know the LORD. On that day I will answer, says the LORD. I will answer the heavens and they shall answer the earth; and the earth shall answer the grain, the wine, and the oil. . . . And I will sow him for myself in the land. And I will have pity on Lo-ruhamah [Not-Pitied], and I will say to Lo-ammi [Not My People], "You are my people"; and he shall say, "You are my God."

This exceedingly powerful passage embraces salvation and restoration for all facets of life. God has reinstated not just a loving marriage but also peace and plenty. Justice has returned, and the entire ensemble of creatures has been reintegrated into a cosmic covenant. The prophet Isaiah announces a similar picture of hope: the end of militarism for the sake of food production and education for peace (Isaiah 2:4; see also Micah 4:3-4). Indeed, Israel's covenant with God originated in divine radical love manifesting itself through liberation from slavery and the provision of good land, progeny, and fullness of life. Such is the full meaning of the famous Hebrew word *shalôm*, and it is the embodiment of a restored covenant. Much like the older traditions, the prophetic hope envisioned a world based on justice, solidarity, plenty, security, and peace. Liberation theology has contributed substantially to the rediscovery of these central motifs in the Hebrew Scriptures.

The Messianic Tradition

Christians have insisted that Jesus is the Messiah. This particular term, so common on Christian lips, has habitually been misunderstood and used in a fashion that shears it from its Biblical roots in the Hebrew text. The word itself, messiah (*msh*), means "anointed one" and refers to the monarchical lineage of the house of David. It is a faith-tradition never universally accepted by the covenant people. The entire nation emerged from the liberation traditions of the promise to the ancestors, the Exodus, and the giving of the land, but it had no such unanimity surrounding the monarchy. Some viewed it as a blessing or liberative act of God, while others saw it as a curse of tyranny that resulted from Israel's inability to trust God. The stories surrounding the creation of the monarchy reflect this polarization (see I Samuel 8:1-9:26). David, the second king of Israel (c. 1000-961 BCE), marked the high point of kingly success. He embodied a combination of military and administrative skills and was able to alter radically important elements of Israel's faith-tradition. Religiously, he linked national pride and success with the ancient covenant faith. Jerusalem became the monopolistic religious centre, and David established his own priesthood. His attempts to build a temple and redivide Israel based on tax districts rather than the older tribal boundaries were less successful. His son and successor Solomon built the temple, but his pride, ambitions, and luxurious life at the expense of the populace sowed the seeds of disaster. Shortly after Solomon's death the young empire split into two parts, with ten rebellious tribes setting up their own kingdom called Israel and the two remaining tribes holding Jerusalem and its surroundings for the heirs of David. Only this rump kingdom of Judah kept the Messianic tradition alive (see the narratives from I Samuel 8:1 to I Kings 12:24).[2]

Despite the turbulence and the subsequent tyranny of the Davidic monarchy, sectors of Israel's faith viewed David as a liberator appointed by God, a liberator who would be God's paradigm for deliverance in times of deep darkness. For such people, God had not only anointed David to rescue the chosen people but also established an eternal covenant linked to the continuity of David's line on Israel's throne (II Samuel 7:8-16). In short, this salvation motif surrounded the Davidic covenant and remained a tradition of liberation upheld by the southern kingdom through good and bad times. In contrast to a clear acknowledgement of the sins and betrayals of this monarchy, the people of Judah also posited God's sure promise, a covenant based on steadfast love and fidelity. They did not abandon the old liberation traditions. Instead, they tied God's promise to David intimately with the promise given to all the people. The Messianic belief asserted that God would uphold David and his heirs while all Israel would be planted in safety and security. In short, the liberation traditions of the older tribal confederation incorporated the divine promise made to David and his heirs. This phenomenon is spelled out with great clarity in the context of the nation's life of worship. The king is enjoined "to judge the people with righteousness" and "the poor with justice" and to be the patron of prosperity for all, especially for "the poor and those who have no helper. . . . From oppression and violence he redeems their life" (Psalm 72:1-7, 12-14, 16).

The hope, then, attached to mighty David and his successors was steeped in liberationist language. Once again it embodied justice, abundance, land, food, peace, and freedom from oppression. David and his heirs were Messiahs, anointed ones, called by God to ensure that Israel's liberation traditions remained characteristic of the nation's daily life. When the kings failed, as they did so often, the prophets of this southern kingdom reproached them for betraying God's covenant to David and held out the promise of a new day and a new David who would indeed embody the liberation mandate of God's Messianic covenant (Ezekiel 34:23; Jeremiah 23:5-6a; Micah 5:4-5a).

The prophet Isaiah, Micah's contemporary, spells out the content of this hope. The new epoch will embody "endless peace for the throne of David and his kingdom," because David "will establish and uphold it with justice and with righteousness from this time onward and forevermore" (Isaiah 9:7). Isaiah paints this coming glorious age under the reign of the Davidic Messiah in glowing detail. He sees the new king as the defender of the poor and meek as well as a harbinger of plenty (Isaiah 11:1-9). This powerful hymn of hope had an older ring as well. Isaiah associates his vision not only with a new David, a Messiah, but also with Israel's more fundamental traditions. God charges the person of the Messiah to undertake the people's earlier covenant of liberation.

The values asserted by liberation theology, then, are firmly embedded in the fundamental "salvation" traditions of what Christians call the Old Testament. The priority concern for the poor and marginalized, the task of joining them in struggle against their oppressors, and the sense of commitment to justice and abundance for all are not incidental concerns of the traditions found in Hebrew Scripture. They stand at the very heart of the covenant. The individual's relationship matters in ancient Israel's faith, but it is always found within the wider context of the fundamental liberation traditions embodied in the pledge to the ancestors, the Exodus from Egypt, the giving of the land, and the anointing of David. The new age promised by the prophets both reflects these earlier experiences and carries them forward.

Liberationist Roots in the Christian Greek Scriptures

Within the Christian Greek Scriptures, commonly called the New Testament, the issues are not always as clear. Indeed, a significant number of passages and positions seem to emphasize individual forgiveness of sins and individual salvation. Here, the liberationist tool of "hermeneutical suspicion" offers solid service in challenging some habitual perceptions.

The Johannine Tradition

One of the most famous and oft-quoted verses emphasizing individual salvation is "For God so loved the world that He gave his only Son, so that everyone who believes in him may not perish but may have eternal life" (John 3:16). The statement seems clear enough: individuals are called to believe in Christ, and if they do they will be saved by receiving the gift of eternal life. While it has some truth, and John's Gospel has a clear otherworldly character, the approach is by no means individualistic. Nor does it advocate the kind of bifurcated Christianity found frequently among North American Christians. It does not link individuals being "born again" and material success. American-dream Christianity has no basis in John.

As well, one finds in the fourth Gospel a stance that is both communal and anti-world. Most frequently this document views the Christians not as individuals to be rescued but rather as God's alternative community brought collectively out of the world by Christ. This becomes apparent in the introductory Prologue (John 1:10-13). Still, the notion of people being "born again" (a term used in John 3:3) one by one is not rejected out of hand, but nowhere is it definitively spelled out in such a way. Rather, this Gospel emphasizes collective rescue from terrestrial life. Jesus' prayer before departing the world (John 17) concentrates on concerns that God uphold the fledgling community that bears Christ's name. The motif is collective, not individualistic. In the previous chapters Jesus speaks to his disciples as a corporate entity. The Spirit Advocate will be sent to them as a group (John 14:25-27; 16:7-15), and the resurrected Jesus empowers them as a group (John 20:19-23). Indeed, they constitute an outlaw community. The earlier Christian Church was illegal in Roman eyes. Although it was not out to overthrow its imperial masters, as far as the writer of John was concerned, it was an alternative to the world ruled by Rome and separate from it (John 18:36). Indeed, Jesus enjoined the Christian community to be one of service, a service he embodied by washing his disciples' feet (John 13:1-9). Further, John's Jesus advocates an otherworldliness characterized by radical love for each other. Ironically, this love serves to inflame the world's hate for this new community (John 15:12-15, 17-19; I John 4:20).

Thus, the fourth Gospel offers nothing to those Christians bent on individual conversions that embrace the American dream. He gives no support for those athletic stars, worldly successes, or rich corporate barons who link their prestige and prosperity to God's blessing because of their devotion to Christ. Instead, John's community of Christians separates itself from and is scorned by these very kinds of people. Liberationists may not be able to draw all their convictions from John's writings, but they find no opposition here either. A serving love and an emphasis on community they share with these writings. Those who oppose such principles find even less support for their ideas in the Johannine material.[3]

The Gospel according to Paul

The letters of Paul, much like John's Gospel, create the initial impression of emphasizing an individual and otherworldly salvation. Along these lines Protestant Christianity has used Paul to proclaim the dialectic of radical sin and radical grace, traditionally called "justification by grace alone through faith alone." Even Roman Catholics have drifted towards an individualistic and spiritualized interpretation of Paul. Both traditions point to well-known passages in Romans that use such phrases as "no human being will be justified in his sight by deeds prescribed by the law" (Romans 3:20). One account asserts that God is indeed "righteous and justifies the one who has faith in Jesus" (Romans 3:26). These words would appear to indicate that God's justificatory work is parcelled out to individuals and that justification concerns itself primarily with the forgiveness of sins as this applies to individual believers. Such a perception seems to be enhanced by Paul's description of his internal moral struggle between sin and grace (Romans 7:15-19, 24-25).

Another way of looking at Romans provides a dimension more in keeping with Paul's social and cultural setting. Although the apostle does use highly personalized language, especially in chapter 7 of this major epistle, he does so only in his construction of a wider collective context. That setting is the conflict between Jews and Gentiles in the Christian communities. For Paul, as a Jew raised in a Greek-speaking milieu, the world is divided between Jews and Gentiles. The Jews remain the people of the law; the Gentiles stand outside this tradition. Yet, as a convert to Christianity, Paul judges that all of humanity, for him collectively made up of Jew and Gentile, has fallen under the sovereignty of sin. For him, Christ emerges as the only source of rescue and freedom, the only source for both Jews and Gentiles collectively. Paul draws attention to the individual within this broader reality because both Jews and Gentiles enter the new community as individuals or in small groups. Hence, for him, the cosmic struggle between the powers of sin and liberation is manifested also in the very inner reaches of every Jew and every Gentile. Yet in Paul the individual is set in the context of the communal reality of the sin-liberation conflict.[4]

Within this Pauline worldview are concrete examples of how the apostle's thought and practice resonate with liberationist perceptions. One of the most radical of these emerges in his letter to the Galatians (3:28): "There is no longer Jew or Greek, there is no longer slave or free, there is no longer male or female; for all of you are one in Christ Jesus." New Testament scholar Elisabeth Schüssler Fiorenza views this passage as an older baptismal formula employed by Paul to make a point. She indicates that Paul himself had trouble practising this summary of principles, but she hastens to add that this brief phrase is loud proof of a radical social egalitarianism in the communities that bear the name of Christ.[5] This does not obscure the fact that Paul's churches consisted of a mix of people from different cultures and class backgrounds. In such a context, then, it is not surprising that the radical equality of Galatians 3:28 would be faced with challenges, such as the food hoarding and gluttony conflict, referred to in I Corinthians 11, in which members of the Christian community argue over how to serve the Lord's Supper. In many other situations Christianity struggled to uphold its radical social egalitarianism in the face of pressure to compromise with the wider culture. The early church's ambivalence with respect to the equality of women stands out in this regard.[6]

In the same correspondence Paul presents yet another example of the ministry that had radical implications. He takes the position that apostles have every reason to expect the churches to support them materially (I Corinthians 9:1-14). The statement marks the beginnings of the concept of a paid and established clergy, and this is an economic connection that can dampen considerably the more radical and prophetic thrust of the gospel. Recognizing this, Paul refuses to be so bound. He will not accept such support. Of himself and Barnabas, he says, "We have not made use of this right, but we endure anything rather than put an obstacle in the way of the gospel of Christ" (I

Corinthians 9:12). Instead, Paul takes up a tent-making job and thus earns his living in the manner of an artisan, a "commoner" trade well-represented in his churches. In this way he lives a solidarity with those on society's margins.

One final instance of radical egalitarianism in Paul occurs in those sections of his letters that deal with his fund-raising activities for the struggling and impoverished Jerusalem congregation. The apostle cites Christ himself as example par excellence of radical material generosity: "Though he was rich, yet for your sakes he became poor, so that by his poverty you might become rich" (II Corinthians 8:9). Paul follows this thought with a statement supporting blatant social equality within the believing community: "For I do not mean that others be relieved while you are in distress, but rather that this [be done] by equality so that at the present time your abundance be for those who are lacking and that latterly their abundance may supply your lacking. Thus there might be equality" (II Corinthians 8:13-14). This passage indicates not only the existing inequality among Christian congregations but also the pressure to rectify that inequality through a shared program of material equality.[7]

The Book of Acts

Two passages in the early chapters of Acts contain brief summary statements describing the norm for and model of Christian community (Acts 2:41-46, Acts 4:32-35). In both texts such communities are put forward as axiomatic bodies based on what some have called "Christian communism." A number of characteristics of these early Christians emerge.

The first passage underscores the fact that these communities structured themselves along "house church" lines. It appears as if their meals have a deep religious meaning that, at least in part, involves eating practices based on sharing. And *all* of them share their goods in common — an egalitarian sharing based upon need. For the most part today's churches are timid by comparison, although exceptions do exist, among them the Hutterites, small Christian communes such as the Sojourners of Washington, D.C., and the consciousness-raising Latin American base-Christian communities. These exceptions remain "the still small voices" of a tiny minority.

The second passage is even clearer on the church's practice of communal ownership:

> Now the whole group of those who believed were of one heart and soul, and no one claimed private ownership of any possessions, but everything they owned was held in common. . . . There was not a needy person among them, for as many as owned lands or houses sold them and brought the proceeds of what was sold. They laid it at the apostles' feet, and it was distributed to each as any had need.

This facet of early Christian life was so critical, both for believers and as a model to the outside world, that the following text (Acts 4:36-5:11) portrays one example of those who proved true to that principle (Barnabas) and one example of those who did not (Ananias and Sapphira).

James and Revelation

The two New Testament books of James and Revelation contain strong strains of thought reminiscent of the great prophets of the Hebrew Scriptures. Calls for justice and the denunciation of the wealthy and powerful emerge from both these testimonies. The book of Revelation (also called the Apocalypse of John) was written in the context of a mass organized campaign by the Roman Empire to destroy Christianity. The document's attitude towards Rome reveals a striking contrast to Paul's more optimistic assessment in Romans 13:1-7. According to the writer of the Apocalypse, no good existed in the Roman system. Rome was Babylon the whore, satiated with the blood of godly martyrs. It was a realm that formed military alliances with all the world's kings to do battle against the people of God. It embodied the evil of commercial wealth and luxury, an entire economic system found wanting (Rev. 18:11-24). When God finally destroys evil, a newly renovated Earth will emerge and "mourning and crying and pain will be no more" (Revelations 21:1-4).

In words echoing the older Hebrew prophets, James rails against the rich in no uncertain terms (5:1-6):

> Come now, you rich people, weep and wail for the miseries that are coming to you. Your riches have rotted and your clothes are moth-eaten. Your gold and your silver have rusted, and their rust will be evidence against you, and it will eat your flesh like fire. You have laid up treasure for the last days. Listen! The wages of the laborers who mowed your fields, which you kept back by fraud, cry out, and the cries of the harvesters have reached the ears of the Lord of hosts. You have lived on the earth in luxury and in pleasure; you have fattened your hearts in a day of slaughter. You have condemned and murdered the righteous one, who does not resist you.

In James's starkly written account, the rich fall under a scathing attack. They are excoriated for agrarian oppression — unjust wage manipulations, persecution of the righteous, and ostentatious living. Even wealthy Christians are not spared his cutting words (James 2:1-6a):

> My brothers and sisters, do you with your acts of favoritism really believe in our glorious Lord Jesus Christ? For if a person with gold rings and in fine clothes comes into your assembly, and if a poor person in dirty clothes also comes in, and if you take notice of the one wearing the fine clothes and say, "Have a seat here, please," while to the one who is poor you say, "stand there," or, "Sit at my feet," have you not made distinctions among yourselves, and become judges with evil thoughts? Listen, my beloved brothers and sisters. Has not God chosen the poor in the world to be rich in faith and to be heirs of the Reign that [he] has promised to those who love [him]? But you have dishonored the poor. Is it not the rich who oppress you?

Here James underscores with graphic detail what liberationists call the priority for the poor and oppressed both within and outside the community of faith. Indeed, the rich stand condemned as the enemies of the gospel and the poor as its special people. This condemnation of wealthy oppressors has direct links to the story of Jesus' encounter with the wealthy young man in Mark's Gospel (10:17-22). Indeed, it is worthy of note that James's message bears a striking comparison to the radical "Reign of God" announced by Jesus in the first three Gospels.

Jesus and the Reign of God

A close examination of Jesus' preaching and his ministry reveals why the most radical elements of Christian history have gravitated to his understanding of the "Reign of God" (usually referred to as the "Kingdom of God"). The Canadian and U.S. social gospel movements represent two recent examples, and current liberation theologians are similarly attracted to this approach. This Reign of God material resides almost exclusively in the first three Gospels. For over a century a majority of New Testament scholars have agreed that these three documents, called the Synoptics, contain our best sources for understanding what Jesus taught and did.[8]

The three Gospels of Matthew, Mark, and Luke contain only two summaries of Jesus' ministry. The first of these is in the parallel passages of Matthew 11:4-5 and Luke 7:22, which do not emphasize individual salvation and eternal life for those who have faith in Christ.

Instead Jesus offers a concrete summary of Scriptural notions of *shalôm*. These notions include physical healings, especially among society's pariahs, and the priority of ministry to and with the poor. In the second summary passage, the inaugural sermon in "home-town" Nazareth, Luke has Jesus reading from the Isaiah scroll (Luke 4:18-19): "The Spirit of the Lord is upon me, because He has anointed me to bring good news to the poor. He has sent me to proclaim release to the captives and recovery of sight to the blind, to let the oppressed go free, to proclaim the year of the Lord's favor."

Once again, according to this representation the ministry of Jesus is clearly physical and intimately linked to convictions espoused by liberationists almost two thousand years later. In his words we hear the priority for the poor, an emptying of the prisons, physical healing, and liberation for the oppressed. Jesus' reading ends with a curious reference to "the year of the Lord's favor," which alludes directly to the notion of "jubilee" spelled out in some detail in Leviticus 25 and 27. Jubilee was a programmed-time arrangement, designed under Israel's covenant with God, in which laws ensured that land distribution and debt would not be allowed to create a permanent ruling class and underclass. In short, jubilee was set up to produce a rough equality of the land. Hence, in announcing his commitment to jubilee, Jesus displays his character as a rural or agrarian revolutionary.[9]

In addition, Luke contains another summary announcing the radicalism of Jesus and his ministry. This time the Gospel writer places it in the mouth of Mary (Luke 1:47-55). In this hymn she announces the coming of God to set things right, a coming based upon God's earlier promises of liberation. Mary speaks of a societal reversal in which God will bring down "the powerful from their thrones" and lift up "the lowly," fill "the hungry with good things," and send "the rich away empty" (Luke 1:52-53). In these three summaries, common themes emerge. The ministry of Jesus does not concentrate on individualistic forgiveness of sins or on a personal faith in Christ that ensures eternal life. Rather it centres upon a radical coming of God's reign that will overthrow the old order and set things right. In this vision the rich and powerful will be levelled, and the poor and oppressed will be restored to freedom and security. These features appear again and again in Jesus' ministry of word and deed, as a few key examples indicate.

~ ~ ~

JESUS WAS INSISTENT THAT GOD'S REIGN WAS IMMINENT, RIGHT AROUND the corner, and that it involved a massive conflict between the forces of right and wrong. His confrontational casting out of demons is a direct manifestation of this approach (see Luke 10:18-19; 11:15-23). The notion of an unequivocally pacifist Jesus does not easily fit into this framework. Jesus operated in a context in which his people were both socially oppressed and politically subjugated. The milieu of his ministry, at least at its inauguration, was that of the poor and crushed Galilean peasantry. His contemporaries were not just Pharisees and Sadducees, but also the armed Zealots and the separatist Essene radicals, who had views paralleling his own. Jesus, perhaps, was more inclined to the notion that there would be an overthrow of the old order by direct divine intervention. Less clear is his view on the role of "sword-bearing" among his own disciples. He speaks of turning the other cheek rather than retaliating, and he enjoins his followers to love their enemies (Matthew 5:43-48), but in other instances he uses the language of hostile confrontation (Matthew 10:34; Luke 12:49). He urges his disciples to collect money and buy weapons (Luke 22:35-36), and he seems to have close ties with Zealots and important elements of their program (Luke 12:29-31; Luke 16:1-8a; Matthew 18:23-35; Luke 6:15; Acts 1:13). At the very least, Jesus' "pacifism" has a highly aggressive character. What becomes most readily apparent is that his view of the imminent coming of God's reign remains militant in character; it involves a project of overthrow and reversal. Certainly, Jesus' physical decimation of the Temple merchant booths seemed to be bloodless in character, but it was far more confrontational and aggressive than many Christian pacifists would like it to have been (Mark 11:15-17).

~ ~ ~

WITH STUNNING CLARITY JESUS ENTERED INTO A DIRECT SOLIDARITY WITH the powerless, marginalized, and oppressed of his society, a solidarity that placed him up against the economic, religious, and political elites of his day. This point of view emerges graphically through his words against the wealthy and for the poor. In Luke's Gospel Jesus pronounces God's favour upon the poor and broken (6:20): "Blessed are you who are poor, for yours is the Reign of God." Correspondingly he lambastes the rich and comfortable (6:24): "But woe to you who are rich, for you have received your consolation." Jesus directly reflects the divine reversal sung by Mary in the Magnificat in these words of solidarity with the oppressed and the contrasting judgements against the oppressors. Following his encounter with the rich young man, Jesus states, "It is easier for a camel to go through the eye of a needle than for someone who is rich to enter the [Reign] of God" (Mark 10:25).[10] This critique of the wealthy and preference for the poor emerges clearly in the story of Zaccheaus (Luke 19:1-10) and in the contrast between the contributions of the rich and that of the widow who gave all that she had, the equivalent of a penny (Mark 12:41-44). For Jesus, wealth stood as the very antithesis of serving God. In the famous passage, "You cannot serve God and wealth" (Matthew 6:24), Jesus makes a direct link between riches and idolatry. Many have since tried to defend the accumulation of wealth as long as this pursuit was not allowed to divert people from God's will. This does not square with Jesus' preaching. For him wealth, which was not radically distributed, remained rank idolatry.

This condemnation of wealth and solidarity with the poor emerges graphically in the notion of agrarian jubilee, a notion fundamental to his message. He consigns to the wrath of God an agrarian "capitalist" who uses his abundant harvests for personal profit and aggrandizement (Luke 12:16-20). A similar condemnation falls upon those who place profitable business transactions above an invitation to come to the Great Banquet (Luke 14:16-24). It was the rich man who was tormented in Hades, but humiliated poverty-stricken Lazarus was taken to be with Abraham (Luke 16:19-31). In the parable called "The labourers in the vineyard" (Matthew 20:1-15), wages are based upon need rather than work done, values inherent to jubilee notions of relative social equality. The condemnation of the slave by the king in Matthew 18:23-34 (the parable known as "the unforgiving servant") reflects this point as well.

So important to Jesus is this radical redistribution that he concerns himself mostly with its reality and less so with its motivation. In the parable of "The unjust steward" (Luke 16:1-8a) an agrarian overseer, caught in acts of fraud, was told to render an account of his work and join the ranks of the unemployed. His last act lightened the debt load of the peasants at the expense of his boss, the wealthy landowner, an act that Jesus finds to be commendable. Similarly, in Luke 18:1-8, a persistent widow wears down a less-than-desirable judge until she receives justice. There resides the issue: not feeling just, but rather rendering justice.

~ ~ ~

JESUS' IDENTIFICATION WITH THE POOR AUGMENTS THROUGHOUT HIS ministry to include all the marginalized and discarded of his society. This radical inclusiveness stands out as perhaps the most unique and revolutionary facet of his entire ministry. One clear example of this is the accusation by his foes that Jesus was "a glutton and a drunkard, a friend of tax collectors and sinners" (Matthew 11:19). In Jesus' society the tax collectors were the notorious publicans. Although they were Jesus' own countrymen, they collected taxes for the hated Romans. Their living consisted in any moneys they expropriated above and beyond what Rome expected of them. In such a system these tax collectors were both thieves and traitors, but Jesus embraced them, broke bread with them, and reached out to them so that they might join his ranks (see Mark 2:15-17; Matthew 9:9; Matthew 10:3; Luke 19:1-10).

Jesus violated taboos by his direct relationships with women. The term "sinners" was sometimes a euphemism for prostitutes. Similarly, Jesus kept company with these women on a regular basis. His meal-sharing with them was an intimate accepting act that scandalized virtually all members of his society (for example, see Mark 2:15-17; Matthew 11:19). Such radical behaviour spilled over into his dealings with women, who were accepted only within the confines of a highly patriarchal society. Jesus' openness with women contrasted sharply with societal mores, and it was especially shocking when he was so open to those women who were outsiders for additional reasons. The prostitutes received a welcoming, and he showed preferential care for women caught in adultery (John 8:2-11). He engaged women in conversation, and in the instance of the Canaanite woman, he received much-needed instruction himself (Matthew 15:21-28). Mary and Martha befriended him (Luke 10:38-42), and the woman at the well, with whom Jesus had a deep and extended conversation, was both loose-living and a foreigner (John 4:7-39). This radical acceptance by Jesus of political traitors and marginalized women is summed up in his harsh judgement against society's righteous (Matthew 21:31b): "Truly I tell you, the tax collectors and the prostitutes are going into the Reign of God ahead of you."

Lepers and foreigners made up two other groups embraced by Jesus and rejected by his own society. Lepers were feared pariahs in ancient Palestine. Not only was leprosy viewed as a divine punishment, but also people were terrified of contracting the disease from someone who had it. Jesus plunged into the midst of this ostracized group, embracing and healing them (Luke 17:11-19; Luke 5:12-14; Mark 1:40-44). He ate with lepers (Mark 14:3), and he praised one leper he healed, a foreign Samaritan, because that person showed faith, unlike nine other cured lepers among Jesus' own countrymen (Luke 17:11-19). Part of Jesus' ministry was defined as the healing of lepers

(Matthew 11:5, and parallel), and his commissioning of disciples involved an injunction for them to do the same (Matthew 10:5-10). As for the hated foreigners, Jesus incorporated the heretical Samaritans into his orbit, including the woman at the well (John 4) and the faithful leper (Luke 17). His shocking parable of the good samaritan (Luke 10:29-37) portrays a compassionate hero who was an outcast. Members of the religio-political establishment had turned away from the robbed and beaten man. Likewise Jesus embraced the Gentiles, even if with initial caution (Matthew 15:21-28). His harsh words of judgement against the self-righteous in Matthew 8:11-12 and Luke 13:28-29 are marked by an open-door policy to the entire Gentile world.

Jesus' notion of eating and drinking at the table of God's Reign was key to his ministry. The banquet at the end of the age embodied plenty, solidarity, joy, and full sharing. It reflected jubilee and *shalôm,* the fullness of life so promised by Israel's ancient prophets. A meal meant intimacy and solidarity; it was a harbinger of divine things coming. Hence Jesus' breaking of bread with the outcasts of society enacted a profoundly liberating solidarity as opposed to a charitable deed. In Jesus' parable of the great banquet (Luke 14:16-24), the prosperous were too busy with financial and personal matters to attend the meal, at which point the banquet host reached out to society's rejects. "Go out at once into the streets and lanes of the town," he said, "and bring in the poor, the crippled, the blind and the lame. . . . Go out into the roads and lanes, and compel people to come in, so that my house may be filled" (Luke 14:21b-23).

Jesus' message was fundamentally radical and revolutionary — liberationist. Like the prophets before him, he railed against the rich and powerful of his society — the religious, political, and economic elites. In the name of God's in-breaking reign and jubilee he sided with the poor and all the oppressed of his society. He promised a radical reversal of the entire social order that would result in a prime place at God's banquet table for all those who had been rejected and pushed to the side. But this message was so threatening that Jesus delivered a warning to his disciples. Following him and carrying out such radical solidarity would demand the payment of a heavy price: the abandonment of worldly promises of security (Matthew 6:25, 33; 10:7-14).

Jesus' expectations for discipleship, for commitment, were high — not just in relegating security to a lesser concern, but also in the virtual assurance that persecution would dog the steps of so radical a journey (Matthew 10:16-22). God's reign of revolutionary justice and equality would face sharp resistance by both established religious elites and those who controlled the repressive forces of the state. Even loved ones would stand against the disciples of jubilee. In the midst of this fearful persecution, Jesus warned his friends of the consequences of risky discipleship. "If any want to become my followers," he said, "let them deny themselves and take up their cross and follow me" (Mark 8:34).

Liberation against oppression emerges as central to the entire message of Jesus. He demonstrated it in his healings, in his solidarity with the poor, in his intimacy with every marginalized sector of his society, and in his agrarian radicalism embodied in the notion of jubilee. In these respects he represented both the heritage of liberation found in ancient Israel and the subsequent beliefs and practices of the early communities that would bear his name. Jesus, in his message and ministry, highlights the central focus of Biblical teaching, namely, that God makes common cause with the oppressed and vulnerable in their struggles against those who would crush them.

Liberation theology is today's most significant effort to recover those primordial Biblical traditions. Canadian author Pierre Berton summarized that reality in this description of Jesus' ministry:

> In the beginning, Christianity was anything but a respectable creed. Its founder moved among the outcasts of society — among the prostitutes, racial minorities, political traitors, misfits, vagrants, and thieves; among "the hungry, the naked, the homeless and the prisoner." He himself was considered a religious heretic and a traitor to his nation, an enemy of the status quo, a man who broke the Sabbath, a dangerous radical, a disturber and a malcontent who fought the establishment and whose constant companions were the sort of people who are to be found today in the skid-row areas of the big cities. When he stood trial, there was an element of truth in the charge under which he was found guilty: "He stirreth up the people."[11]

But the Scripture of the Old and New Testaments is not the sole source of liberationist roots. Precursors of liberation theology populate the landscape of Christian history after the New Testament period. Highlights of such liberationism emerge from every epoch of the church's history.

The Early Church: A Host of Martyrs

For the first three hundred years of its existence Christianity stood outside the law and was subject to awesome persecution. Consequently the young communities of people who followed Jesus remained vulnerable in societies that oft demanded uniformity. Rome, with its political and military might, tolerated private and internal religious variety, but it would not abide a public religion that refused to grant full authority to the empire and its Caesar. Christianity devoted itself to an alternative world and was viewed understandably by the imperial centre as a competitor for ultimate loyalty. Because of its inconsequential size, it tended to be ignored, though it nonetheless remained vulnerable to outbursts of persecution. In the Gallic towns of Lyons and Vienne in CE 177 the populace rose up against Christians, and about fifty of them were tortured, burned to death, or thrown into the arena as food for carnivorous beasts. In much of the populace's collective consciousness the outlawed Christians were an odious sect, viewed as promiscuous, secretive and dangerous.[12]

The opinions of the pagan intelligentsia towards Christians were not markedly better. Around CE 180 the pagan scholar Celsus stated that the followers of Jesus were "able to convince only the foolish, dishonorable and stupid" of their brand of the truth. No wonder, he mused, for these muddled faithful were "only slaves, women . . . little children . . . wool-workers, cobblers, laundry-workers, and the most illiterate and bucolic yokels, who would not dare to say anything at all in front of their elders and more intelligent masters."[13] The Latin writer Lucian gave his view of those who followed Christ (c. CE 165): "They hold all things alike in contempt, and consider all property common, trusting each other in such matters without any valid security."[14] Even in their antipathy, these pagan foes of the Jesus movement show us that the early Christian communities consisted of the rejected and oppressed sectors of society, of faithful outlaws, radicals and egalitarians who practised the communal sharing of property. Such a movement was vulnerable to the elitist, militaristic, and success-oriented culture embodied in the Roman imperium.

Although the imperial power, when unthreatened, would often ignore these tiny groups that bore the name of Jesus, the emperor and his entourage had only contempt for these outlaw Christians. For example, the Roman governor of Bithynia in Asia Minor (c. CE 111), Pliny the Younger discussed with his imperial lord Trajan how to handle cases brought to trial by pagan citizens against Christians. Pliny himself practised a relatively merciful approach: "I asked them [those brought forward] whether they were Christians. If they confessed, I asked a second and a third time with threat of penalty. If they persisted I ordered their execution, for I do not doubt that whatever it was that they profess, certainly their stubbornness and inflexible obstinacy deserved to be punished." Trajan upheld his governor's policy.[15]

In at least four instances the Roman imperium lashed out officially against Christians. Nero turned against the Nazarenes of Rome after large sections of the city were destroyed by fire (CE 64), and Emperor Domitian (CE 90s) inaugurated an empire-wide persecution against Jesus' followers. One generation before Constantine legalized Christianity, his predecessor Diocletian (CE 284-305) organized a massive program to wipe out Christianity root-and-branch. In CE 250 the situation was infinitely more critical. The emperor Decius was upon the throne, determined to enforce patriotic harmony and religious uniformity throughout the land. Part of this project included a concerted effort to pressure the Christians into conformity, which represented a turning point for the new faith. The pressure on Christians to compromise their faith and fall into line was greater than it had ever been. Many succumbed, but many also held to their convictions and paid the price with their lives. Among these martyrs were many significant leaders of the church. Perhaps the most famous was Cyprian, the bishop of Carthage in North Africa.

Events like these over the three-century period of Christian illegality prompted the early church to develop a detailed theology of martyrdom. So inspired were the early believers by those who faced torture and death with steadfast faith that stories of the martyrs were collected and told again and again. The tradition doubtless helped prepare others to face the hostility and persecution from both their fearful neighbours and the Roman state.

The early Christian communities comprised mostly commoners living on the margins of a reasonably cultured and urbane society, a society that valued success, reason, fairness, and patriotism. The Roman world honoured military might and territorial expansion. For most of the populace this imperialism simply reflected a greater reason for patriotic pride. Today the United States, Canada, and the West in general mirror these qualities with chilling accuracy. Christians in the early centuries repudiated these values quite openly.

They refused to endorse or enlist in the military. In essence, they were what we would now call draft-dodgers or conscientious objectors. The North African church leader Tertullian asked, "Shall it be held lawful to make an occupation of the sword, when the Lord proclaims that he who uses the sword shall perish by the sword?"[16] Two generations later Hippolytus, a leader in the Roman church, gave specific instructions to those who were preparing to join the Christian faith: "A military commander or civic magistrate that wears the purple must resign or be rejected. If a catechetical student or a believer seeks to become a soldier, they must be rejected, for they have despised God."[17]

The early Christians continued Jesus' radical critique of wealth. Cyprian spoke out on such matters, much like the prophets of the Hebrew Scriptures: "But those, moreover, whom you consider rich, who add forests to forests, and who, excluding the poor from their neighborhood, stretch out their fields far and wide into space without any limits, who possess immense heaps of silver and gold and mighty sums of money, either in built-up heaps or in buried stores . . . such a one enjoys no security either in food or in sleep."[18]

The Constantinian Betrayal

The illegal and radical character of Christianity did not lead to its obliteration. Instead of being decimated by the Roman sword, it was subverted by the Roman olive branch. Lured by social peace and the twin promises of prestige and power, the radical Christian communities were co-opted by the emperor Constantine (CE 306-337). Some church propagandists, however, view Constantine as the embodiment of Christian empire, the God-ordained marriage of the Christian gospel with Roman might. They point to his legislation to allow Christians freedom of worship and to his promotion of Christians to a status of privilege within the empire. Clergy became exempt from taxation, bishops were entrusted with positions of secular administration, the church was given wealthy legacies, and favourable legislation emerged to promote Sunday Christian worship. In this process the emperor became the ruler of the church, and refined theological debate about doctrine replaced the life-and-death issues faced by Christians barely a generation earlier. An outlaw faith, through Constantine, became pivotal to the Roman establishment.[19]

Constantine's reign had a great impact upon early Christianity, establishing the faith's subsequent relationship with the Roman imperium and becoming one of the most critical watersheds in Christian history. The radical religion of Jesus and his followers, a community of and for the poor and marginalized, a community of resistance and martyrdom vis-à-vis the Roman state, was virtually obliterated and redefined in less than a generation. What torture and the sword had been unable to do came about through massive and often subtle bribery. The religion of the poor and vulnerable became the religion of the prestigious and powerful. An illegal faith became the established faith, and the oppressed became the oppressors.

Voices of Protest (CE 300-600)

The new Constantinian brand of the faith never did succeed in holding total sway over practising Christians. Although its perception of Christianity has dominated the church's tradition for the last seven centuries, significant voices of protest have always emerged to call the institution back to its radical origins. These voices began to be heard as early as the days of Constantine himself, when they were reflected largely in the monastic movement. More rigorous Christians, disgusted with the massive domestication and co-opting of the faith, protested by a form of withdrawal. Communal monasticism, the dominant pattern of Christian retreat from the world, was based upon earlier models of resistance to the dominant culture during the centuries when Christianity was an outlaw religion. Thus, in a conscious fashion, the monks preserved an earlier protest component of the churches, but they did so in a new fashion and under new conditions. They formed communities that lived the simple life and shared all goods in common. One practical example of this emerged with the renowned monk Basil of Caesaria, who refused to conform to the requirements of imperial Christianity. When confronted by an official threatening him with "confiscation, exile, tortures" or "death," Basil replied,

> Think of some other threat. These have no influence upon me. He runs no risk of confiscation who has nothing to lose, except these mean garments and a few books. Nor does he care for exile who is not circumscribed by place, who does not make a home of the spot he dwells in, but everywhere a home whithersoever he be cast, or rather everywhere God's home, whose pilgrim he is and wanderer.[20]

Words like these represent a continuation of the alien character of the faith in the eyes of the ruling cliques, even when those cliques assume the identity of Christian. Basil passionately defended the communal life against more individualistic alternatives. "I think that the life of several in the same place is much more profitable," he stated, because "God has so ordered all things that we are dependent upon each other. . . . The solitary life has only one goal, the service of its own interests. That clearly is opposed to the law of love."[21]

These monks, who lived together communally, were not isolationists, however. They separated themselves from society in order to better serve that same society. Despite the church's compromises with the Roman imperium, the monks continued to love the church and work within it. In this sense they stood as a voice of prophetic outrage, a tendency that emerges most clearly in their radical denunciation of wealth. For Basil the goods of this world belonged to all, especially the poor: "Where does all your wealth come from? Care for the poor absorbs all available resources. . . . So whoever loves his neighbor as himself owns no more than his neighbor does. But you have a great fortune. How can this be, unless you have put your own interests before those of others?"[22]

Other monastic leaders echoed Basil's concerns. Jerome excoriated the wealthy in his maxim that "all riches come from injustice," and John Chrysostom, an Eastern father of the church, espoused similar sentiments: "Do not say, 'I am using what belongs to me.' You are using what belongs to others. All the wealth of the world belongs to you and to the others in common."[23] Such opinions are not the exception. They are common to the great monastic leaders of both the Eastern and Western churches. Within such communities survived a prophetic and radical voice that countered the massive capitulation of the church to the values and rewards offered by the emperor Constantine and his successors. These monks were largely responsible for engineering the transition of organized Christianity into what came to be called the medieval period.[24]

Medieval Voices of Liberation

It would be a colossal distortion to suggest that medieval Christianity was characterized chiefly by liberationist values and practice. Most often, the practice continued the Constantinian or triumphalist model. Nonetheless, the liberationist light was not snuffed out. Once again, a radical stance emerged regularly in various forms of the monastic movement.

Francis of Assisi

A particularly striking example of the liberationist survival was that of the Franciscans, who originated in response to the urbanization of thirteenth-century Europe. Francis of Assisi was born into a family of wealthy merchants, but while still in his twenties he abandoned his

prosperous and safe existence for a religious vocation. He was converted to a radically Christian life by certain words in Matthew's
Gospel: "Everywhere on your road preach and say, the reign of God is
at hand. . . . Carry neither gold nor silver, nor money in your girdle,
nor two coats, nor sandals, nor staff: for the worker is worthy of his
hire." The young Francis accepted these words and the life of Jesus
with utmost seriousness, taking on voluntary poverty and a full identification with the lepers and beggars of the urban slums. These lived
principles were embodied in the monastic rule that Francis created and
in the lifestyle followed by the Franciscan brothers. Franciscans were
"by no means to receive coin or money," not even for the manual
labour their leader expected them to undertake. In return for their toil
they were permitted to receive only such payment as would satisfy
their simple material needs. Indeed, their top priority was to ensure
that the needs of the poor were satisfied.[25] So strict was this monastic
rule that the brothers could own nothing; even the clothes on their
backs mirrored the coarse and simple variety worn by the commoners.
Leonardo Boff, once part of a Franciscan order, points out:

> The liberation achieved by Francis consisted in being a rich young
> man, the flower of the bourgeois society of Assisi, who took on the
> condition of the poor and lived like a poor man. He served the poor,
> touched them, kissed them, sat at the same table with them, felt
> their skin, lived in physical communion with them. These contacts
> humanize misery; they give back to the poor the sense of their
> human dignity, never lost but negated by the society of the healthy.
> Francis created a fraternity of brothers open to the world of the
> poor.[26]

The Voice of Women

The monastic life of medieval Europe also provided an opportunity for
women to operate outside of the rigidity of the patriarchal society as
defined by the Latin church. This is not to suggest that female religious
did not suffer oppression from a male-dominated and hierarchical
world. Still, they could, in the "set apart" life of monasticism, find a
space to exercise leadership and creativity. In that process they provided a broad and freeing vision that has inspired Christian feminists in
our own day. This can be seen especially among the women mystics.
Mechthild of Magdeburg, for instance, belonged to the Beguines, a
group of commoner lay women who did not marry and lived together
communally. She and her sisters worked for a living, prayed and

worshipped together, and gave priority service to the poor. Her notions of justice sound like contemporary liberationism: "Justice demands that we seek and find the stranger, the broken, the prisoner and comfort them and offer them our help."[27] As well, she broadened the perception of the divinity by using feminine as well as masculine language for God. "God is not only fatherly," she stated. "God is also mother who lifts her loved child from the ground to her knee."[28]

This use of feminine imagery to speak of God reached its height in the British anchoress Juliana of Norwich (1373). In her revelations she experienced the Trinity as "fatherhood, motherhood and lordship," with Christ being described as "our Mother, Brother and Saviour": "But [Christ] is our Mother also in mercy. . . . Thus our Mother describes the different ways in which he works, ways which are separate to us, but held together in him. In our Mother, Christ, we grow and develop."[29] To these descriptions Juliana adds the notion of liberation. Not only is Jesus the keeper "of our Sensuality," but he is also responsible for "our restoring and liberation." Thus she calls Jesus "our Mother, Brother and Liberator."[30] To be sure, these notions of liberation were understood from within the individualist mysticism of this anchoress; nonetheless, her very language provided a breakthrough from the rigid hierarchical and patriarchal dominance of the Latin Christianity of her day.

Peasant Uprisings

Towards the end of the medieval period the apparent stability of previous centuries was unravelling. A combination of urbanization, increased commerce, plague, and social breakdown proved devastating to feudal rigidity. Commoner discontent exploded throughout the fourteenth century and in many instances met with marked success. Even in times of relative peace a language of resentment existed, directed by the artisan and peasant commoners towards the rich and powerful. The popular stories of Robin Hood recapture some of these sentiments. The rural poor viewed the figure of Mary, central to medieval piety, as one who stood with them. In this context she was called "the Madonna of rogues."[31] In general these commoner revolts of the fourteenth century display the continued existence of a militant "grass-roots" Christianity during the Middle Ages.

Throughout that period a combination of wars, plagues, famine, tax increases, lower wages, and oppressive working conditions inspired protests in the form of artisan strikes, tax revolts, and street demonstrations, with some of these events giving way to violence. In a number of cases rebellion created temporary alternative societies prepared to include the poor in the process of governing. Influenced by radical Franciscans, Cola di Rienzo took over the city of Rome and proceeded to tax the nobility class in the name of the people. Called the "candidate of the Holy Ghost" and the "liberator of the city," he led popular militia in the confiscation of noble lands, which he turned over to the use of the wider populace. In France, reverses in a war with England brought to a head the smouldering discontent of the poor against the rich. Beginning as a middle-class revolt led by the merchant Etienne Marcel, the protest grew rapidly into an alliance of bourgeois reformers with more radical urban artisans and the armed peasantry of the surrounding countryside. Finally, towards the end of the century, a peasant uprising in England led by Wat Tyler met initial success in its radical endeavours. Tyler, with an army of about sixty thousand peasants, marched on London and forced the monarchy to free land tenants from their financial burdens, drop trade tariffs, and abolish serfdom.[32]

In all these instances the rebels viewed their protests through the lens of Christian values. This is particularly clear in the sermons of the radical priest John Ball, who supported the British uprisings. His outcries against the rich landowners parallel the later Diggers during the Reformation period.[33]

The Reformation and Liberation (1500-1700)

Commoner protests based upon a Christian worldview spread beyond the Middle Ages. They were endemic to the initial years of the Protestant Reformation, when, in many respects, they continued to pursue unresolved grievances from previous eras. Nonetheless, rebellious peasants attached these earlier demands to the emerging critical spirit so characteristic of the more moderate and well-known Protestant reformers. The most celebrated example of this synthesis emerged in the series of peasant uprisings in the German territories associated with the new Lutheran tradition. Although attuned to Reformation principles of Biblical authority and religious freedom, the revolutionary peasants and their leaders linked these often privatized theological notions to broader social and economic concerns. For instance, the "Twelve Articles of the Pesants," a document promulgated before the outbreak of war in spring 1525, cried out, in the name of the Christian faith, against the oppression heaped upon the peasantry. Certain articles protested the removal of feudal rights that had allowed the peasantry to use certain "common" lands for subsistence needs such as fishing, gaming, and collecting wood fuel (see Articles 4, 5, and 9, for example). But others made radically unprecedented demands in the name of such Reformation principles as freedom and the priesthood of believers. These included the right of "the entire community" to "choose and appoint a minister."[34] The peasants also demanded that the traditional tax of the tithe should be taken from the elite classes and turned over to the commoners in the believing communities, both to pay the minister and to care for the poor. Most radical of all was the document's demand for the abolition of serfdom: "It has been the custom hitherto for men to hold us as their own property, which is pitiable enough considering that Christ has redeemed and purchased us without exception, by the shedding of His precious blood, the lowly as well as the great. Accordingly, it is consistent with Scripture that we should be free and we wish to be so."[35]

Other statements presented by organized and protesting sectors of the mid-European rural classes abound, with content strikingly similar to the "Twelve Articles." As well, the protesters gathered into armed bands named after the commoner footwear called the *bundschuh*. Their flags often bore this symbol and such slogans as "God's justice alone." One of their songs (*Die Gedanken sind frei*) proclaims:

> And should tyrants take me
> And throw me in prison.
> My thoughts will burst free
> Like blossoms in season.
> Foundations will crumble,
> And structures will tumble.
> And free men will cry
> *Die gedanken sind frei*.[36]

Rural rebels were not the only commoners seeking significant social change in the name of the gospel. Day labourers and artisans of the towns were also crushed by the religio-social oppression of the epoch, and they too pushed for liberation under the umbrella of Christian teaching. This was especially true among the masses of journeymen who were unemployed or marginally employed at best. All of these people provided the grass-roots support for the Protestant Reformation in the towns.[37]

Towards Pacifism, Voluntarism, and Community Solidarity

The ultimate failure of the popular armed revolts did not destroy those Christian "grass-roots" communities that identified with the marginalized and oppressed sectors of sixteenth-century Europe and seventeenth-century England. On the continent these groups were termed Anabaptists because of their insistence that membership in the Christian community was a matter of choice ("believers' baptism") rather than automatic citizenship provided by a "Christian" culture ("infant baptism"). This notion, viewed today as essentially a point of theological debate in a religiously pluralistic society, proved a matter of life-threatening import in sixteenth-century Western and Central Europe. Catholics and most Protestants believed in a holy alliance of church and state, the Christendom model established by Constantine in the early part of the fourth century CE. Baptism served not only as a record of citizenship but also as a permanent filing system from which tax lists emerged. Hence to violate this system by the voluntarism of "believers' baptism" was an act of both heresy and sedition, punishable by exile or often death. To be sure, most of these Anabaptist groups were pacifist, but this did not erase concerns about their subversive rejection of the socio-religious establishment for a more just and more liberated alternative society. Thus, to varying degrees, they refused to serve in the nation's armies, pay war taxes, hold civic office, or pledge allegiance to their respective states. Such behaviour led many of them to torture and execution. This loss of life was so common to these radicals that they produced in 1660 a massive volume celebrating those who shed blood for the faith (*The Bloody Theater or Martyrs Mirror*). Today's Mennonites are heirs of this tradition.[38]

The Hutterites formed a particularly interesting Anabaptist group during the Reformation epoch. They adopted and lived out similar convictions and had their share of martyrs as well. They took the Anabaptist commitment to community to its most radical conclusion, namely the communal ownership of all goods. Basing their position on the primitive communism of the Book of Acts, they developed this notion theologically along the lines of God's creation of the world for all to share and the notion of radical, egalitarian Christian love. To this day the Hutterites practise this form of voluntary communism in spite of the petty and legal persecution they encounter with some frequency.[39]

In seventeenth-century England during the Puritan protests, a number of radical Christian groups advocated notions of liberation from both royalists and mainline Puritanism. Notable among these were the Levellers and the Diggers. In many respects the radically democratic Levellers built upon an earlier Christian heritage to promulgate more modern principles of liberty and republicanism. They called for widening the vote to include all males over the age of twenty-one, and one of their leaders in the army, Colonel Thomas Rainborough, insisted that women be granted the suffrage as well. Levellers wanted to outlaw the legal profession and promulgate all laws in simple English so that everyone could understand them. They demanded annual parliaments, civilian control of the military, the right of a fair trial before one's peers, freedom of religion, congregational choice of clergy, and economic and tax reform. Finally, they insisted that members of parliament be allowed to serve only one term. The Diggers proved to be even more radical. Their constituency emerged almost exclusively from the poorest of the poor, those peasants forced off the land by agrarian capitalists. In turn, they were organized by such figures as the radical artisan Gerrard Winstanley. Using the Biblical language of oppression and liberation, he and others called for the confiscation of public grasslands in urban areas by the poor, based on the notion that the Earth was created by God for all. A handful of Digger takeovers occurred, and even some planting of crops was begun before these small groups of rebels were swiftly crushed, and the Diggers passed into history.[40]

Magisterial Reformers

What about the middle-class Protestant leaders? Where do such recognized figures as Luther and Calvin fit into Reformation "liberation theology"? Are they and their churches "oppressors" or "liberators"? The answers to these questions remain complex, but it is important, nonetheless, to hazard a response. Reformation Europe consisted of two struggling groups: an oppressed bourgeois sector competing against a political and ecclesiastical feudal aristocracy in both church and state; and the peasant and artisan masses crushed by economic, social, political, and religious tyranny. Amidst this turbulence the Protestant rebels were a mix of reformers and radicals, with conservative or limited reforms often unleashing radical forces. For their part, the mainline Protestants such as Luther and Calvin maintained the unity of church and state in their reformations. They were rebels against Catholicism, but in their own political jurisdiction they were part of the establishment. Consequently, the legacy of both Lutheranism and Calvinism in the oppression-liberation polarity is fraught with ambiguity.

Almost every Protestant tradition honours Luther as the inaugural hero of the Reformation, but since World War II historians have come to acknowledge the cruel and oppressive side of this great religious figure. His brutal tirades against the peasant rebels of 1525 and his vicious anti-Semitism are no longer denied.[41] Despite such grim reminders, some Lutherans and other Protestant Christians find that Luther's life and thought contain elements that fit neatly into the liberation camp. Although Luther soon became part of an authoritarian religious establishment and recommended to his princes the suppression of religious dissent, he had both consciously and unconsciously inaugurated vast waves of political and religious transformation that would sweep across Europe. Despite even his own conservative personality, Luther's contributions to his time and subsequent history were those of a rebel, as manifest particularly in his three provocative pamphlets of 1520.

In *To the Christian Nobility,* Luther calls upon the German princes to undertake religious reform by wresting power away from the established church. Such efforts included a radical overhaul of the existing tax structure and the reversal of important elements of political control. In his *The Freedom of a Christian*, the reformer heightened the full equality of all Christians under Christ by the radical doctrine of justification by grace alone through faith alone. As a traditionalist of the Middle Ages, he was opposed to the emerging values and practices of nascent capitalism. He decried the amassing of riches through interest gains, price gouging, and the placing of financial profit over people. In this context he called money and property "the most common idol on earth."

Certainly Luther was a member of the clerical and academic elite. Nonetheless, his insights and inaugural efforts challenged existing oppressive systems. Where he held back from the radical implications of his reformation, others moved forward, giving his ideas the liberationist deepening they so richly deserved.[42]

In the English-speaking North Atlantic world, John Calvin and his followers had a deeper and wider influence than did Lutheranism. Calvin's disciples in France and England used basic Reformation principles to overthrow the tyranny embodied by monarchs and feudal aristocracies. The Protestantism that spread from Geneva to France and England sought to subvert more conservative establishments in these lands. Calvinistic propaganda linked with artisan and intellectual revolts in French towns to promote a religious movement dedicated to the overthrow of feudalism and Catholicism. Even when rebellious nobles took over the leadership of French Calvinism, the revolt against centralized monarchy continued. These Calvinist aristocrats employed Geneva-trained pastors to promote ideas of Biblical liberty that attempted to move France towards a constitutional monarchy with elements of bourgeois democracy.[43]

In England and Scotland the Calvinists proved more successful than their French counterparts. During the latter part of the sixteenth century, figures such as John Knox and Christopher Goodman raised the call of reformation revolt against both Catholicism and monarchical autocracy. In exile they learned to build those small consciousness-raising "base-Christian communities" akin to Latin American liberationist models today. They developed a notion of Christian citizenship that helped to create organized groups ready to engage subversively in civic life in the name of the gospel. As well, they constructed a political and religious justification for the overthrow of tyrants.

By the seventeenth century large numbers of the rising landed gentry and merchant classes had come to identify their fortunes with the Calvinistic wing of the Anglican Church. Called Puritans, these reformers built a strong political base in parliament, where they opposed the royalist absolutism of James I and Charles I in the name of religious reform and the values of Christian and covenantal liberty. These Puritans, a rising wealthy elite group, became the avant-garde of that capitalism that would make England a global power, and they developed values and structures that would tyrannize even further the oppressed underclasses of British society. Nonetheless, they were also the forerunners of human rights and the democratic tradition.[44]

The Modern Period (1650-1990)

The epoch of Western history from the mid-seventeenth century to the present is uniquely different from the previous eras of the Christian tradition. From the end of the Thirty Years War (1648) and the British Glorious Revolution (1688) to the present, the Christian religion in the West has experienced a decline of its import in the face of massive secular and alternative value systems. Principles of science, reason, and "the rights of man" emerged in the Enlightenment and competed directly with Christendom's worldview. The revolutions that followed this ideological assault undermined even further the power and prestige of the established churches. In short, the faith's traditional "triumphalism," established by Constantine, has disintegrated rapidly over the last three hundred years. Strangely enough this trend also provided the occasion for explosions of Christian creativity, many of which mirror the liberation Christianity that we recognize today.

Christians for Democratic Liberation:

For the most part the Christian churches resisted the movement towards democracy in the eighteenth and nineteenth centuries, especially on the European continent. However, some noteworthy exceptions emerged, including the Christian denominations located in the rebellious thirteen American colonies. In the Protestant tradition these churches had grown out of the Pietistic tradition found on the European continent and within British Methodism. Pietism's emphasis on the priesthood of believers, its commitment to Christian community, its social compassion, its notions of Christian equality, and its educational reforms all contributed to the emerging democratic spirit of the eighteenth-century North Atlantic world.

Pietism found highly receptive soil in the thirteen British colonies on the eastern shores of the North American continent. From the beginning these colonies reflected a Christian pluralism found nowhere else in the world of that time. A less tolerant Britain used these lands as a dumping ground for its own religious dissenters, which included Puritans, Congregationalists, Quakers, and Catholics, among others. Even the strict Puritans produced dissident heralds of religious freedom and toleration, chief among them being Anne Hutchinson and Roger Williams of Rhode Island. For their day Williams and the Quaker William Penn in Pennsylvania developed constitutional societies that embraced principles of religious freedom far in advance of the European nations. In such a way they laid the foundation for emancipatory principles guaranteeing the freedoms of conscience, speech, and religious practice. Finally, on the eve of the American Revolution the colonies received a new burst of unity occasioned by a massive Protestant and Pietistic revival known as the Great Awakening. It was ecumenical in spirit and committed to reaching the "grass-roots" populace through revivalist preaching. The Awakening's stirring of masses of people, along with the spirit of independence found on a colonial frontier, did much to fuel the protests against England that led to the Revolutionary War (1776-83).

The rebellious colonies were not the only locus of the democratic spirit. Its principles had emerged strongly among the varied Enlightenment philosophers of the eighteenth century. Thinkers such as John Locke and Voltaire or the more radical Thomas Paine and Jean-Jacques Rousseau set the tone with their cries for liberty and the "Rights of Man." To be sure, behind the noble language of the most conservative of these *philosophes* lay the property-amassing agenda of the rising bourgeoisie and a somewhat callous attitude towards the poor.

Nonetheless, theirs were voices for liberation. At the very least, they advocated liberty for their own class, which was resisting the hierarchical rigidity of declining feudalism and the divine right of monarchs; and Enlightenment radicals such as Paine and Rousseau put forth the call for a much wider equality as well as making perceptive attacks on the oppressive character of property ownership. Finally, this emerging democratic tradition enshrined the belief that revolution against tyranny was a fundamental truth written on the very heart of divinity itself.

Few would deny that the democratic tradition liberates far more than it oppresses. However, it was largely the product of non-Christian values. Most established churches during the democratic outbursts in Europe sided with the antirevolutionary forces of reaction. Nonetheless, a minority of Christians stood out as allies of the democratic protestors. In England this opposition emerged largely in the left wing of the Methodist movement. One example was the New Methodist Connection, which its foes called the "Tom Paine Methodists." This democratic impulse in British Methodism is not surprising given the working-class influence within the movement as well as its large number of lay preachers. The success of the campaign to abolish the slave trade in Britain resulted largely from the work of artisan and working-class Methodists, who organized protests and petitions to end this traffic in human beings. As well, Methodist preachers and lay leaders struggled within the Chartist movement for universal suffrage in Britain from the 1830s through the 1840s.[45]

Although they were not as numerically prominent as the oppositional British Methodists, democratic protesters within the Catholic tradition of Enlightenment and revolutionary France proved critical to the successful emergence of the French Revolution itself and laid the groundwork for the Christian Democratic movements of the nineteenth and twentieth centuries in Catholic Europe. Middle-class Enlightenment protest, linked to debt and economic privation, erupted into the series of outbreaks known collectively as the French Revolution. In less than five years (1789-93) France moved from an absolute monarchy through a constitutional kingdom to a radical republic marked by the execution of Louis XVI and his family. These actions made France a symbol for democratic radicals and their dreams for well over half a century, while for reactionaries and elitists the French Revolution and its principles embodied a diabolical nightmare. Among the foes of the revolution stood the Roman Catholic Church, although Catholicism was by no means monolithic. From the Enlightenment to the European revolutions of 1848 small numbers of bold Catholics played an active role among the democratic revolutionaries in France and elsewhere. As early as the salon debates of the eighteenth century, a number of priests espoused the democratic principles of such figures as Diderot and Rousseau. At a more grass-roots level impoverished priests organized to protest their own oppression by demanding a greater voice in ecclesiastical decision-making. Further, a large number of priests in the Revolutionary Assembly voted to give up their feudal privileges. The most notable of these clergy was Henri Grégoire, one of the most advanced democrats of his time. He had helped found France's first abolitionist organization, and in 1794 his insistent voice led the National Assembly to abolish slavery in France and all its possessions. At the same time he pressured the revolutionary parliament to grant citizenship to French Jews, thus abrogating centuries of anti-Semitic legislation created and endorsed by the church. In spite of the changing political fortunes of radicals in France, Grégoire retained both his Christian faith and radical republicanism until his death in 1831.[46]

Shortly before Grégoire's death another priest in France had taken up the democratic call. Féli de Lamennais, born in 1782, was nurtured in the Catholicism of his native Brittany. As a passionate papalist he endorsed the absolutism and antirevolutionary attitude of most of his church in the wake of the disillusionment and collapse of radicalism following the French Revolution. By 1830, with the founding of the newspaper *L'Avenir*, de Lamennais had embarked on a career of democratic advocacy. His views were decidedly to the left of the cautious constitutionalists who advocated a monarchy with limited suffrage. Instead, endorsing the entire range of liberties promulgated by the earlier French Revolution, he called for a republic. All this he did in the name of the Christian gospel. He called for a church stripped of its privileges that, based upon Jesus' teaching of the reign of God, would act in solidarity with all freedom fighters and the oppressed poor. Although de Lamennais was rejected by his church, the values he lived and proclaimed were taken up by increasing sectors within Catholicism until their official adoption at the Second Vatican Council in 1962.[47]

Abolition and the Christian Gospel

The Biblical maxim "there is neither slave nor free" (Galatians 3:28) was not lost on notable Christian radicals. Father Grégoire in France had given much of his life to the abrogation of black slavery, and "grass-roots" Methodists provided the popular base of the abolitionist drive in England. In the United States, where a whole regional economy was built upon the backs of slaves, radical Christians created a vast drive to erase this blemish from history. The Friends Society, better known as the Quakers, had taken a leading role in the anti-slavery movement ever since the American Revolution. Quakers such as John Woolman and Anthony Benezet prompted that religious body to expel its slaveholding members the very year of the Declaration of Independence (1776). Just twelve months earlier a group of Philadelphia Quakers had organized the first abolitionist society of modern times. By the early decades of the nineteenth century abolitionism was a well-organized effort pressuring the churches, government, and society to liberate the black slaves. Journalists such as the New Englander William Lloyd Garrison refused to back down and even faced imprisonment for the cause. John Greenleaf Whittier and other poets rallied to abolitionism as did a number of novelists. None performed a greater service than Harriet Beecher Stowe, who believed that God had guided her hand in writing the explosive *Uncle Tom's Cabin*. Such massive pressure from black and white and male and female Christian radicals did its part to produce the abolitionist Republican Party of the 1850s, the party that would catapult Abraham Lincoln to the presidency in 1860.[48]

Christian abolitionism did not limit itself to legal protest. The slave Reverend Nat Turner led a revolt of his peers in 1831, and many Christians black and white proved instrumental in the illegal "underground railroad," which created an effective network to help slaves escape from their bondage and flee to freedom. The rifle-toting Harriet Tubman was called Moses by her people. Perhaps the most renowned of the armed abolitionist preachers was John Brown, the scourge of pro-slavers and moderates and a saviour for the oppressed. In the hope of leading black and white armed abolitionists on a military offensive through the slave-holding southern states, Brown made a lightning strike on the military arsenal at Harper's Ferry, Virginia (now West Virginia). For this action Brown was tried and hung for treason.[49] But before he died he prophesied that his death would fuel the inevitable liberation of the slaves. He was right. To a tune that would inspire both the Union soldiers in the Civil War and the later labour movement, these words were sung: "John Brown's body lies a-moldering in the grave, but his soul is marching on."[50]

Black Christianity and Freedom

Since the beginning of the American republic, free and slave blacks were at the forefront of the liberation movement, and most of these freedom fighters were fuelled by their Christian faith. Undoubtedly white slavers and their allies used the Christian faith as a means to control the slave population, but oppressed blacks found in the new religion the liberationist faith that came to spread fear in the hearts of their oppressors. In brush arbours the slaves gathered to hear the Bible stories that stirred their souls and made them freedom bound. Among the great abolitionists was another ex-slave, Frederick Douglass. Using the pages of his newspaper *The North Star*, Douglass raised the voice of freedom for his enslaved people.[51]

The struggle for full black liberation continued after emancipation. Again and again prophetic voices emerged from oppressed Afro-American communities to challenge the status quo. Reverend George Washington Woodbey, an ex-slave, openly advocated a socialism inspired by the Christian gospel, so much so that he became one of the American Socialist Party's leading militants. His work *The Bible and Socialism* serves as a classic forerunner of recent liberation theology. Woodbey asserted, "What is said of the poor and their oppressors in the Bible is but a history of the class struggle. And the Bible stands with the Socialist party in the defense of the poor."[52]

In the twentieth century one of the most able voices among black liberationists was the founder of the National Association for the Advancement of Colored People (NAACP), William Edward Burghardt Du Bois. Bard for the crushed black soul, his heartrending manifestos laid the groundwork for the entire civil rights movement of the 1950s and 1960s. And many, many others sowed the seeds of discontent in the name of justice. They bore fruit in the 1950s and 1960s in a vast civil rights movement that reverberated around the world. The leading voice of this liberative outburst was a young southern Baptist preacher, Martin Luther King Jr. Although his goal of integrating blacks and whites, along with his commitment to non-violent direct action, was repudiated by increasingly militant approaches, King and his Southern Christian Leadership Conference remained the central embodiment of the movement for black liberation in the United States until his martyrdom in spring 1968. Initially he sought to win individual rights for Afro-Americans, but he moved gradually from attacks on segregation to an indictment of his nation's pervasive racism. By the mid-1960s he had branched into attacks on U.S. imperialism through his outcries against the Vietnam War, and he was building a broad multiracial antipoverty coalition when he was murdered in Memphis, Tennessee in 1968.[53]

The movement for black liberation was by no means uniform. Malcolm X formed a sharp contrast to King, not only by the espousal of an alternative religious faith but also by his willingness to meet violence with violence. Younger black leaders emerging from the Student Non-Violent Coordinating Committee (SNCC) became impatient with King's more moderate integrationist approach, instead emphasizing the need for Afro-Americans to develop self-pride, find strength within themselves ("Black Power"), and push more militantly towards the goal of full equality. Perhaps most symbolic of black militancy during the late 1960s and early 1970s was the Black Panther movement, which grew out of the urban ghettos of the land.[54]

A number of prominent black preachers and theologians adopted these more militant stances. Some were involved in the drafting of and support for "The Black Manifesto," which was presented in 1969 to the well-known Riverside Church in New York City by the Rev. James Forman, the document's chief architect. "Our fight is against racism, capitalism and imperialism," the statement affirmed, "and we are dedicated to building a socialist society inside the United States where the total means of production and distribution are in the hands of the State, and that must be led by black people, by revolutionary blacks who are concerned about the total humanity of this world."[55] The Rev. Albert Cleage, one-time candidate for the presidency of the U.S. National Council of Churches, is most well-known for his insistence upon the "blackness of Jesus" and for his Detroit pastorate at the Shrine of the Black Madonna. As a supporter of "The Black Manifesto," Cleage declared: "Salvation is saying, 'I believe in the revolutionary struggle which Jesus, the Black Messiah, inaugurated.'"[56]

More recently these values have been espoused and expanded by James Cone, one of North America's most articulate and militant theologians, who has made a direct link between black and liberation theology. In *A Black Theology of Liberation,* Cone asks: "Is [Christ's] presence synonymous with the work of the oppressed or the oppressors, blacks or whites? Is he to be found among the wretched or among the rich? . . . Jesus was not for and against the poor, for and against the rich. He was for the poor and against the rich, for the weak and against the strong. . . . To speak of him is to speak of the liberation of the oppressed."[57]

Women's Liberation and Christianity

The radical formula asserting the full equality of women and men in Christ (Galatians 3:28) has been honoured more in theory than in practice throughout most of Christian history. Nonetheless, the voice of female Christians has echoed down the years and especially in the modern period, when the radical Christian gospel has forged links with secular movements of emancipation organized in the nineteenth and twentieth centuries. Christian women both joined as militants in broad emancipatory struggles and poured their creative energies into more focused and specific battles for the liberation of women.

In the nineteenth-century, American Christian female leaders became advocates both for themselves and for other oppressed groups, a tendency that the abolitionist movement made quite apparent. Well-known women's rights advocates Lucretia Mott and Elizabeth Cady Stanton were militants in the movement to end black slavery and grounded these efforts upon their own Christian faith. Their activism for abolition led them to denounce the oppression of women as well. In 1848 they organized a pioneer female rights convention at Seneca Falls, New York, where the delegates demanded a full range of equal rights, including the suffrage.[58]

Stanton and Mott took their struggle into both the public and ecclesiastical arenas and were joined there by their friend Susan B. Anthony, who had been arrested in 1873 for voting illegally in Rochester, New York, along with twelve of her "sisters."[59] As well, many of the women at Seneca Falls pressed for full equality within the Christian churches. Stanton herself affirmed, "The most powerful influences against women's emancipation can be traced to religious superstition." She, Mott, and others appealed to modern Biblical scholarship over the prevailing tradition that used the Bible to defend a lower status for women. In 1898 they produced *The Woman's Bible*, a massive scholarly effort to remove elements of sexism from the Scriptures and to highlight the role of women leaders in the sacred texts.[60] As well, many ex-slaves, active in the abolition crusade, cried out against the oppression of women. Sojourner Truth was a recognized figure in this camp.

Within the urban squalor of America's rising industrial capitalism, Christian militant women brought their own feminist consciousness to bear through their leadership in social reform movements. Jane Addams, a social radical most remembered for her settlement house programs, sharply criticized conservative Christianity. Frances Willard was the chief voice of the Women's Christian Temperance Union. This abolitionist, suffragette, and socialist led her organization away from a narrow abstinence perspective to a more broad-based movement geared towards substantive political and social reform. Both Willard and Addams are representative of grass-roots activism in the social gospel movement.

The contemporary women's movement has built upon the foundations laid by these ancestors, and this is no less true among female Christian liberationists. Dorothee Soelle and Rosemary Radford Ruether are just two of the renowned scholar activists who combine their feminism with liberation theology. From the insistence on inclusive language to advocacy for all the poor and oppressed, these women represent one of the most vital elements currently found in global emancipatory efforts. Increasingly, minority Christian women are becoming prominent in the wider movement, adding their own unique experience of oppression, struggle, and hope.[61] The feminist New Testament scholar Elisabeth Schüssler Fiorenza is also an avowed liberationist: "Only when theology is on the side of the outcast and oppressed, as was Jesus, can it become incarnational and Christian. Christian theology, therefore, has to be rooted in emancipatory praxis and solidarity."[62]

Christian Militancy, the Working Class, and the Church Response

By the early nineteenth century England was in the midst of a pervasive industrial revolution. Within a hundred years the factory system, with its mass production, wage labour, and urban squalor, would characterize all the major Western powers, and the capitalist mode of production, distribution, and financing would be well on its way to dominating the globe. This was also the period during which the working class emerged and began to suffer the injustices and oppression so endemic to capitalist production. For the church this new reality posed an unprecedented challenge. Institutional Christianity was based sociologically and ideologically on more traditional socioeconomic and political values and thereby proved ill-equipped to respond to the industrial revolution.

When the church did respond, despite many failures and half measures, it managed to fashion some creative approaches. The North American social gospel emerged as Protestantism's most influential response to the ravages of capitalism and industrialization. In the United States the Baptist theologian Walter Rauschenbusch gave the social gospel its most articulate voice. Through his publications he condemned capitalism, indicted the churches for their timidity, and called upon Christians to follow Jesus' teachings on the Reign of God by a profound solidarity with the working class.

In opposition to capitalism, which he described as "fundamentally unchristian," Rauschenbusch heralded the labour movement as incipiently Christian and a force for good.[63] But, above all, the renowned "social gospeller" posited Christianity against capitalism, God against Mammon:

> Christianity teaches the unity and solidarity of men; Capitalism reduces that teaching to a harmless expression of sentiment by splitting society into two antagonistic sections. . . .
>
> Jesus bids us strive first for the Reign of God and the justice of God, because on that spiritual basis all material wants too will be met; Capitalism urges us to strive first and last for our personal enrichment. . . .
>
> Christianity makes the love of money the root of all evil, and demands the exclusion of the covetous and extortioners from the Christian fellowship; Capitalism cultivates the love of money for its own sake and gives its largest wealth to those who use monopoly for extortion.[64]

Rauschenbusch espoused the socialist vision as representative of those "Christian principles of equal rights, democratic distribution of economic power, the supremacy of the common good, the law of mutual dependence and service, and the uninterrupted flow of good will throughout the human family."[65] He and his allies, in the early decades of our century, thus embodied a Protestant form of radicalism akin to liberation theology.

It was the Catholic Church, however, that developed Christianity's most comprehensive response to the forces unleashed by the industrial revolution. In France and Germany especially, avant-garde Catholic priests and members of the laity began the process of forging links with the working class. The turning point came when the pioneer papal encyclical *Rerum Novarum*, promulgated in 1891 by Leo XIII, called for social concerns to become an integral part of Catholic life. Built upon a blend of reactionary and conservative notions, this letter advocated justice for the worker based largely on a paternalistic medievalism and religious defence rather than socialist thought. Despite these serious limitations it began what has come to be known as the "social doctrine of the church."

Especially creative responses to *Rerum Novarum* and its successor documents emerged in the French Catholic Church. There social Catholic pioneers created a number of experiments designed to mitigate the oppressions of the industrial system. Count Albert de Mun was the chief representative of a more conservative brand of social Catholicism. Operating from a sense of *noblesse oblige*, this aristocrat organized worker circles and a youth club and for decades (1870s-1914) fought for pro-worker legislation as a deputy in the French parliament. Although possessed of both passion and dedication, de Mun and those he inspired were no liberationists. They sought justice, and they were social reformers, but their perspective was that of the social paternalist.[66]

The younger Marc Sangnier represents a radical break from de Mun and the more traditional brand of social Catholicism. In his youth movement (called Sillon), Sangnier not only advocated "for" the workers but also forged alliances "with" the workers. He held as his Christian conviction that democracy and social egalitarianism were the historical forms through which the gospel would achieve its salutary impact upon society. Towards this end he encouraged his *Sillonistes* to create co-operatives, form popular universities in urban ghettos, and join the more revolutionary trade unions found in the France of his day (1890s-1910). He upheld the right to strike, acknowledged the reality of class struggle, and defended the necessity for "the free and conscious worker [to] possess in common the instruments of their work." Thus did Sangnier advocate socialism, though he refused to use the word itself. Despite the pope's condemnation of him in 1910, Sangnier continued his social radicalism under other forms until his death in 1950. It was Marc Sangnier and those like him who developed a social Catholicism of the left that well deserves the name "liberationist."[67]

Sillon directly influenced subsequent efforts at a social Catholic radicalism. One such effort, the Jeunesse Ouvrière Chrétienne (JOC), was the pioneer in what came to be called specialized Catholic Action. Based on the notion that "like must minister to like," the JOC was a movement of working-class youth who were believing Christians. From the 1930s on they pursued a lifestyle of full identification "with" the workers because they were, in fact, workers themselves. These adolescents and young adults made their presence felt in their factories and neighbourhoods by organizing for social reform and transformation. Although at times the JOC has acted in timidly reformist and divisive ways within the working class, it has also contained an incipient radicalism at the grass-roots level, a radicalism that increasingly linked itself with more revolutionary working-class efforts. The organization's work included resistance to fascist aggression and alliances with Marxists and others who militated for social transformation.[68]

In the United States Peter Maurin, an ex-Sillonist, enlisted Dorothy Day, a recent convert to Catholicism, to help him create a radically Christian anarchist body called the Catholic Worker Movement. Their alliance was a fortuitous one. Reaching a wider public through their newspaper *The Catholic Worker*, the movement has been a beacon of Catholic radicalism and spirituality committed to a liberation of all the poor and marginalized. The organization's militants live a life of communal sharing in the midst of the poor found in America's urban ghettos. There, in the Catholic Worker's humble dwellings, the marginalized are welcomed to share food and lodging. Not only do the Catholic Workers live among the human refuse of the cities but they also advocate for social transformation. Over the years they have demonstrated and been arrested with trade union radicals, communists, black activists, feminists, and members of the peace movement.[69]

Post-World War II France saw an explosion of creative Catholic radicalism. The Cardinal Archbishop of Paris, Emmanuel Suhard, called this epoch a "new Pentecost." From around 1943 until 1954, when the Cold War and the Vatican suppressed many avant-garde Catholic experiments, France produced a grand variety of Catholic efforts to forge links with the nation's working class and its advocates. During this time the JOC renovated itself, and a number of adult counterparts appeared. Parishes in urban ghettos and rural poverty pockets adapted themselves to meet the needs of marginalized populations, and a seminary, the Mission de France, began to train priests for this specialized type of vocation. The Catholic press had increasingly progressive examples, such as *Témoignage Chrétien* and newspapers like *La Quinzaine,* and teams like the Jeunesse de l'Église published resolutely pro-working class statements and allied themselves openly with Communists. Increasingly France's most noteworthy theologians sided with such progressives. They included figures such as Emmanuel Mounier, Henri de Lubac and the Dominicans Yves Congar, Maurice Montuclard, and Marie-Dominique Chenu. These last two could be classified as liberationists although the term would postdate them by fifteen years.[70]

Perhaps the most radical and most creative French Catholic effort to reach France's industrial workforce was that of the worker-priests. Recognizing that the factory workers lived in a world outside of the Christian faith, a few of France's more progressive bishops sent a number of priests to live fully as workers themselves. Roughly one hundred of them entered the factories, lived in the poor neighbourhoods, ate the same food as their factory comrades, and experienced the same joys and privations. Soon they found themselves active in the more radical trade unions led by militant Communists. The worker-priest had become the priest-militant, much to the embarrassment and chagrin of more conservative Catholics. Worker-priests were elected to union positions, led strikes, edited strike newspapers, fought for neighbourhood reform, and were arrested in peace demonstrations. In the final years before their condemnation by the hierarchy in 1954, they called for radical reforms within the church. Though barely a decade old when Pius XII closed them down, the worker-priests had made their impact. In their brief journey they not only brought God to the marginalized and oppressed, but also, more importantly, found God already there. They themselves were transformed. "I have not preached the gospel to the poor," said worker-priest Joseph Robert. "It is the poor who have preached the gospel to me."[71]

Other examples of liberationist forerunners abound, but this summary of emancipatory movements indicates that contemporary liberation theology is not without significant ancestors. Subsequent chapters will highlight Canadian examples. Christian history gives ample testimony to the survival of Biblical radicalism. Regardless of "Christendom's" efforts to promote a success and prestige-oriented gospel — a "gospel" enamoured with the powerful and blind to the poor — both the Biblical witness and the testimony of church history demonstrate that liberation theology and its allies are rooted at the heart of our tradition. The very gospel itself demands of us a life given in solidarity to the Christ who calls us out of the Egypt of oppression and into the promised land of liberation.

3   The Oppressors in Canada

CANADA EXISTS AS A NATION BUILT ECONOMICALLY UPON THE capitalist system, a system based on investment for the purpose of personal gain or profit. In contrast to the notion of "a day's wages for a day's work," capitalism thrives on gain above and beyond the original investment of time, money, or labour. Biblically this very foundation of capitalism stands condemned as a violation of God's covenant of liberation: "If your brother . . . falls on evil days and is unable to support himself . . . you must support him as you would a stranger or a guest. . . . Do not make them work for you, do not take interest from them. . . . You are not to lend them money at interest, or give them food to make a profit out of it" (Leviticus 25:35-38). Modern capitalism, however complex, remains fundamentally flawed at its very core, because its values are based on personal or private gain, greed, and competition. William Irvine, the great Alberta social gospeller, stated it succinctly in 1920: The social gospel "denounces a system of society that makes paupers by the millions and millionaires by the score."[1] No matter whether it is called capitalism, the free market, globalization, neo-liberalism, neo-conservatism, or the free-enterprise system, this international economic structure feeds upon values that are the very antitheses of the Biblical *shalôm*.

Moreover, capitalism remains infinitely more than the warlike values it puts forward as either natural or virtuous. It is fundamentally a system in operation and has massive pragmatic implications. Its concrete manifestations assault us daily. Perhaps its most overwhelming characteristic is its division of the world's population into a few wealthy and powerful owners and a vast global population of marginalized and oppressed masses. Thus the world and Canada are subdivided into the "haves" on one side and the "have-nots" and "have-a-littles" on the other.

The Concentration of Wealth and Economic Power

For scoundrels are found among my people. . . . They take over the goods of others. . . . they have become great and rich, they have grown fat and sleek. — *Jeremiah 5:26-29*

The growing concentration of wealth and economic power that evolved in Canada throughout the twentieth century clearly demonstrates this intensive polarization. At the beginning of the century entrepreneurial capitalism became transformed into corporate capitalism, with massive industrial concentrations in mining, steel, paper, and textiles. Between 1900 and 1920 about 200 consolidations absorbed in the neighbourhood of 440 firms. The period also saw the entry of U.S. branch-plants into Canada: from 1900 to 1905 the number of U.S.-owned firms doubled, a harbinger of things to come. The emergence of major financiers, such as Max Aitken (Lord Beaverbrook), brought corporate concentration to the point at which less than fifty men controlled more than one-third of the nation's material wealth. Railways became a major locus of such investment. The railways controlled the marketing of wheat, Canada's chief resource for the international capitalist market.[2]

From the Great European War to the Second World War, the corporate and financial elite increased its control of the wealth and industry of the land. The misery of the Depression was instrumental in this growing consolidation. Just prior to the economic collapse, U.S. capital investment and industry in Canada had come to supersede the British input, and that trend has continued with little abatement to the present. By 1930 almost all major U.S. manufacturing firms had plants in Canada, accounting for roughly one-third of the nation's manufactured goods. In certain major industries U.S. firms controlled a majority proportion of Canada's manufacturing: rubber (64 per cent), automobiles (82 per cent), and electrical apparatus (68 per cent), for example. International Harvester Company alone accounted for about 40 per cent of Canadian sales.[3]

Such economic elitism and colonialism was compounded in the case of Quebec. Much like Ontario, Quebec had joined the Atlantic market by the mid-nineteenth century, but unlike its Confederation partner the francophone province was colonized not only by economic outsiders from the United States but also by the resident British economic elite. Thus endured the legacy of control that dated from the defeat of France by Britain in the Seven Years War. More recently, textiles, mineral extraction, and pulp and paper, among the major arenas of the Quebec economy, fell into the hands of U.S.-based companies.

Quebec thus mirrored the wealth and power concentration found in
the rest of Canada, though in this case outside control was intensified
by a long-term anglophone colonialism.[4]

World War II and its aftermath witnessed a rapid expansion of earlier developments in spite of worker gains and an almost three-decade
era of unparalleled prosperity for most Canadians. Massive capital concentration and increasing U.S. control of the national economy continued and intensified rapidly after the cessation of hostilities. At the peak
of the nation's postwar "boom," 183 corporations accounted for
between 40 and 50 per cent of gross production in manufacturing. The
amassing and control of resources were enhanced by the tight circle of
the nation's economic elite. Most came from the traditional Anglo-
Saxon families that have reigned over Canada's major financial institutions for generations, though they did little to protect these resources
from outside intrusion.[5]

By the 1950s, compared to the United States, Britain had become
a minor investor in its former colony. In 1952 U.S. investment in
Canada amounted to 77 per cent of the total, and U.S. capital sources
owned almost 50 per cent of the gross value of manufacturing corporations. The growing U.S. absorption of Canada manifested itself also in
Quebec, where, from the end of the war until the outbreak of the Quiet
Revolution, U.S. capital investment rose from $7 billion in 1946 to over
$22 billion in 1960. These figures translated into an increase in U.S.
control over Quebec's economy of from 40 to 60 per cent. The percentage was markedly higher in the natural resource sectors. Continentalism, or the full integration of Canada into the U.S. economy, stood out
as a virtual *fait accompli* by the 1970s.[6]

Although a Trudeau minority government produced legislation
(the Foreign Investment Review Agency, FIRA) to curtail this American-
ization, and although the Quebec Liberals of the 1960s achieved much
in reclaiming their province's economy, both U.S. control and capital
concentration moved inexorably forward. By the end of 1971 the top
113 corporations dominated the national economy, with many of these
giants based in the United States. In the financial sector corporate control amounted to 90 per cent of assets and 91 per cent of revenue in
banking, and 86 per cent and 81 per cent in insurance. The manufacturing sectors exhibited similar concentration in the hands of a few
companies.[7] By the end of 1973 the United States alone accounted for
79 per cent of all foreign direct investment in Canada.[8]

By the 1990s the almost three-decade-old economic boom following the wartime antifascist alliance had fallen on hard times. Keynesian

economic policies, promoted especially by social-democratic parties and benefiting from economic expansion, had generated full employment and created advanced welfare states throughout the Western world. In what has been called "the Deal," North American capital and the major labour unions forged an alliance in which workers made substantial economic gains, including job security, and promised industrial peace in return. All this began to change in the 1970s, with the great oil crisis and the Nixon government's abdication of the wartime Bretton Woods Agreement (1944). According to political scientist James Laxer the corporate elite, in Canada and abroad, abandoned even the pretense of Keynesianism and began an unprecedented assault on the welfare state in the name of a naked free-enterprise ideology. We face this corporate counterattack in all its fury under the name of globalization, neo-conservatism, and neo-liberalism, terms that appear interchangeably in the pages ahead.[9]

Despite the business elite's rhetoric of competition, cost-cutting, and efficiency, the essence of globalization remains strikingly simple. Laxer points out that the unfettered marketplace is the god of this neo-liberalism, and towards that goal the "neo-cons" seek "to reverse the movement towards greater social equality that occurred to varying degrees in every industrial country during the postwar decades." Laxer states: "The rationale for reversing the tide is always the same: because of heightened competition, society can no longer afford social democracy, so expensive social and educational programs must be curtailed in order that we can resume healthy economic growth."[10] This new capitalist aggression has an all-too-familiar ring. It represents a continuation of a system that places profit ahead of democratic structures, social justice, and fundamental human need. Nonetheless, this neo-liberalism reflects three new and especially devastating realities that underscore its enmity with Biblical *shalôm* in an unprecedented manner.

First of all, globalization embodies elements of power and control that qualitatively exceed any of capitalism's earlier phases. More than ever before, the Canadian business elite now represents only a piece of a huge global power bloc of capital that plans and acts beyond the regulatory power of the nation-state. The might of "big business" emerges in the transnational corporations (TNCs), institutions that embody an increasingly planet-wide infrastructure. The world's seventeen largest TNCs employed 4.3 million people by 1989 and amassed profits of over $1 trillion in U.S. currency. In that same year international conglomerates exceeded the production of the world's forty-one poorest countries, with a population in excess of 2.9 billion. Concentration of wealth globally within the thirty-five thousand transnationals is staggering. In the area of consumer goods, five transnationals account for 70 per cent of sales. The top five companies building cars and trucks sell 58 per cent of the world's production, and the five largest electronics-components firms make up 53 per cent of global sales. Throughout the 1980s an international merger mania took hold. The amount of money spent in such acquisitions totalled more than the annual economic output of the United Kingdom. This concentration of wealth and power worsened in the 1990s. By 1996 the combined sales of the globe's two hundred largest TNCs far outweighed the combined sales of one hundred and eighty-two countries, all but the largest nine. As well, 85 per cent of the globe's Gross Domestic Product is owned by the richest 20 per cent of its population.[11]

Canada has not escaped the effects of this global concentration of capital. In Canada less than 1 per cent of all enterprises control 74.9 per cent of all assets, while a full 99 per cent of the nation's half-million companies own a mere 14.6 per cent of corporate assets. At the same time none of the hundred largest TNCs is headquartered in Canada; fully one-third of them base their operations in our powerful neighbour to the south. The role of U.S.-based corporations has intensified markedly in less than a decade. Foreign-dominated firms received 43.3 per cent of all non-financial industries' profit in 1984, with a full 53.2 per cent of such profits accruing to the top five hundred of these companies. By the early 1990s, within the top five hundred corporations in Canada, 38 per cent were foreign-controlled and 28 per cent foreign-owned. Such an infusion of U.S. control of the Canadian economy creates a mammoth trade dependency. Canada's sales to the United States account for 20 per cent of the nation's total, as compared to a mere 3 per cent for our U.S. counterpart. Economic colonialism of this magnitude has intensified a massive outflow of capital from Canada to the United States: $3.5 billion (1984) to $5.6 billion (1990). This economic imperialism has continued apace with the NAFTA accord and will reach devastating proportions with the Multilateral Agreement on Investment (MAI). *The Third World Guide 95/96* states the matter bluntly: "No other major western economy maintains a trade imbalance of such magnitude; it is comparable only to the dependence of the countries of the South with relation to the industrialized countries."[12]

Even more chilling than this corporate concentration is the emergence of a transnational infrastructure designed to supersede the capacity of nation-states to regulate capital. The growing numbers of regional and global trade blocs exemplify this; examples are the

General Agreement on Tariffs and Trade (GATT) and its successor, the World Trade Organization, and the European Economic Union; and, closer to home, the Free Trade Agreement (FTA) and the North American Free Trade Agreement (NAFTA). The globalization of finances, exemplified by the International Monetary Fund (IMF) and the World Bank, presents an especially grim example of the extent of corporate domination of capital and investment. These institutions manifest a control of the global economy engineered from board rooms run by Western elites. For example, the United States, with only 5 per cent of the world's population, holds 16 per cent of the vote at the World Bank, while Japan, with less than 2.5 per cent of the world's population, commands 9.4 per cent of the bank's voting power. All told, the industrial nations control 60 per cent of the vote on the World Bank's executive board. The World Bank remains an instrument of the rich and powerful used to dominate the poorer, more vulnerable nations of the developing world; and it manages this partly by forcing debtor nations into Structural Adjustment Plans (SAPs) that undermine the fragile social-safety networks in the poorer lands.[13]

Second, neo-liberalism has radically altered its investment strategy. In *Turning the Tide: Confronting the Money Traders,* John Dillon of the Ecumenical Coalition for Economic Justice describes this shift in chilling detail. Economic growth is measured more and more in terms of "an increase in the money economy," and "investing is shifting from the production of goods and services to financial speculation." Every day about $1.3 trillion dollars exchanges hands globally, and financial transactions now top merchandise trade by a multiple of seventy-two. Add currencies, stocks, bonds, and commodity futures to this, and the total daily exchange amounts to roughly $4 trillion U.S. Today's computer technology can send in the neighbourhood of $13 trillion U.S. around the globe with unprecedented speed. Such "cybermoney" further enhances the instability of a worldwide market that some appropriately call a "global casino." Capital becomes abstracted in this new reality where money is used primarily to generate more money, and speculation replaces not only production and service but, even more important, jobs and human needs. Such Biblically condemned usury has taken control in the brave new world of globalization.[14]

With this shift to a new, more speculative phase of capitalism, governments fall under tremendous pressure to adapt. Business expects political leaders to relinquish governments' regulatory functions, thus allowing capital free reign to invest globally without barriers. Policies of high interest rates, a boon for financial gamblers, stand as another given for neo-liberalism's speculative phase. One immediate effect of this is the inability to use older Keynesian economics to balance governmental budgets. Hence business elites put additional pressure on governments to get their fiscal houses in order, and they demand that they do this by becoming "more competitive." To the corporate leaders this means draconian cuts to social programs and further deregulation by government in the economic arena. The vicious cycle only tightens. Within the last few years the global financial community has treated Mexico, for instance, with a particular ruthlessness, underscoring the antihuman character of this brand of globalization. Mexico became the locus for high-level speculative investment, and when the crash occurred, global financial institutions and the U.S. government closed in to impose SAPs.[15]

Canada has fallen under the weight of the new financial aggression. Debt and the demand to reduce public spending via social program cutbacks represent the antigovernmental agenda of the "neo-con" ideologues. The massive increase of our foreign debt gives credence to the corporate "deficit crisis" cry of alarm. By 1995 the debt had tripled to $339 billion from 1980. As well, the nature of the debt had changed from the more stable pattern of direct investment to the more volatile portfolio investment. Nonetheless, the reasons cited by the corporate elite for this massive government debt, namely too much social spending, shield the public from the reality of the matter. Rather, the corporate elite and the governments it supports are the guilty parties. High-interest policies, pursued by the Bank of Canada for years and demanded by the corporate sector, stand as the single most important cause of the massive debt. Another problem is the fact that a large portion of this debt is held by non-Canadian sources. Social spending, which has fallen in relation to our GDP since the 1970s, has virtually nothing to do with the nation's debt. Responsibility falls almost exclusively on the shoulders of the corporate elite and its allies.[16]

Third, the rapid movement of capital globally, through the use of "cybermoney," connects with the introduction of pervasive technology into the global economic system. Computers and other forms of new technology result in layoffs, other job losses, and underemployment. The instantaneous transport of capital through cyberspace and the so-called "information highway" have redefined production and the nature of work, thus producing a new brand of Taylorism. With their commitment to speculative investment and quick profit flow, the corporate chiefs generate quick gains by eliminating workers and reorganizing production around the new technology.[17]

Jeremy Rifkin's book *The End of Work* describes in depth the new world of technology and how it is destroying and will destroy the global infrastructure. Rifkin compares the public relations promises offered via this "cyberworld" with the reality of the destruction of jobs and entire ways of life left in its wake.

In *Whose Brave New World?* Heather Menzies does for Canadians what Rifkin has done for a largely U.S. audience. She speaks of a new era of rapid and decentralized production based upon computer efficiency and fewer and fewer workers located in various nodules of production distant from each other. Using existing examples and projecting from them into the future she lists several outcomes of this new brand of Taylorism: the collapse of work, underemployment, jobless growth, decline of skilled workers, collapse of labour unions, computer monitoring of the workforce, and technological piecework — in short, a return to a "sweat-shop" reality computer-style.[18] Menzies describes the impact of this "neo-con" heaven on people's lives:

> The marginalization of people and the downward drag of earnings and benefits will continue in lockstep with jobless economic growth. Meanwhile, the new working rich and what's left of the middle class will be kept busy at the core of the new economy, putting in ten-hour and twelve-hour days — or up to twenty hours in the four-month "product-development" season of the high-tech sector — feverishly engineering the next generation of products, and finding clever new niches for them in the ever-expanding empire of cyberspace.[19]

Globalization represents an unprecedented and increasingly successful assault on postwar Keynesianism. The full employment epoch, with its significant commitment to social welfare, has buckled under the hammer of a corporate offensive of unparalleled magnitude. Biblical *shalôm* joins the list of victims. And our political leaders? Where do they stand in the midst of this crisis?

The Corporate Control of Canada's Political Life

> Their hands are skilled in evil; the official demands . . . the judge gives judgment for a bribe, the powerful pronounce as they please.
> — *Micah 7:3*

The profound link between the nation's corporate elites and its politicians is not new. Confederation emerged from such an alliance. John A. Macdonald's coalition of the major political groupings in Upper Canada and Georges-Étienne Cartier's *bleus* in Lower Canada embodied an

alliance of the landed, financial, and railroad elites who had an economic power stake in how Canada would be constructed. Nation-build-
ing reflected at least as much a capitalist enterprise as it did a patriotic
one. Essentially the Canadian people had invested in a capitalist railroad project that would further enrich the wealthy elite and give them
control over the sole link that held the nation together.[20]

Domination of Canadian politics by the nation's business and
financial barons continued unabated well into the years of the Great
War and beyond. The experience of linking the Prairies to the Ontario-
Quebec heartland reflected this continuing exploitation. Federal immigration policy, the control of "King Wheat" by the railroads and the
nature of urban development in the new provinces all played a part.
The federal government under Wilfrid Laurier devised an extensive
immigration program to build up the Prairie labour force so that virgin
territory could be transformed into a source of financial profit. The
man behind land development and immigration in the west was Clifford Sifton, Laurier's minister of the interior. Sifton, with the support of
William Van Horne, the chairman of the CPR's board, mounted a mammoth promotional campaign to lure land-hungry immigrants from
Europe and elsewhere to people the Prairies, and he utilized his own
Manitoba Free Press to praise his person and his policies. Like the Tories
before them, Laurier's Liberals governed the nation for the benefit of
private economic elites.[21]

In the first years of the new century wheat emerged as Canada's
single most important commodity traded on the international market.
Only in its initial cultivation did the farmers themselves have any say
over what they produced. On the day they took their wheat to market
they turned control of the crop over to grain-elevator monopolies, the
railways, and the Eastern banks and financiers. Both of the old-line
parties, whether provincial or federal, refused to inaugurate substantive changes. Their links with the economic overlords prevented such
actions.[22]

From the beginning, urban centres on the Prairies arose in
response to capitalist needs. Winnipeg, the "Gateway to the West," was
fundamentally a railroad centre that served to send raw western goods
(chiefly wheat) to the east and to bring back expensive manufactured
implements (highly protected by tariffs) needed by the farmers. As the
Prairie's chief manufacturing centre, Winnipeg depended upon its huge
railroad yards for its chief industrial endeavours. The city also became
the West's centre of speculation and banking.[23]

Winnipeg's political and social life was characterized by an alliance of the political and socioeconomic elites, who in the years before the Great War were often synonymous. The mayor's office, for instance, was held by forty-one men between 1871 and 1914. Of these, 39 per cent were merchants and businessmen; 37 per cent were in real estate and/or finance; 14 per cent were in manufacturing or the construction industry; and 10 per cent were from the professions. No worker or artisan held the post throughout that period. A similar situation was reflected in the city's Board of Control, which was under the tutelage of the local commercial elite at the high level of about 90 per cent. These political elites were tied directly to such business organizations as the Winnipeg Board of Trade, the Real Estate Exchange, and the Winnipeg Development and Industrial Bureau. These "civic leaders" also belonged to such national bodies as the Canadian Manufacturers' Association and the National Association of Real Estate Exchanges. They maintained ties with both the federal Liberals and Conservatives, the two mainline parties linked to the railway interests. This control of city life by the wealthy was cemented by property qualifications for voting. In 1906, when its population was over 100,000, Winnipeg had only 7,784 registered voters.[24]

This use of municipal politics to serve the goals of the city's socioeconomic elite was manifested in both the town's "booster" campaigns and in its programs of urban reform. The "city fathers" used the call for civic pride and patriotism to promote the railways, recruit immigrants to labour in the various trades, attract industry, and encourage real estate development. They used the very newspapers they controlled to trumpet these values and goals in a promotional way.[25] Even issues of urban reform fell under the sway of the business interests. Ultimately it was the elites who championed the cause of public ownership of hydroelectricity, transit systems, fire fighting, and other utilities. This tendency was by no means a matter of municipal socialism; rather, it involved the use of public revenue to finance the necessary infrastructure for private industry to flourish.[26]

The alliance between the tiny economic elite and the civic leaders of the nation continued through the Great Depression. Neither R.B. Bennett for the Tories nor the ubiquitous William Lyon Mackenzie King for the Liberals was inclined to seriously confront the misery caused by the Depression, and both leaders were steeped in the values of big business and aligned with its interests. King, prime minister for most of the period, had earned his stripes as an employee of John D. Rockefeller by advocating company unions in place of autonomous labour organizations. For his part, Bennett had garnered his daily wages as a prominent corporate lawyer. King adored power and powerful men, and Bennett, who distrusted democracy, felt that political power should be exercised by the elite. This same elite would people Bennett's cabinet. All but two of these senior members were part of the nation's Eastern financial establishment. From such men, whether Liberal or Tory, one could hardly expect substantive humane responses to the tragedies that emerged in the Depression's wake.[27]

During these crisis years the politicians did little or nothing to violate the vested interests of the nation's economic elite. Both of the ruling federal parties called for stock solutions, such as supporting business to hire the unemployed as opposed to the creation of any substantive social programs. Relief was habitually thrown back upon the provinces and municipalities. When progressives, church figures, and assorted leftists offered creative solutions or acted upon them, they met the resistance of the federal government at every turn. The Bennett government's response to the "On-to-Ottawa" trekkers is a case in point. In the name of anticommunism, a standard ploy of established elites in the century, Bennett violated provincial rights and used force to crush a well-organized and peaceful democratic protest in Regina in 1935. This police riot resulted in one policeman dead, scores of trekkers injured, and even more were jailed. Often provincial politicians were no better. Both Maurice Duplessis of Quebec and Mitch Hepburn of Ontario used the "anti-Red" shibboleth to pass antidemocratic legislation or use police against legitimate trade union activity.[28]

The immediate postwar years in Canada reflected a period of unprecedented prosperity throughout the industrialized nations in general and Canada in particular. Governments, committed to Keynesian economic policies, brought advanced social welfare states to their fruition for almost thirty years. Business and labour eked out a compromise that provided full employment and job security for workers and labour peace for the corporate elite.[29] During this period Mackenzie King's Liberal government enjoyed a progressive reputation. Fearful of the ascendancy of Canada's major socialist party, the Co-operative Commonwealth Federation (CCF), a party that had come to power in Saskatchewan in 1944, Mackenzie King adopted a series of social programs that co-opted elements of the socialist platform and brought the Liberals to power in the first postwar election. On a more aggressive note, by the end of the 1940s the nation's politicians and press had picked up on the "red-scare" mood south of the border and used anticommunist hysteria to divide and weaken the trade union movement. The effects were most apparent in Quebec, where successive governments led by Maurice Duplessis combined authoritarian politics, government patronage, union "bashing," and pro-corporation economic strategies to control the province in favour of their friends and against all their progressive foes. Although there had been significant federal social legislation, the economic elite maintained its hold on the political forces of the land.[30]

During the Trudeau years, despite a sense of euphoria and the progressive image promoted by the prime minister's government and surrounding his person, a strengthening of corporate and elitist control over political life occurred. The upper-class elites were most visible at the higher levels of political power, namely in federal cabinet positions, especially those dealing in economics and finance. Provincial premiers with wealth were not uncommon: Richard Hatfield, Frank Moores, Peter Lougheed, Robert Stanfield, and Robert Bourassa, for instance. The politically well-positioned wealthy abounded in both major political parties.[31]

Indeed, the entire twentieth century witnessed a direct connection between federal governments — whether Liberal or Conservative — and the corporate elite. The Tory Robert Borden (1911-20) was a corporation lawyer, director of the Bank of Nova Scotia, and a co-founder of the Crown Life Insurance Company. Arthur Meighen was a lawyer who served Toronto's financial community. Louis St. Laurent, Mackenzie King's successor, made his living as a corporate lawyer. Before entering politics he served as a director of Metropolitan Life and the Bank of Montreal. John Diefenbaker, a criminal lawyer, had more humble origins, as did Lester Pearson, but both these men had strong corporate support during their years in power. Pierre Trudeau's financial independence is also well-known. As for federal cabinets, 70 per cent of Bennett's ministers represented the business community, and for Diefenbaker's cabinet the figure was 62 per cent. Between 1935 and 1957, 64 per cent of the Liberal Party ministers held important business posts before and/or after their political stints.[32]

It would be an act of sheer credulity to surmise that such corporate control of political life was motivated exclusively or chiefly by philanthropy and civic pride. Evidence from the 1970s tends to support a less charitable interpretation, namely that the wealthy elite has used its political influence and control to push its own private agenda. For example, when the government set up its advisory boards, especially on economic matters, it populated these boards with the members and allies of the economic elite.[33]

The governments that followed the Trudeau years intensified their "big-business links." Neither the Mulroney Tories (1984-93) nor the Chrétien Liberals (re-elected in 1997) deviated from the corporate agenda.

The leadership of both parties has direct connections with business barons. The Liberals of the 1990s and their predecessor Tories benefited handily from the largesse of the wealthy and powerful. Between 1984 and 1989 the corporate elite passed over in excess of $52 million to the Mulroney Conservatives. The Chrétien Liberals added more than $11 million to their party coffers in 1994, half from corporations and half from wealthy individuals. The banks top the list as major contributors to both parties.[34]

Personal ties cement the connection between "big business" and the federal Liberals and Tories. Brian Mulroney served as chief executive officer of the Iron Ore Company of Canada, a U.S.-based firm, immediately before his election as Conservative Party leader, and the leading light of the Chrétien government remains Paul Martin, well-known for his corporate connections and values. Although Prime Minister Chrétien poses as the "little guy from Shawinigan," his deep ties to "big business" rest barely below his superficial populism. His career as a lawyer was linked exclusively to corporate firms, and his daughter's marriage to the son of the corporate baron Paul Desmarais underscores those ties. Indeed, the senior Desmarais has been called "the godfather of the Canadian political communities" because of his intimate connections with Trudeau, Mulroney, Chrétien, and Paul Martin Jr. The very marginalization of the "social Liberals," especially Lloyd Axworthy, and the advancement of the pro-corporation Martin and Roy MacLaren to the key economic posts in the Chrétien government signalled that the corporate agenda held top priority for Mulroney's successors.[35] The net results of these connections amounted to a veritable alliance in which corporate Canada called the shots.

This unholy linkage has resulted in the adoption by first the Conservatives and later the Liberals of the big-business agenda of globalization. Both the Business Council on National Issues (BCNI), an organization of 160 chief executive officers (CEOs) directed by Thomas d'Aquino, and the pro-corporation "think tanks," exemplified by the C.D. Howe and Fraser institutes, have promoted the neo-liberal corporate program for the past two decades. The Mulroney Tories and the Chrétien Liberals have pushed it relentlessly in the political realm. Internationally this drive took the form of the two trade deals, the FTA passed by the Tories in 1989 and the NAFTA legislated into place by the Liberals in 1994.[36]

In spite of the golden promises surrounding the free-trade deals, they have proved devastating to most Canadians. Duncan Cameron and Mel Watkins, in *Canada under Free Trade*, produced an avalanche of evidence chronicling this human cost. During the two years prior to the enactment of the FTA, 803,000 new jobs were created in Canada, but the first two years of the deal saw a precipitous decline — only 13,200 new jobs in 1989 and a net job loss of 7,400 in 1990. From January 1989 to the end of June 1992 the number of Canadians who lost their jobs increased by a total of 583,000. By June 1992 the unemployment rate had risen to a staggering 11.6 per cent, with a total jobless figure in excess of 1.6 million workers. Plant closures multiplied at an alarming rate, with manufacturing companies relocating in cheap labour havens like the U.S. South and Mexico. National indebtedness also escalated in the wake of the FTA. Canada's trade accounts plummeted during the Mulroney years. The nation had a trade surplus of $6.7 billion when he became prime minister; by 1991 Canada had fallen into the "red" to the tune of over $77.8 billion. Debt and deficit were products of the ruinous linking of Canada to U.S. capital.[37]

NAFTA has served to intensify an already grim situation. Despite Mulroney's and Chrétien's promises of "jobs, jobs, jobs," NAFTA exacerbated the unemployment situation. Massive profits and words of "recovery" notwithstanding, NAFTA opened the door to an increased flight of capital and high-paid manufacturing jobs to points south where cheap labour abounds. Even the United States and Mexico experienced massive job losses in the wake of NAFTA. Almost all the new employment that has occurred in the FTA/NAFTA years has been in the form of low-paying, insecure "McJobs," while 280,000 full-time jobs were lost in 1995 and 1996. From the early 1990s to 1996 the unemployment rate held at around the 10 per cent mark despite soaring profits; the proportion of the working-age population holding jobs fell from 62.4 per cent to 58.6 per cent; the ratio of part-time jobs rose from 13.9 per cent to 18.6 per cent; the gender gap in wages increased for the first time in thirty years; and the proportion of young families living in poverty climbed from 28 per cent to 45.1 per cent. NAFTA also strips from our citizens control over our natural resources and culture. The agreement has transferred realms that have a major impact on our lives — culture, environment, social welfare — into the hands of pro-corporation bodies that don't have to answer to the normal democratic process. The result in Mexico was the Chiapas rebellions. The corporate free-trade agenda has lined the pockets of the few at the expense of the many. As elections and polls showed, the majority of Canadians did not want these deals. Before their elections, both Mulroney and Chrétien opposed the agreements. Before the voter they said one thing; before their corporate masters they did another.[38]

Both the Mulroney Tories and Chrétien Liberals have echoed and enacted the corporate barons' cries of a deficit crisis that, in their opinion, demands massive government spending cuts, especially in the arena of social legislation. Otherwise, they argue, Canada will not meet the competitive standards required in the new global marketplace. Economist Mel Watkins and writer Linda McQuaig have revealed the corporate "scam" that lies behind the actual deficit crisis, without denying the reality of the problem.[39] Since the mid-1970s the combined indebtedness of all three levels of government has doubled, and the cost of financing the federal debt, as a percentage of gross domestic product (GDP), rose from 3.2 per cent in 1980 to 6.3 per cent in 1991. The costs to the governments have escalated as represented by the percentage of the annual budget used for such payments. In 1980-81 that figure amounted to 16.8 per cent; in 1990-91 it was 28.4 per cent. The large annual deficits continued to build in that period, and they were lumped onto an already staggering debt.[40]

Despite this reality, the deficit has become a political weapon used by government and its corporate allies to weaken the social infrastructure of the nation, to dismantle Canada's social-safety network, to strengthen public support for the rich and powerful, and to open Canada to the globalization campaign of the transnational corporations. This is the crux of the matter. The lie is not the assertion that Canada has run up a dangerous deficit and we need to do something about it. Rather, the scam is that Canadians in general, and especially the poor, are blamed for the problem and are expected to pay to relieve it. But it was the wealthy elite that created the debt, and they should be the ones held accountable for balancing the ledger. First of all, the massive debt arose chiefly out of corporate and government investment policy. The greatest cause for the massive debt remains the interest that must be paid to service it, and the size of these payments results directly from a high-interest-rate policy set in place during the last decade. These rates were not the "natural results" of unalterable economic laws, as some would have us believe. They were, rather, a political-corporate choice designed to serve the profit interests of the wealthy. To make matters worse, this "high-interest" policy led to increasing foreign investment in both debt and equity. For example, in 1978 foreigners held only roughly 15 per cent of Canadian government marketable bonds. By 1991 they held 38 per cent. This reality enhances the nation's economic captivity to others, especially the United States. In the years from 1986 to 1991 the government would have been operating in the black had it not been for ruinously high interest rates. The possibility of a surplus was obliterated by interest payments on the debt that amounted to $206 billion. The monetary policy of the Tory government and its corporate allies saddled our nation with its debt problem.[41]

The intimate ties with the corporate elite of both the Mulroney Tories and the Chrétien Liberals emerge in their respective taxation policies, policies that favour the rich at the expense of the poor and middle classes. Historically public expenditures have been met through taxing a nation's citizenry. In theory the government renders necessary services to its residents. These services are paid for by the public at large through a taxation system. The issue is not whether to tax or not, but whether the taxes are sufficient to the task — and are they fair?

The problem has never been the payment of too many taxes used to support too many unwieldy social programs. Historically the real issue has revolved around fairness. Throughout its brief existence the nation's taxing policy has mirrored injustice. The tiny elite of rich and powerful have been and remain the direct beneficiaries of a taxation system designed not just to protect their wealth but to increase it. Only with the rise of popular protest, largely in the farm movements of the Prairies, were concerted efforts made to render the tax system more equitable. Under such pressure a tepid personal income tax emerged, as much a result of wartime exigencies as a response to agrarian pressure.[42]

Although the Canadian government set in place, from the 1940s on, a graduated personal income tax, corporation taxes, and even an inheritance tax, the wealthy elite has avoided or weakened the payment of these equitable dues through its ties with the two major political parties. This cozy arrangement was threatened by the 1967 report of the federal government's Royal Commission on Taxation chaired by Kenneth Carter, a managing partner in one of the nation's leading accounting firms. The report sent a shock wave throughout the business community. The document spoke of an unfair system in which the middle and poorer sectors of the populace paid more than their share of taxes while the rich paid less. Contrary to the wishes of the corporate elite, the Carter Commission's report called for taxation of capital gains and inheritances as well as the closing of some significant corporate tax "loopholes." Carter and his courageous committee members were excoriated by their "high-rolling" colleagues, both at work and in their social life.[43]

Under the barrage of business protests generated by the Carter Report, the new Trudeau government was forced to place tax reform on its agenda. Its initial White Paper sought to find a middle ground between the Carter proposals and the business community, but no one was pleased by this compromise. Although it softened most of the Commission's proposals, it still insisted on capital gains taxation. The major corporations pressured provincial governments to demand that Ottawa back down, and the elite-dominated Senate turned up the heat as well. By June 1971, when the Trudeau government tabled its tax bill, it had not only abandoned Carter's principles, but also compromised even its own White Paper. Capital-gains taxes were softened, personal and corporate taxes were not integrated, tax breaks were given for corporate takeovers, and the estate tax was erased. Nothing had changed by the time Finance Minister Marc Lalonde brought down the 1983 budget of Trudeau's final government. It was a document of extensive tax breaks for the rich in the form of tax credit and relaxed tax rules for investors.[44]

The following Conservative and Liberal governments built on this already existing unjust tax system. The Tory government placed its tax load heavily upon the middle class and poorer consumers while lightening the obligations for the wealthy to pay. Personal taxes rose rapidly while corporate taxes went into a precipitous decline. In 1980-81 personal income tax represented 40.6 per cent of all federal budget revenues; the corporate share was 16.6 per cent. By 1991-92 the personal income tax portion had risen to 49.6 per cent, while the corporate portion had plummeted to a mere 6.8 per cent. This deepening contrast can be found in provincial governments as well. These statistics reflect clear government policy designed to provide tax-break windfalls for the major corporations. For example, Mulroney's so-called tax reform of 1987 reduced the federal corporate tax rate from 36 per cent to 28 per cent. In 1989 Canada's industries paid only 17.8 per cent, significantly less than the 25.2 per cent average noted for members of the Organization for Economic Co-operation and Development (OECD). From the time that Mulroney took power until 1992, personal income taxes rose in the neighbourhood of $17 billion and corporation taxes augmented by a mere $2 billion. About forty years earlier, in 1950, individuals and corporations paid a roughly equivalent percentage, but by 1991 the individual portion had risen to nine times that of the corporate allotment.[45]

This transfer away from corporate to personal income taxation is not unfair at all, it has been argued, because Canadians in general have a progressive income tax system. The approach is supposed to guarantee that the rich pay their fair share. The reality is that individual taxes are either regressive or progressive. When they are regressive everybody pays the same amount regardless of ability to pay. Regressive taxes include the sales taxes both provincially and federally, and the Goods and Services Tax (GST), legislated by the Mulroney government. These types of indirect and regressive taxation account for 38 per cent of total taxes; of the G-7 countries only England has a higher rate. All revenue raised this way is a bonanza to the rich and an assault on the poor.[46]

The personal income tax is progressive in theory, but so riddled with loopholes that the rich pay very little; the poor pay through the reduction of social services; and the increasingly strapped middle class pays the major portion. The refusal to tax capital gains and corporations helps wealthy individuals to avoid paying their share of income tax. For example, from 1980 to 1987 the nation's banks made profits of $7.64 billion (with record profits in the mid-1990s), but paid income taxes at the rate of only 2.48 per cent. During these same years the entire Canadian financial sector amassed profits of $54.818 billion while paying taxes at the rate of 11.2 per cent. In 1987 alone corporations owed an estimated and whopping $10 billion in unpaid taxes. Wealthy individuals, the immediate beneficiaries of the vast profits and unpaid taxes, are the very ones who hire tax attorneys and accountants to use the provided loopholes to further reduce what they must pay the government. These escape hatches include such things as deferments, write-offs of capital costs, depletion allowances, capital gains exemptions, protective legislation, government low-interest loans and grants, foundations and trusts, and other tax shelters. Shockingly, this often means that the very wealthy pay no taxes at all, and in most cases they pay very little. Even tax cuts supposedly carried out in the name of fairness tend to benefit the wealthy. In the mid-1980s Michael Wilson proposed tax cuts amounting to $3.1 billion. But only $257 million of that amount (a mere 8 per cent) would be redistributed to the poorest 26 per cent of the Canadian public. The top income group (2 per cent of the population) would receive 12 per cent of that total, or $379 million. Such a prejudicial system in favour of the rich and powerful translates into a revenue loss of between $35 billion and $50 billion annually.[47]

In spite of rhetoric to the contrary, Jean Chrétien's Liberals proved to be clones of the previous Tories when it came to taxation issues. Just as they abandoned their anti-Free Trade policies, they also turned their backs on promises to scuttle the regressive GST. Even worse, their government recommended that a sales tax on food and prescription drugs be added to the existing system. Liberal tax policy in the late 1990s continued the Tory practices of loopholes, deferrals, capital-gains cuts, and tax rate deductions for the wealthy and their institutions, showing yet again that the nation's two traditional parties were funded and controlled by big business.[48]

The alliance of the corporate and political elites, as exemplified by a system of unjust taxation, is a moral outrage. It directly attacks the poor and vulnerable and stands as a violation of Biblical *shalôm*. Neil Brooks and Linda McQuaig provide an apt critique of the Canadian approach to tax legislation:

> The issue is no longer "fairness," but "competitiveness." This tends to obscure class issues, leaving the impression that we are all struggling together to help Canada maintain its place in world markets. . . .
>
> Certainly, abandoning the goal of progressive taxation lends credence to the belief that differences in income and wealth represent deserved differences. . . . We utterly reject this approach, arguing instead that the way the market distributes resources has no moral justification.[49]

The NDP Betrayal

> O you who turn justice to wormwood, and cast down righteousness to the earth!
> — *Amos 5:7*

The New Democratic Party (NDP) and its predecessor, the Co-operative Commonwealth Federation (CCF), have built their reputations on being the voice of the neglected majority of the nation. Arising from the grass-roots protests of oppressed farmers and workers in the first three decades of the twentieth century, the CCF and later the NDP have championed left-wing and social-justice causes for the better part of the last sixty years. However, under the rubric of trying to win elections and run provincial governments, the NDP has experienced a serious erosion of principle in the name of pragmatism. In so doing it has lost the confidence of the marginalized and the grass-roots militants that gave it both its strength and integrity. It has also reduced the public discourse to cosmetic social change and retired the vision of a radical social transformation laid out at the founding CCF convention at Regina in 1933.

This trend has become most glaringly apparent in recent NDP provincial governments. Certainly these governments have put important reforms in place and have made genuine efforts to save industries and jobs. They have set programs in motion to put the unemployed back to work. They have introduced pay equity measures. As a result of NDP leadership, Ontario pays the highest minimum wage in Canada. New Democrat governments, despite the economic pressures, have outspent previous governments in such critical areas as non-profit housing, rent control, and child-care. They have made efforts to place significant numbers of women in high profile positions throughout the government sector. The Ontario NDP passed important pro-labour legislation.[50]

Not surprisingly the business elites and the corporate-controlled media have excoriated these governments and have been unable to contain their glee when presented with NDP blunders. That response was to be expected, but what remains most disheartening has been the NDP's capitulation to the corporate agenda in both language and program. NDP governments have jumped on the bandwagon of "deficitophobia," insisting that costs and programs must be reduced and more revenue raised to fight the debt. Further, the fashion in which provincial NDP governments have tackled these issues echoes the programs promoted by the business community and its partisan allies in the other major parties. Social programs have been cut, leading to job losses throughout the public sector. The Ontario NDP's "social contract" legislation negated collective-bargaining agreements with the public-sector unions and, by so doing, invited employers to do the same.[51]

NDP timidity in power has wounded thousands upon thousands of grass-roots militants. Its brand of realism is a barely warmed-over version of the economic public-relations scam manufactured by the barons of Bay Street and their allies. We expect that scam of the elite, but when it comes from the leaders of the party of J.S. Woodsworth and Tommy Douglas, it can only be seen as a betrayal.

Corporate Control of the Media, Culture, and Education

> You [people], why shut your hearts so long, loving delusions, chasing
> after lies.   — *Psalm 4:2*

For about a century, radicals and progressives have wrestled with the question of why masses of the oppressed have permitted a tiny elite to manipulate and crush them year after year. Certainly the element of fear — fear of job loss, fear of arrest, torture, and even death — stands out as a critical factor. This ever-present hint of terror should never be underestimated. But there are more sophisticated means of manipulation that the wealthy and powerful have used to subjugate the majority of the population. These means have often taken the form of corporate control of the mechanisms that create, shape, and sustain the prevailing ideology of any given society. Habitually this involves the elite's domination of the mass media, education, and popular culture.

In Canada, before Confederation, issues of survival were paramount, and the handful of educational institutions during that epoch made certain that culture and information remained under elitist domination. With Confederation and the building of national railway lines came the development of mass schools and newspapers, realities that opened the doors of information and learning to the majority of the population. Nonetheless, these very opportunities were subject to the control and manipulation of the elites. A truly popular press emerged only with grass-roots protest movements, but these newspapers never had the financial resources to compete with those owned by newspaper magnates.[52]

The evolution and development of Canada's school system reflected a similar ruling-class bias. The school promoters of the early years viewed education as a means of success and advancement, as a road towards social mobility. Training in the social mores of polite middle-class Victorian society was a must. The system inexorably linked education and refinement. A person could achieve civility through the possession of capital and property. To be sure, educational reformers, such as Egerton Ryerson, were also committed to broadening the educational system to include workers and the poor, but these leaders were blinded by the illusions of middle-class democratic values. Their inclusion of the underprivileged was advocated in the name of transforming the uncouth and rebellious attitudes of the commoners into the more civilized behaviour and values of their social betters. However, many of the nation's children could not take advantage of schooling for very long in their young lives. From the end of the last century until Canada declared war in 1939, the exigencies of family survival demanded that working-class children leave school early to toil in the factories.[53]

Even before World War II popular culture had been co-opted by the moguls of the growing mass media. Popular magazines, pulp novels, radio, and movie theatres pandered to adventure, fantasy, and various forms of escapism designed both to indulge and sedate the populace. These same media were also replete with the dominant values of the social and financial elites.[54]

In the decades after the Second World War, control of mass forms of education and communication by the wealthy and powerful grew to lethal proportions. Opportunities for alternate forms of media and education were reduced by a combination of the wealthy's increasing ownership of prewar media and elitist control of television and the emerging computer revolution. The "hegemonic" control of this phenomenon can be divided into three parts: the educational system, the mass media, and popular culture.

1 The educational system

The use of education to mould and control the population along the lines devised by the wealthy and powerful has not changed since Egerton Ryerson's day, nor has the promulgation of a broad blend of middle-class values including hard work, competition, success, patriotism, and middle-of-the-road rationalism. These establishment values undergird the entire school curriculum; and they are imbedded in a patriarchal and hierarchical system modelled along the transmission lines of factories characteristic of the age of industrialization. In this system teachers are treated like workers hired to produce a uniform product, namely students moulded into producers and consumers prepared to replicate the ideology of the dominant system through their lives and their labour. This is not to say that Canada's educational institutions do not employ many creative teachers who are dedicated, in their very teaching, to systemic and even radical change that would serve the interests of the so-called underclasses of our society. Nor am I suggesting that there are not some innovative programs already in place that do just that. But as a whole the existing system is controlled by elites and the ideology that those elites want the public to espouse; and this very oppression has been accepted as normal and appropriate by the vast majority of the populace. One radical educational critic, Sandro Contenta, suggests by way of contrast the need for an education that encourages decentralization, rebellious thinking, a co-operative emphasis, a partnership between teachers and students, and experiential learning through storytelling and the creation of new myths.[55]

In the midst of such internal contradictions our schools have also fallen under the corporate attack. The existing educational system, with its blend of failures and creative efforts, has become subject to assaults from a business and political alliance of the right. Increasingly our schools are expected to intensify ideological allegiance to the big-business worldview and to produce students shaped to the labour needs of that corporate "brave new world" known as globalization. The school itself is fast becoming a blatant marketplace of products being hawked before a captive audience of students. As governments adopt the privatization agenda and cut back grants to education, schools are forced to solicit and accept corporate moneys with the attached strings that come with these "gifts." Such eroding of the public sector in education invites a two-tiered system of favoured educational facilities for the well-to-do and inferior schools for the poor and working-class families.[56] Instead of genuine reform, as suggested by Contenta and others, our schools suffer the obliteration of humane values from our classrooms. Teachers and their unions reel under corporate-governmental alliances while more direct domination of the educational system and its curricula by the business elites intensifies at an alarming pace.

2 The mass media

Although the prewar mass media were controlled by society's elite, the over fifty-year period following the Second World War has been marked by a phenomenal increase and concentration of corporate control of the media, including newspapers, magazines, radio, and television. Concentration and ownership by a corporate elite rise exponentially given the important role of advertising in these media to meet cost and profit needs. For example, from 1954 to 1968 revenue from advertising in the television industry rose by an astonishing 1,272 per cent. By 1971 in the newspaper and periodical business a full 73.3 per cent of revenue came from advertising, a figure that rose to over 80 per cent by the 1990s. In radio broadcasting advertising picks up 100 per cent of the cost. This reality plays an important role in shaping news content to fit the wishes of the major companies who buy ad space from the media.[57]

Outside of the ability of corporate advertisers to influence content, the very escalation of media control by a handful of the corporate elite is staggering. James Winter has documented this chilling reality in his book *Democracy's Oxygen*. In television, by the mid-1980s, over sixty per cent of the eighty-one private commercial stations were operated by business groups owning more than one station, and half of them were held by groups possessing three or more stations. By the mid-1990s this concentration had intensified with the media expansions of Rogers Communications. With its takeover of Maclean Hunter, the Rogers conglomerate increased its cable audience by 71 per cent, and its holdings came to include the Home Shopping Network, seventy video stores, thirty-one radio stations, four television stations, a youth specialty channel, one-third share in Unitel, the Rogers Cantel cellular phone company, ten new newspapers (*The Financial Post*, the Toronto Sun Publishing chain, and some weeklies) and five of the ten top-selling magazines in the country. Not surprisingly Rogers contributed slightly under $100,000 to the Liberal Party in the very year that the corporation had sought approval from the CRTC for its acquisition of Maclean Hunter. Though not a substantial figure by U.S. standards, certainly it seemed to be enough to get the job done.[58]

The newspaper industry has gone through a similar process of concentration, and this despite well-documented warnings by the Kent Commission (1981). In 1980 the Thomson chain bought out F.P. Publications, thus reducing the major newspaper chains to two, and the 1990s have witnessed the success of Conrad Black's Hollinger Inc. in cornering the Canadian newspaper market. Hollinger owns 60 out of 105 Canadian dailies, or 71 per cent, and reaches 43 per cent of the national readership. Most other Canadian newspaper readers fall under the proprietorship of a few other corporate giants, such as Ken Thomson and Paul Desmarais. In New Brunswick the K.C. Irving chain controls the province's four English-language dailies. Cross-media ownership is now the norm, as in the case of Ted Roger's acquisitions.[59] Linda McQuaig summarizes the net impact of such media control:

> At the most basic level, we must always remember that virtually all media outlets are owned by rich, powerful members of the elite. To assume that this fact has no influence on the ideas they present would be equivalent to assuming that, should the entire media be owned by, say, labour unions, women's groups or social workers, this would have no impact on the editorial content.[60]

Control of the media by the elite remains most publicly damaging in the arena of content. The ownership by a few guarantees that the corporate agenda dominates the content of the mass media. The very basis of standard reporting is the fundamental worldview shared by the big-business magnates. Communications researcher James Winter demonstrates in great detail how the media have adopted a series of truisms that constantly parade before the public and are never or rarely criticized. He lists fifty-four of these truisms. They include, for example:

- the unfettered free market system is the fairest and best guiding principle;
- we all pay far too much in taxes, thanks to overspending by bloated governments;

- a small group of radical feminists is constantly whining about problems that either don't exist or are relatively small; and
- labour struggles are senseless, avoidable contests created by unions' unwillingness to negotiate in good faith.

Given that the mass media remain the most fundamental means used to establish consensus, it is easy to see how important is the reality of "social hegemony." We are shaped daily by the very media that are controlled by and operate for the tiny corporate elite of our society. The mass dailies, periodicals, and especially television socialize us constantly, or in the words of critic Noam Chomsky, they "manufacture consent." By contrast the alternate forms of public discourse tend to be invisible.[61]

The corporate-owned media exclude systematically high-profile news items that receive dominant attention only in the alternative publications. Each year an organization known as Project Censored Canada (PCC) announces its ten most important "underreported" stories. The 1995 list included "American-style health care is coming to Canada," "Social spending not cause of deficits, debt," and "Canadian media mum on human rights in Mexico." The PCC demonstrates how the mass media control the flow of information by assaulting the reading, listening, and viewing public with quantities of more trivial or more sensationalist news, designed to titillate rather than inform. In 1995 these "overcovered" stories or "Junk Food News" items included "The O.J. Simpson trial," "Actor Hugh Grant nabbed with prostitute," and "The Paul Bernardo trial." As these findings show, the corporate-owned media control the flow of information in a manner that replicates and promotes the elite's narrow agenda. Democracy emerges as the most significant victim in such a shrinkage of the public discourse.[62]

3 Popular culture

In its positive sense, "popular culture" refers to alternative sources of communication and expression generated from grass-roots sectors of the populace. The folk music of rural Quebec or Cape Breton Island, ethnic dances and costumes, and the powerful poetry emerging from working-class life are examples from the Canadian scene.[63] This culture survives as a voice of liberation in an increasingly oppressive society. On the negative side, though, is the "popular culture" designed by the corporate establishment to create a mass consensus that will support the big business agenda, or at least not threaten it. The entire society suffers endless bombardment with these messages. They offer success financially, personally, and sexually. They promise to make a person beautiful, and they hold out a virtually painless and pleasure-filled world. Advertising and vapid television "sit-coms" tell us to buy our way to a consumer heaven, to surround ourselves with gadgets designed to bring us this earthly paradise—the right home, the car that will change our lives, the VCR, the computer, Nintendo games, beer, deodorant. Our needs are constantly defined for us, with products readily available to fulfil them—all at a marketable price. This is not "popular culture." Better we call it "pop culture," a manufactured and manipulative product designed to control and co-opt. Even genuine popular culture is frequently absorbed and marketed by entertainment capitalism. Jazz becomes big business, the garb of protest is sold at exorbitant prices in trendy boutiques, and the militant folk music of the sixties degenerates into the multimillion-dollar industry of the eighties and nineties. The Bank of Montreal's use of Bob Dylan's "The Times They Are a Changin'" exemplifies this trend. Such is oppression at its very deepest—a domination etched on our being by a subtle blend of stimulation and sedation.[64]

Control of the Churches

> For all, least no less than greatest, all are out for dishonest gain;
> prophet no less than priest, all practice fraud.   — *Jeremiah 6:13*

Where does the church fit in all this? Although the church has long played a role in resisting and fighting oppression, there is, tragically, another side to the story. The church has also been an oppressor, and this role has dominated much of its institutional life since the Constantinian compromise of the fourth century CE. In the name of God the church has pursued bloody crusades against Muslims, Jews, so-called witches, and heretics, and it used religion as justification for keeping the poor "in their place." Even the liberating forces of the Reformation left their harsh trails. In modern times the church has linked itself with the established power against progressive movements both reformist and revolutionary. In short, the church has played a substantive role throughout its two millennia history as an ally of oppressive forces against the poor and marginalized. That has remained its greatest shame.[65]

Organized Christianity in Canada, from its beginnings in New France, has borne the stigma of these contradictions. Until the post-World War II epoch, the church joined with the schools (many of which were its own) and the mass media to generate those fundamental social values and public order promoted by the dominant classes. The

Protestant mainline church was an established and privileged part of anglo-bourgeois culture, and much of its passion from Confederation to the 1920s was used to create and shape a nation along the narrow lines of that culture. In Quebec the francophone Catholic Church had a long history of control and privilege that it strove mightily to maintain against more modern and secular forces both oppressive and liberating.[66] The Christian churches have consistently and brutally mistreated Canada's aboriginal peoples.

In the twentieth century the Christian church continued to play an ambiguous role in the tension between oppression and liberation. Protestantism's most prophetic churches — the Methodists, Presbyterians, and Anglicans — were also the most privileged ecclesiastical institutions of English Canada. The barons of industry and finance, as well as leading politicians, populated these churches' pews and exercised lay leadership in various ecclesiastical institutions. Boosters of urban expansion in the Prairies were the pillars of the mainline Protestant churches in the "boom" cities of the West. A prime example was Winnipeg's "Merchant Prince" and one-time mayor, J.H. Ashdown. He and his compatriots were "rugged individualists," imbued with the Protestant work ethic and committed to the ideals of private property and the free-enterprise system. Ashdown himself, an active Methodist, chaired the board at Wesley College, where young seminarians trained for the ministry of their church. On the board Ashdown joined J.A.M. Aikins, the town's major corporate lawyer, the businessman R.T. Riley, and the Tory premier of Manitoba (1900-15) Rodmond Roblin.[67] These Protestant barons were not motivated by cruelty or naked acquisitiveness alone. Their hunger for profit and power grew out of their distinctive brand of patriotism and Christianity. Their devotion to the faith, however genuine, upheld the existing capitalistic worldview. Indeed, they used their Christianity to justify their economic power. These men and their faith-perceptions dominated the institutional churches, and their money remained the chief source of ecclesiastical funds.

As men used to power and influence, they were not prepared to tolerate opposition, even if it came from the pulpits of their churches. As a result Ashdown and his allies turned against the prophetic voices in their own churches. Over a period of a few years they were able to marginalize the Methodist radicals on the left wing of the social gospel movement. James Shaver Woodsworth, Canada's most noted social gospeller, was edged out of the ministry, and Reverend A.E. Smith of Brandon was not supported by his conference or the national church when he sought to form a string of labour churches across the west.

The "social gospel" chair of the Methodist Department of Evangelism and Social Service co-operated with the RCMP in spying on and reporting about these labour churches. As early as 1916-17 Ashdown and the board dismissed the renowned progressive and popular professor of Wesley College, Salem Bland, along with another social gospel advocate, and an Ashdown-favoured conservative emerged as principal. A counteroffensive erupted at McDougall Methodist Church in Winnipeg against its controversial pastor William Ivens. His advocacy of pacifism, especially during the war, and his outspoken support of labour causes led members of the parish to seek his dismissal.[68]

Despite progressive pro-labour rhetoric promulgated by Presbyterian and Methodist conference meetings, the churches' own record as an employer contrasted shamefully with its professed convictions — as the dismissal of the most outspoken Methodist leaders illustrates. Another involved the reaction of the social gospel denominations to the printers' strike of 1921. Virtually every church voice spoke out against the strikers, who were seeking a forty-four-hour workweek. Although Methodist progressives pressured the church to uphold the strikers' demands, the Methodist publishing firm hired scab labour and continued operations.[69]

In Quebec most of the church's energy from the rise of industrialism to the Quiet Revolution of the 1960s was spent in defending and enhancing its power and control throughout the province. Justice for the worker and the poor received a lower priority and often took the form of paternalistic charity. Quebec francophone elites were virtually all practising Catholics, and the church's hierarchy remained deeply enmeshed in political, educational, and social welfare matters. When the church did support working-class organizations, such as the Confédération des Travailleurs Catholiques du Canada (CTCC), a trade union federation, and the youthful Jeunesse Ouvrière Catholique (JOC), these were often arms of hierarchical politics controlling working-class life. To be sure, both the CTCC and the JOC increased their militancy over the years, but this was due more to working-class realities and their grass-roots membership than to the express desires of ecclesiastical leaders.[70]

Paralleling the Protestant establishment in the Prairies, the Quebec Catholic Church persecuted its radicals, waffled in its support for unions, and acted as a strikebreaking employer in critical labour disputes. The very values it promulgated within the CTCC were forthright indications of what could be expected from the church hierarchy in labour disputes. Class collaboration was part of the divine order of things. The church was committed to "industrial peace" and a "good social order." This meant a world devoid of strikes, actions that would only lead to disruptions of the social peace desired by the bishops. Behind this attempt to circumscribe labour's struggle within the boundaries of ecclesiastical social conservatism was a profound belief in natural inequality. Said CTCC Chaplain Father Hébert: "The Church has always maintained inequality, founded upon nature, as a dogma, because such inequality is desired by God and conforms to the providential nature of things. . . . To strive to suppress class inequality and replace it with a deceptive and illusory equality is to go against God's plan and wish to put a human order in place of God's order."[71]

It would be unfair to accuse the Québécois church of either cynicism or direct collusion with the barons of industry and finance. In fact, Quebec Catholicism was simultaneously naive and in an ambivalent position. On the one hand, it believed sincerely in the possibility of effective class collaboration with justice. On the other hand, it was a major part of elitist power in Quebec and saw the world from that perspective. However, its genuine commitment to working-class justice led it to taste a good dose of harsh reality. In spite of episcopal attempts to arbitrate labour disputes, the bishops increasingly discovered the intransigence and greed of the industrial barons. This growing awareness of class reality came to a head in the famous Asbestos Strike of 1949, during which large sectors of the church acted in solidarity with the workers. Included among the supporters was the archbishop of Montreal, Joseph Charbonneau. His public sympathy for the strikers so infuriated Maurice Duplessis that the premier used his influence with Rome to ensure the dismissal of the archbishop from his post. Although the Quebec church developed more avant-garde credentials after the Quiet Revolution, its evolution has been by no means unequivocal, as demonstrated in the well-publicized Tour Dominicain conflict of the early 1970s. This institution for the elderly, run by Dominican nuns, employed twenty-seven lay workers. Protesting low wages and the refusal of the sisters to allow them to unionize, these laity went out on strike. As in the earlier printers' strike of the 1920s, the church found itself in an awkward vacillating position. Its general inclination was to support an ecclesiastical institution, even though that institution exploited its own workers. At the same time, a more radical Catholic minority advocated for the workers.[72]

The situation today is markedly different from earlier times when the church was a major voice of the establishment and the general culture. Organized religion now finds itself increasingly marginalized. Our secular and consumer culture views the church as less and less relevant to its perceived needs. Ecclesiastical institutions display a sense of considerable desperation as they seek security and stability in a newly emerging Canada increasingly indifferent to traditional Christianity. Congregations and advocates of church growth struggle frantically to design parishes "with appeal" to once again fill pews and bring back overflowing offering plates. Reginald Bibby's recent book on the churches, *Unknown Gods*, reflects this marketplace mentality. Organized Christianity stands no longer as a powerful force for the status quo; instead it has been relegated to a minor backwater. Still, church radicals are not immune to attack from within ecclesiastical ranks. The activism of Catholic Tony Clarke against the FTA cost him his job with the Canadian Conference of Catholic Bishops, and in 1997 the Catholic archdiocese of Toronto banned "Exposing the Face of Corporate Rule," a poster produced by that city's Jesuit Centre.[73]

An Outrageous Lifestyle

> Alas for those who lie on beds of ivory, and lounge on their couches, . . . who sing idle songs to the sound of the harp . . . who drink wine from bowls, and anoint themselves with the finest oils, but are not grieved over the ruin of Joseph!   — *Amos 6:4-7*

Canada's corporate elite has extended its control not only over the financial and productive sectors of society but also over the political, social, cultural, and ecclesiastical realms. The overlords underscore their power through the profligate lifestyles and ethical values they promulgate and practice in direct opposition to Biblical religion. The personal salaries and income of this tiny elite are outrageous. At least twenty-five Canadian CEOs collected over $1 million in salaries, bonuses, and stock options in 1993, a figure which had escalated to fifty by 1996. That same year, Lawrence Bloomberg of First Marathon Inc. alone received $6.9 million, while four other Canadian CEOs (including Conrad Black) pulled in over $2 million. By 1996 Bloomberg had fallen to twelfth place, with Laurent Beaudoin of Bombardier Inc. raking in a compensation package of just over $19 million. Retirement benefits are just as shocking. In 1993 Paul Stern took away $6.1 million from Northern Telecom when he retired, while Cedric Ritchie of the Bank of Nova Scotia and David A. Nichol of Loblaw managed packages of $2.6 million and $2.3 million respectively. This profligacy contrasts scandalously with other wages within the society. The realm of what Ed Broadbent called "ordinary Canadians" reveals a much diminished picture of wages: autoworker ($52,700), coal-miner ($48,800), federal civil service manager ($42,500), nurse ($38,000), truck driver ($29,850), shoe salesperson ($14,600), and barber ($14,100). These statistics show that the media message of inflated salaries for unionized labour and public employees is a massive distortion.[74]

Yet Corporate Canada remains unembarrassed by the disparities. Justifications abound. Ian Delaney, CEO for Sherritt Inc., reacted to the debate on high corporate salaries by stating:

> And that brings me to Lawrence Bloomberg. Lawrence recently set a new high-water mark in executive compensation and has suffered intense criticism as a result. . . . One of Canada's less endearing qualities is our ability to deride success. We have developed the politics of envy to the highest degree. Consider: Lawrence comes from a modest background. . . . He did well. About 13 years ago he put together a small group of partners and established his own small business. In the intervening period, he has built that small firm into one of the largest independent investment dealers in the country.
>
> He has assumed all the risks an entrepreneur is supposed to accept. One of his rewards is public derision. Are we no longer prepared to let people win?[75]

Delaney's views are not exceptional. The values of aggression, competition, success, and "winning" blaze forth as virtuous, as if our national economic and social life were merely a football game in which winners deserve the spoils and losers suffer merely the dejection of a lost athletic contest. Such principles parade as "axioms," fundamental and unassailable laws of the universe. Such is the arrogance of wealth and power.

A quick perusal of business-oriented magazines on the shelves in corner convenience stores or of books marketed in the business sections of the few Canadian bookstore chains reveals a mythology of success and greed displayed as universal virtue. The June 1994 issue of *Success: The Magazine for Today's Entrepreneurial Mind* carried the laudatory cover story "From Mailman to Millionaire: How Steve Geppi Built a $250 Million Empire." Geppi made his fortune in the relatively superfluous medium of comic books, in contrast to the production of more socially useful items, such as food, clothing, or shelter; but this fact in the general scheme of things becomes irrelevant. The central focus remains success, the "rags-to-riches" heroics. Parallel stories dot *Profit: The Magazine for Canadian Entrepreneurs*. The table of contents in the June 1994 issue includes "The Winner" ("Our No. 1 company was founded as a sideline by a precocious coin-collecting ex-law professor") and "Selling Secrets" ("Growth companies know the key to successful marketing today: redefining their relationships with suppliers, clients and customers"). Our bookstores display a plethora of "win through riches" books, titles (picked at random) such as Bob Fifer, *Double Your Profits in Six Months or Less*; Charles J. Givens, *Wealth without Risk for Canadians*; Ted Levalliant, *Achieving Wealth for Canadians*; Mark Newsome and Jeffrey Zahn, *Taking Control: Your Blueprint for Financial Success*; and Gordon Pape, *Retiring Wealthy*. A title that is particularly striking is Wess Roberts's best-selling book, *Victory Secrets of Attila the Hun*. Attila the Hun, a symbol of barbarism and ruthless military action, has now become a business hero. The book's cover says it all: "1,500 years ago Attila got the competitive edge. Now he tells you how you can get it, too — His way."[76]

These dominant values — wealth, success, profit, power, all sought after virtually for their own sake — are the foundation of a veritable secular religion. In the Bible this faith system stands condemned again and again as idolatry. Jesus himself stated unequivocally, "You cannot be the slave both of God and money (Mammon)" (Matthew 6:24). Yet the ideology of wealth and success has marked the ruling elite's philosophy since the dawn of the capitalist era in Canada.[77]

The scandal of this elite moves beyond simply the control of wealth and power. Indeed, it spills over into daily living. The conspicuous consumption of the very wealthy is marked often by multiple cars, mansions and cottages, exclusive clubs, yachts, personal jets, extravagant parties, affairs, bribery, corruption. Still, society's "shakers and makers" cannot be categorized so simply. Some are satyrs, others are white-collar criminals, and still others are blatantly greedy without any will towards the betterment of society. However, the sin of the elite's lifestyle, in the fundamental Biblical sense, remains social rather than motivational. It is the destructive ideology and the arrogance that wealth and power produce that remain at issue, as well as the individualistic ethos that emerges from this. For over a century many of Canada's corporate barons have advocated their own brand of social betterment and have been active patrons of culture, philanthropy, and political and social reform. They stood as dominant forces within their nation and communities acting for their programs of "human improvement" to the exclusion of more grass-roots approaches. In fact, their very philanthropy proved profitable to them, both financially and in terms of public relations. At best, their good will has produced some charity but virtually no justice. Corporate magnates, for instance, have been among the strongest supporters of food banks, which became a common feature in the recession-ridden 1990s. The retail grocery conglomerates, who endorse food banks, use them to unload unsold perishables, to encourage the charitably minded public to buy more food for those in need, and to present themselves as concerned for the needy (a marvellous advertising gimmick). In the entire process few ask the more fundamental questions about maldistribution of income, taxes, and global food distribution. The well-known Ronald McDonald Houses found near some major hospitals reflect a similar strategy. They are publicized as havens for suffering families to use while they visit loved ones in hospitals. That the families are encouraged to pay for the rooms is downplayed, as is the tax benefit accruing from this "donation." This highlights the "public relations" character of this philanthropy. That McDonald's is notorious for its low-wage and anti-union policy is lost in the brilliant PR campaign to present the hamburger chain as a model corporate citizen.[78]

Although some members of the elite exude compassion and care towards others, that is not the point. The issue remains the very inordinate wealth and power of this tiny group, a wealth and power that allow its members to control the economy, politics, culture, media, and even definitions of charity found in the society. Such excess remains unacceptable to Biblical religion; it stands condemned as idolatrous. It is oppression, and they are the oppressors. The cost of their excess emerges in the endemic manipulation and misery heaped upon the oppressed masses in Canada and abroad.

4

The Oppressed in Canada

[God] expected justice, but saw bloodshed; righteousness, but heard a cry! Ah, you who join house to house, who add field to field, until there is room for no one but you. . . . Ah, you who are wise in your own eyes . . . who acquit the guilty for a bribe, and deprive the innocent of their rights. — *Isaiah 5:7b-8, 21, 23*

MISERY AND INJUSTICE REMAIN THE LOT OF MOST OF THE WORLD'S people and, to varying degrees, for all too many Canadians as well. Various sectors of Canada's populace fall under the yoke of oppression generated directly or indirectly by the concentration of wealth and power in the hands of the few. A glimpse of these harassed groups past and present provides graphic commentary on the human costs of the oppression. Certainly those people who are crushed by the juggernaut of the tiny elite of oppressors embody a pluralism of backgrounds, characteristics, and experiences. Their skin colours vary, as do their ethnic backgrounds. They embrace both genders; they live in rural and urban settings. They include the employed and the unemployed. Most are heterosexual, but many are gays and lesbians. Their ages range from infancy to the very elderly. Some are "have-nots." Others are "have-a-littles." Some have modest "nest-eggs" that provide a sense of security. These differences are important, because they shape people's lives individually and collectively.

The oppressed also share fundamentals in common. They fall individually and as an aggregate under the heel of the oppressors who control Canadian society, and among them we seek the necessary solidarity to challenge the nation's overlords. As well, almost all these groups exist as part of a larger collective that can be called, for want of a better word, *workers*. Given the central character of wage labour in our society as a definition of both self-worth and remuneration, I define workers as that majority of our population that depend upon revenue granted to them on the basis of what they produce with their labour.

This remuneration usually takes the form of a paycheque or, in the case of family farmers, or self-employed (including homeworkers), money paid for goods produced. In short, they have only their labour or labour products to sell in a vast marketplace created, defined, and owned by others, and usually they remain only a paycheque or harvest away from marginalization and poverty. But, as well, some workers integral to the system receive little or no remuneration save for a "pat on the head," if that. Volunteer service, child-rearing, and "house work," all tasks overwhelmingly performed by women, illustrate the patriarchal dimension of a wage-labour and class system of exploitation. Even those professionals who are usually called "middle-class" might only be able to stave off economic disaster for a few months if they lose their jobs.

The challenge of examining this vast majority globally and nationally demands a twofold perspective. First of all, there is the descriptive issue. We need to honour both what we share in common and what stands as unique to each identifiable group within the marginalized. Beyond this essential task lies the structural concern of organizing this description in such a way that it leads to a fair and accurate integration of each category utilized. The framework I use in this chapter, though hardly unique to me, represents one possible approach in a continuing dialogue among those victimized by the system of power and oppression as described in the previous chapter. To make a greater claim for this model would embody an ideology seeking to impose itself for its own sake, and that, of course, smacks of oppression. Even worse, a framework etched in marble stands invariably as a source of division, when what needs to emerge is unity.

Our second challenge is the forging of solidarity among the oppressed. Certainly, a tiny elite controls and oppresses the majority of the population through the wealth and structural power at its disposal. But the oppressed have the overwhelming power of numbers. Why then do the oppressed remain the oppressed? Fundamentally, it is because their various sectors also embody elements of their oppressors. Those of us who suffer under the elitist yoke become complicit with it. We respond to corporate power's "divide and conquer" agenda by turning on each other. By a judicious mix of half-truths and lies, we have been manipulated into accepting such either/or positions as jobs or environment; gender equity or job seniority; good jobs or an open policy towards immigrants; growth or unemployment; family values or same-sex benefits; productive citizens or "welfare bums"; growth or aboriginal land claims; public sector versus private; professionals versus workers; urban versus rural; and the list goes on.

The oppressed also fall victim to the elite's destructive ideology. The elite's control of education, the media, and culture bombards us with "oppressor" values, which we internalize — Noam Chomsky's "manufactured consent." Greed, acquisitiveness, and a sense of entitlement infect us all. The "divide and conquer" mentality emerges in the in-fighting generated by such fears as job loss. It also etches itself on our very souls by being internalized, so that it stands as a roadblock to solidarity. The participation by the oppressed in their own oppression is a factor to be kept very much in mind as we struggle to understand the shaping of injustice in Canada. As we do this, whether Christian or not, we will increase our strength and ability to participate in that solidarity so necessary to combat oppression.

Economic and Class Oppression

Perhaps the most obvious form of oppression is economic servitude. Workers, as I define them, embody this category in a broadly inclusive fashion. Yet this larger group contains some variation, and with that in mind, I first consider the role of those traditionally described as workers in both the private and public sectors. From there I turn to the more varied manifestations of this broader category.

The Workers

> I mean to visit you for the judgment and I am going to be a ready witness . . . against those who oppress the wage-earner.
> — *Malachi 3:5*

At the dawn of the twentieth century the situation of the traditional working class proved precarious indeed. Wages were minimal, frequently at subsistence or below. To survive, workers were forced to toil six days a week throughout the year without any vacation or social welfare legislation to meet crises such as lay-offs, sickness, or accident. So vulnerable was the labouring family that often both parents and children had to become wage-earners. The existence of costly, dangerous, and unsanitary housing, coupled with dirty and life-threatening workplaces, added to this grim situation.[1]

Varied situations provided a different spin to working-class life. The "navvies" who built the railroads spoke of their day as "a dog's life." They described an endless cycle of dawn-to-dust toil with the scantiest of meals. Lodging for these railroad workers proved equally grim. Conditions in the mining towns and camps, though different in some respects, were essentially dehumanizing. Wages were uneven, and the work proved dangerous. The housing for miners represented a habitual scene of "domestic squalor." Overcrowded shacks were used for schools, and five or six workers were crowded into small sheds that passed as living space. The lack of sanitary facilities led to deadly epidemics.[2]

The coal miners of Cape Breton, especially in the early decades of this century, were renowned both for the misery of their lives and the oppression heaped upon them by the companies. In 1924 J.S. Woodsworth brought to the attention of Parliament the findings of investigations about the Cape Breton coal towns: "These enquiries and commissions have revealed wretched housing and sanitary conditions, abuses connected with the company's stores, unsatisfactory working conditions, low wages, irregular work."[3]

In Cape Breton itself Dawn Fraser, a labouring poet, described the death of coal miner Eddie Crimmins in this way:

No, not a dream he ever had
That he might work and save —
Was quite content to live and die
And be a working slave.
And yet he starved, he starved, I tell you,
Back in nineteen twenty-four,
And before he died he suffered
As many have before.
When the mines closed down that winter
He had nothing left to eat,
And he starved, he starved, I tell you
On your dirty, damned street.[4]

The working-class ghettos of Canada's major urban centres proved little better than the labouring conditions in the more outlying areas of the nation. An unemployed Winnipeger, shortly after the Great War, shared his fears of the coming winter with Labour MP Woodsworth: "I haven't had a steady job for months. I always could find a job up till a few years ago. But since we were laid off, I haven't been able to get more than a few days. . . . It's not only that the shops are running part time, but the staff was cut right down and lots of the men are out altogether. . . . No railroad should have the power to turn men off that way. That has been my job for years."[5]

With the advent of the Depression, an already appalling situation became worse. The dehumanization of the relief camps was a scandal. Conditions in the coal and steel towns of Cape Breton proved even more desperate than before, and work life in the lignite fields of southern Saskatchewan was even worse. In Quebec from 1929 to 1932 the number of workers decreased from 206,074 to 155,025, a drop of almost 25 per cent. In the working-class ghetto of Saint-Henri in Montreal the drop in employment approached 50 per cent.[6] The bleak statistics of the Depression era take on a poignant character in the words of a Depression wife's reminiscences about her deceased coal-hauler husband:

> He would be strong at the start of winter because in summer they just hauled ice and that was simple, easy, and the pay was the same. Ice door to door was a vacation. But you could just see him running down in winter. How many's the time, oh hundreds, that he has just lain down on the kitchen floor. . . .
>
> In 1939 my man fell and with this load of coal on his back something snapped. The doctor said he couldn't do hard work again. . . . He just kept going down and down and although he was only 33, the army wouldn't have him. He wanted to go, for his country. His own country didn't want him. . . . He died next year. That's how the hard times destroyed my man. And me.[7]

Against such oppression the workers resisted, and their most effective form of protest was the union movement. But corporate power stood resolutely against such militancy. Using its wealth and political influence, the nation's tiny elite produced a legacy of violent repression and legal violence that etched itself upon trade-union memory. Sometimes it operated without much fanfare in the halls of Parliament through the killing and weakening of pro-worker legislation. At other times it involved a blatant brutality through the crushing of mass protests organized by workers. The "Regina Riot" of 1935 was one of many defining worker actions in Canadian history.

Most memorable of such moments is the Winnipeg General Strike of 1919. In the preceding years the wealthy had harvested enormous profits from war-related industries while the working class had made no comparable gains. By spring 1919 the building and metal trades, through the Building Trades Council, were calling for wage increases, an eight-hour day, and union recognition along industrial lines. Management responses took a hard-line approach. Talk of a general strike filled the air, and on May 13 the city's organized workforce voted in favour of that strategy by a wide margin of 11,000 to 500. The strike began on May 15, and for over a month up to 35,000 workers brought Winnipeg to a grinding halt. During this period the Strike Committee ran the city peacefully with the help of the local police, and organized groups of strikers maintained essential services.[8]

Despite the peaceful character of the strike, the corporate and governmental powers moved to crush the protest, using massive legal and military force to do the job. The Winnipeg elite quickly formed the "Citizens' Committee of 1,000," a body with close ties to local, provincial, and federal governments. Using these connections they arranged the dismissal of local police and created a special police force from their own ranks. The Royal Northwest Mounted Police (RNWMP) and units of the regular army also joined in to help crush the strike movement. Between June 16 and June 21 the RNWMP raided local labour halls and arrested strike leaders in their homes. On June 21 a silent parade protesting these arrests was brutally suppressed by the new police force and the Mounties. In the melee one man was killed, and thirty others injured. Although the Winnipeg General Strike did not end officially until June 26, the attack by police on June 21 ended all effective resistance by the strikers. Threats, manipulation, and finally brutality crushed the workers, but behind all these tactics stood the powerful corporate-governmental coalition.[9]

A similar picture emerged in the coal-miner protests of Cape Breton in the 1920s. Between 1871 and 1939 over 1600 workers perished in the mines of Nova Scotia, where corporate power proved especially feudal and brutal. Miners were forced by circumstances to live in substandard unsanitary housing owned by the coal companies and to buy from the "pluck me" company stores, which held a monopoly in the Cape Breton coal towns. Led by J.B. "Jim" McLachlan, a local leader in the United Mine Workers' of America (UMWA) and an avowed Communist, the miners went on strike against their oppressors on more than one occasion. Against their protests stood all the forces of corporate and governmental power. As in Winnipeg, the corporations used "special police," and the government stepped in to arrest the strike leaders. However, unlike Winnipeg, the bosses closed the "pluck me" stores, cut off the water supply to the coal towns, and threw the miners and their families out of their homes. Women and children were attacked, and one miner was killed. Once again, repression, under the guise of legality, had crushed a working-class protest for justice.[10] Yet this struggle enshrined itself upon labour's memory through the songs of the rank-and-file. Dawn Fraser wrote one of these:

So, let us warn the nation's youth
That it's a crime to speak the truth;
They make the law to fit the case,

To lead McLachlan to disgrace.
So crucify him on a cross
Because he dared to sass the Boss,
Because he had the guts to tell
The company to go to hell.[11]

In the mining town of Estevan, Saskatchewan, violence emerged during the Dirty Thirties. When the Depression hit, the coal companies conspired to slash the miners' wages below the subsistence level. As in Cape Breton workers paid exorbitant rates at the company store, and they lived in the unsanitary shacks owned by the company. The mines themselves were dirty and dangerous. Under such conditions even the company's intimidation did not prevent the workers from organizing. The mine owners refused to negotiate, so a strike was called for September 1931. True to form the company owners brought in strike-breakers, enlisted the local police and firemen in the town of Estevan, and sought RCMP help as well. The local press raised the "Red" bogey, and as in Winnipeg in 1919 and later in Regina a peaceful parade was turned into a riot by virtue of a police attack. Today a small monument stands before the Estevan City Hall with the names of the three work-ers who gave their lives on that day, immortalized by working-class poet Cecil Boone:

Three more martyrs for the miners
Three more murders for the boss
Brutal laws, to crush the workers
Who dare fight in Freedom's cause.[12]

In Quebec the Asbestos Strike of 1949 in the eastern counties emerged as a watershed in which oppression met active worker resis-tance. Goaded by anti-union legislation promulgated by the Duplessis government, the Confédération des Travailleurs Catholiques du Canada (CTCC) broke off negotiations and set up picket-lines in the asbestos towns. Duplessis declared the strike illegal and sent in Quebec police to protect scab workers imported by the mining companies. When the CTCC militants tried to block these scabs, the Quebec premier turned the police loose on the protesters. Strikers were beaten, workers and their families intimidated, and even churches invaded. Despite this formidable alliance of government and corporate power, the workers maintained their solidarity and won new respect for the province's trade union movement. "Asbestos" remains one of the great moments in Canadian working-class history and stands as just one more reminder of the perennial collusion of political leaders with the big-business community.[13]

Today Canada's working class continues to live a precarious existence. Even those who earn a decent wage often work in repetitive jobs on some form of assembly line. They are fishers and factory workers, domestics and waitresses, secretaries and hospital labourers. They clean our streets and repair our highways. Although they often differ in colour, gender, sexual orientation, place of birth, and the nature of the toil they perform, they share in common the life of the exploited.

All workers remain victims of the concerted efforts of the corporate and political elite to dismantle our social system, especially when such programs are most needed.[14] More specifically the labouring population has been undermined by chronic unemployment. By March, 1997, the official number of unemployed topped 1.5 million, with a real unemployment rate about four percentage points higher than the official rate of about 10 per cent. Youth unemployment has proven intractable and holds the line at around 17 per cent. So much for the Liberals promise of more and better jobs. The unemployment figure has remained stationary since the federal election of 1993, and the relatively small increases occurred in temporary, low-paying, and insecure work. The figures prove even more grim in various regions of the country, especially Newfoundland. Coupled with layoffs have been massive plant closures; most of the companies involved have moved southward, either to the southern United States or Mexico, places with cheap labour and weak unions.[15]

Behind these statistics lie hundreds of thousands of stories of hurting, flesh-and-blood people. They include laid-off workers, human beings discarded in the rush for profit by a socioeconomic system that treats them as disposable commodities and then contrives to strip away the social service mechanisms that might render their difficult lives slightly more tolerable. Unless we are part of that tiny wealthy elite, such painful realities are also, in some respect, our own — or a friend's, or a son's or daughter's, or someone else's we love and cherish. Alan Mettrick describes this situation:

> Most of the people I write about are not tramps and bums but [people] whose skills we no longer think we need. When [one] steps outside the world [one] knows . . . or is forced out, as most of my fellow travellers were, it is as if [they were] dropped off the world. It is happening to men and women from many walks of life.[16]

Insecurity, generated by radical technological change, capitalist policy, and massive unemployment, has led to a proliferation of part-time, poorly paid, drudgery-oriented, non-union jobs with few if any benefits. These are called "McJobs," a fitting label honouring one of the pioneers in this dubious field of human endeavour. The fast-food chains provide a prime example of the "modern" version of workplace oppression. They rely on teen-age labour, insist on production speed, pay the lowest possible wages, create a stressful environment, and harass any less than compliant workers.[17]

Even jobs in the traditional, unionized, blue-collar sector, characterized by adequate wages and decent social benefits, often defy description as humane employment. They too can be tedious, sometimes demeaning, and hazardous to health and safety. The very nature of the labour often demands that workers become little more than automatons.[18] No one understands the nature of mind-numbing toil better than those who must perform it day after endless day.

Luggage factory

"In forty seconds you have to take the wet felt out of the felter, put the blanket on — a rubber sheeting — to draw out the excess moisture, wait two, three seconds, take the blanket off, pick the wet felt up, balance it on your shoulder — there is no way of holding it without tearing it all to pieces, it is wet and will collapse — reach over, get the hose, spray the inside of this copper screen to keep it from plugging, turn around, walk to the hot dry die behind you, take the hot piece off with your opposite hand, set it on the floor — this wet thing is still balanced on your shoulder — put the wet piece on the dry die, push this button that lets the dry press down, inspect the piece we just took off, the hot piece, stack it, and count it — when you get a stack of ten, you push it over and start another stack of ten — then go back and put our blanket on the wet piece coming up from the tank . . . and start all over."

Auto worker

"I stand in one spot, about two — or three — feet area, all night. The only time a person stops is when the line stops. We do about thirty-two jobs per car, per unit. Forty-eight units an hour, eight hours a day. Thirty-two times forty-eight times eight. Figure it out. That's how many times I push that button."[19]

~ ~ ~

OFTEN, BEYOND THE GREAT MONOTONY LIES DANGER, LIFE-THREATENING danger. Concerns about a healthy and safe environment for workers remain secondary matters to corporations hell-bent on profit at all cost. The Westray coal-mine explosion in Pictou County, Nova Scotia, on

May 9, 1992, is perhaps the best-known recent example: twenty-six miners died in that one incident, bringing the total of mining deaths by explosion in that locale to 272 since 1838. In the same time frame another 330 Pictou miners suffered death by falling rock, crushing by cars, or mangling by the machinery. Such tragedies stand as the inevitable "outcome of a system which puts private wealth creation over public intervention in the economy." As in so many other cases, government and corporate power united to minimize the disaster and the owners' complicity in it. It is especially shocking to realize that in "Canada there is one homicide roughly every twelve hours, but even conservative estimates indicate that a worker dies from a preventable employment condition every six hours."[20]

Even pro-worker governments are pressured into adapting to the corporate agenda of cutbacks in worker safety. For example, in 1992-93, 602 critical work-related injuries occurred in Ontario alone, an increase of 29 per cent over the 466 tabulated for 1989-90. During that same time frame Ontario's ruling NDP cut the number of inspectors by 11 per cent, from 313 to 279, and the number of inspections dropped from 66,404 to 39,837 — a whopping 40 per cent. When actual inspections did take place, the number of workers fined at the end of this three-year period had increased by 308 per cent, while the number of employers and supervisors fined had declined by 33 per cent and 69 per cent respectively. So much for a "pro-worker" government.[21]

Historically the best hope of the working class has arisen out of its own capacity to organize through trade unions — a source of strength that has fallen under consistent attack. These assaults, well-documented, remain part of the present landscape despite media propaganda to the contrary, even though by the early 1990s only 36.5 per cent of the non-agricultural workforce belonged to a union. By that time, too, private-sector unions were experiencing grim times with plant closures, or the threat of closures, and the union movement continued to fight a tough rearguard action against its corporate foes and their government allies.[22]

Given big-business ownership of the media, the negative press coverage of unions should come as no surprise. Journalist Diane Francis is all-too-typical of the mainstream approach to union issues. A frequent columnist for *Maclean's* magazine, she also edits the influential *Financial Post* and writes regularly for *The Toronto Sun*. Recently Francis wrote: "Instead of worrying about a handful of billionaires, who answer to bankers, shareholders and regulators already, Canadians should be concerned that a handful of labor leaders with financial muscle are in a position to run everyone else's lives and inordinately influence political events." Even the more moderate *Toronto Star* takes a pro-business stand against the union movement.[23]

The treatment of unions by governments and before the law further reflects the oppressed status of the working-class movement. Maurice Duplessis' use of the law and brutal repression against Quebec's unions is well-known.[24] With the Quiet Revolution, however, the Quebec union movement entered one of its most visionary and militant stages, especially in the public-sector trades. In their struggles to solidify and expand earlier gains, the province's three major union federations formed an alliance known as the Common Front. Facing this coalition was the pro-big-business government of Liberal Premier Robert Bourassa, who was determined to force the public-sector unions to toe the line according to his policies of economic restraint. In response to this hard-line position the Common Front called a general strike, and over 200,000 workers walked out. The government hastily proceeded to draft Bill 19, legislation designed to force the protesters back to work and thus end the strike. The three union presidents urged their members to defy the law. In retaliation Premier Bourassa had the leaders arrested and sentenced to one year in prison.[25]

That incident stands out as one of the more dramatic moments when the political and legal machinery in Canada was used against organized workers. But such examples are legion, though most instances involve less publicized forms of repression. The nation's courts can and have played a part. For instance, in one of his regular columns in *Maclean's,* Allan Fotheringham contrasted the court's treatment of Jean-Claude Perrot, president of the Canadian Union of Postal Workers (CUPW), with that of Clarence Campbell, once president of the National Hockey League. Campbell, found guilty of bribing a senator to assist him in gaining a government contract in 1980, was fined $25,000 and sentenced to one day in jail. The sentence was subsequently reduced to five hours, and the NHL paid his fine. Perrot was arrested on October 19, 1978, when he defied Parliament's "back to work" legislation, three days after his legal CUPW strike had begun. He was released after serving two months of a three-month sentence. "Different strokes for different folks," Fotheringham concluded. Happily the courts do not always back the corporate agenda. In the 1997 unprecedented teachers' strike against the Harris government's Bill 160, Justice James MacPherson refused to grant an injunction against the strikers and used language favourable to their cause.[26]

Given that the major source of worker strength has been the trade union movement, it stands to reason that corporations have striven consistently to block unionization within their particular sectors. A well-publicized recent counteroffensive of this kind involved the gargantuan effort of the McDonald's fast-food chain to forestall the attempt of high-school student Sarah Inglis to unionize a McDonald's restaurant in Orangeville, Ontario. Her initial success in signing up 67 out of 102 workers was met by a massive campaign of "divide and conquer." Using a "carrot-and-stick" approach, the hamburger chain succeeded in frightening a large number of the vulnerable employees and in isolating Inglis and her more militant friends. McDonald's used parental pressure and threats to close the store to stop high-school employees from supporting a union. On the night before the vote McDonald's held a well-orchestrated closing rally (in a church of all places). The corporate effort proved successful, and the union drive was defeated. Corporate intimidation had won the day, and McDonald's workers everywhere remained under the standard patterns of oppression so common to the fast-food industry.[27]

Sadly, this massive assault on unions by the corporate and political sectors has fuelled internal strife within the workers' movement and intensified divisions between labour and other oppressed groups. Major unions, such as the Steelworkers (USWA) and the Food and Commercial Workers' Union, endorse concentration upon an electoral strategy in alliance with the NDP, while the Canadian Auto Workers, CUPE, and other unions focus on mass alliances with the social movements that have emerged from other marginalized groups. This division emerged increasingly during the Community Days of Action against the corporate-driven Ontario Tories. Even more tragic are those deeply entrenched destructive values, such as racism, homophobia, welfare bashing, and sexism, from which workers are not immune. In Ontario the Harris government came to power assisted by the votes of many working people frightened by and attracted to the leader's rhetoric. Labour's challenge internally involves educating its membership to repudiate divisive and destructive values, healing the divisions within its ranks, and strengthening its growing links with wider social movements while not abandoning its legitimate political links. Although the task is difficult, there are signs of positive trends. Within the CAW, efforts to achieve gay-lesbian benefits in recent contracts with the major automakers, confrontation with the membership over public sexist behaviour, links with wider movements, and attempts to heal the union's relationship with the NDP speak well of labour's capacity to restore the bonds of liberationist solidarity.[28]

The Farmers

> Labourers mowed your fields, and you cheated them — listen to the
> wages that you kept back, calling out; realise that the cries of the
> reapers have reached the ears of the Lord of hosts.   — *James 5:4*

Whether ignored or mythologized, Canada's farm communities remain
a largely exploited sector of the national landscape both historically
and at present. Especially difficult was the life of the Prairie home-
steading wheat farmers towards the end of the nineteenth century.
They lived a dawn-to-dusk existence of toil, with both husband and
wife working full-time, all the while dependent on the unpredictable
course of nature. The settlers knew all this, but they were committed
to the risk in order to build better lives.[29]

The farmers had not prepared, though, for the exploitation they
received at the hands of the global market system that dealt in "King
Wheat." Speculation in wheat caused severe price fluctuations, which
were frequently independent of the nature and quality of any given
harvest. Above all, wheat farmers were subject to the policies of the
railroad monopolies, which controlled the pricing, storing, and loading
of the grain at the point of initial rail distribution. The business interests of the railroads and their allies used this monopoly power to fix
prices and in numerous cases cheat the grain farmers. By 1901 the
farmers had experienced enough of these conditions. That year produced a "bumper" crop, and the railroads had the capacity neither to
store much of the wheat nor to load it before it spoiled. In fury the
farmers organized the Territorial Grain Growers' Association (TGGA),
and the prairie farm movement was born.[30]

As early as the nineteenth century Quebec agriculture had been
integrated into the capitalist market with its vicissitudes, and the rural
people of the Ontario heartland suffered as well. Rural MP Agnes
Macphail noted, "Farmers work 12 hours a day to feed people who
work eight hours and still some people call that a square deal. Too
many are eating 16 hours a day and working eight. Some who eat
three meals a day do not work over one hour."[31]

The structures of oppression faced by farmers have not changed
markedly over the decades, save perhaps in their intensity. In recent
times those Canadians who plough the ground and till the soil remain
one of the most exploited sectors of Canadian society. The so-called
independent or family farm suffers at the hands of a profit-oriented
market system led by the banks and major food and petrochemical corporations. In the last decade and a half matters came to a head in what
journalist have called "the farm crisis." The major banks had

encouraged farmers to borrow heavily, with the value of their land as collateral, for the purpose of modernizing their production. To compete in modern agriculture, it was argued, farmers had to concentrate on mass production, using more mechanization and more chemicals. The crisis came to a head when costs and interest rates spiralled upward to the benefit of investors and corporations but to the detriment of farmers. For them the bottom fell out in the early 1980s with the plummeting prices of commodity goods, followed soon after by bank foreclosures on family farms.[32]

The corporate elites crush the farm indirectly as well through the very "land to mouth" food chain. The first victims of this big-business infrastructure remain the primary producers themselves — the farmers. In essence, today's scene recapitulates that of the "King Wheat" days of the early twentieth century, but a certain reality makes today's injustice even more grim. During the early decades of this century corporate power did not engineer a concentrated attack on the very existence of the farm. Wheat farmers were more or less left alone to grow wheat. In more recent times the conglomerates gobble up farm land, buying out the bankrupt farmers and turning the newly acquired land into profit-oriented businesses. As a result, much turf has been lost to farming altogether. Capitalistic enterprises, best described as agribusiness, have absorbed the remainder. Farming is rapidly becoming a big-business enterprise, guided by the profit motive.[33]

The mass production of cheap food for the consumer is especially insidious. Most Canadians are not farmers, let alone rural dwellers. Rather, they are urban and suburban, and they do most of their shopping at the supermarket chains with their weekly rounds of cheap deals and special coupons. This approach has a deeply oppressive side. By underpricing small owners and producers, large corporations generate monopolistic and semimonopolistic conditions.[34]

Corporation inroads into agriculture emerge also in the arena of technology and chemicals. Industries pushing biotechnology and chemical additives emerge as standard facets of what are rapidly becoming rural industries. Company promoters press for heavy employment of pesticides and chemical fertilizers in crop production and for the use of chemically treated food products for livestock. Food conglomerates, drug companies, government agencies, and sometimes even farmers' organizations engage in blatant forms of propaganda to push such products. So powerful is this pro-corporation coalition that it seeks also to subvert broader efforts to inform the public about alternatives. Even farmers who realize the dangers of this dependence on chemicals can be caught up in adopting the policy in the name of their own survival.[35]

This move towards greater and greater corporate concentration reflects just one more facet of globalization. Agribusiness, with its technological and chemical components, is increasingly transnational, with national governments doing their part to aid this process. Farmers fall victim to this aggression within the bounds of both the GATT and NAFTA. Farmers stand out as a key sector in many lands to fall victim to such accords. Domestic marketing boards, one of the Canadian farmers' mainstays in stabilizing their own markets, have come under increasing attacks in the international agreements. Especially tragic has been the undermining of the Saskatchewan Wheat Pool, which had begun in earnest by the summer of 1994.[36]

Under such an assault against the farm movement's chief sources of strength, rural producers cave in little by little. To further cement their control over agriculture, the major forces of corporate and government power promote an aggressive ideological campaign to bring farmers into their camp. A recent example of this was "Winning in a Global Marketplace: The First Canadian Agri-Food Conference on International Competitiveness" held in Saskatoon in 1992. The meeting was sponsored by the Agri-Food Competitiveness Council, a front organization for such pro-big-business institutions as the George Morris Centre, the Fraser Institute, Agriculture Canada, and the International Centre for Agricultural Science and Technology (ICAST). With Cargill's CEO as chair of its board and with other board members including corporation executives from Nestlé, Weston, and Du Pont, it becomes apparent that ICAST uses a public façade to promote the corporate agenda.[37]

In the face of all this, the infrastructure of rural life is collapsing throughout the land. Local post offices are closing, along with the small businesses that prove so essential to a healthy town and village life. Rural churches are shutting down, frequently with little thought, and many villages are becoming ghost towns. Many community centres have been reduced to decaying buildings no longer in use. Even local farm industries decline or are bought up by major agribusiness corporations. Rural newspapers experience economic trouble, and farm political life falls by the wayside with population decline and a decreasing tax base. The real estate expansion in rural Ontario in the form of commuter or retirement communities is less a sign of rural health than an influx of urban life into the countryside.[38]

Most poignantly, the rural family appears in serious pain despite some continuing strength. One merely has to observe the effects of the farm crisis on women and children. Gisele Ireland published a study, *The Farmer Takes a Wife* (1983), carried out by her organization Concerned Farm Women. Her survey established links between farmers' inability to make interest payments, family stress, and bank pressure. During the banks' offensive against farmers, those unable to pay drank more and physically abused family members with greater frequency. Farm women became increasingly enraged with their plight, and they were more inclined to depression and thoughts of suicide. Under this economic stress couples communicated less with each other, often due to the necessity of both husband and wife being forced to take on additional employment to make ends meet. Couples collapsed in mental fatigue, and children operated farm machinery more frequently with insufficient training.[39] The human side of this pain emerges movingly in a letter from a Manitoba farm wife to her husband:

> I love you and don't ever forget it. Stop blaming yourself for what happened. You had no control over inflation or interest rates. . . . You weren't a poor manager or a lousy farmer. . . . Don't blame yourself. You never took all the credit when things were good, so don't take all the blame now.
>
> You are not a failure. You have not let us down. . . . You stuck it out! That is not failure. You never hurt anyone or took advantage of anyone. That is not failure. You have honesty and integrity! That is not failure. I am proud of you. . . . Your family needs you and loves you very much.[40]

The Poor

> Woe to the legislators of infamous laws . . . who refuse justice to the unfortunate and cheat the poor among my people of their rights.
> — *Isaiah 10:1-2a*

Canada has always had its poor, and it has always had them in large number. They are the refuse of a system that puts profit over people. They are not only the perpetually poor but also those who have fallen on hard times through unemployment, or who work at exploitative "McJobs." Because of both discrimination and vulnerability, a large proportion of the poor include children, the elderly, and women. Indeed, the poor are part of the very nature of capitalism. They are a ready pool of cheap labour when needed or discarded when unnecessary. Their backgrounds vary, as do their skin colours, ethnic heritages, and geographical locations. What they share in common is grim poverty and marginalization.

Pre-Depression working-class Montreal encapsulated this reality. This so-called "city below the hill" reflected a scene of abject misery. Housing was shoddy, expensive, and dangerous; infant mortality was excessively high; educational opportunities were limited in the extreme; sewage and health conditions were abysmal; and the workplaces were dark and dangerous. These, at least, were the conditions before the Depression; after the crash of 1929 the situation intensified.[41]

During the "Dirty Thirties," with its massive unemployment, parsimonious governments controlled by the business and financial elites provided little in the way of economic relief. The welfare that did exist was paltry, dehumanizing, and a bureaucratic nightmare. Especially grim were the work camps set up for the unemployed. Under the impulse of Chief of the General Staff A.G.L. "Andy" McNaughton, the Bennett government created work camps with the twofold purpose of putting idlers to work in a regimented way and keeping the unemployed out of the hands of political agitators.[42] Socialist MP J.S. Woodsworth described life at these camps:

> Picture to yourself a tarpaper shack 79 feet x 24 with no windows, along each side there is a row of double decker bunks, these are spaced off with 8 x 1 board so that there is room for two men in each bunk. The bunks are filled with straw and you crawl into them from the foot end. Along the front of the lower bunk a narrow board is placed upon which the men may sit. The place is very meagerly lighted and ventilation by three skylights. . . . There is a marked resemblance to a hog pen or a dog pound. At times the place reeks of the foul smell and at night the air is simply fetid. The floor is dirty and the end of the shack where the men wash . . . is caked with black mud. The toilet is thoroughly filthy, unsanitary, and far too small.[43]

Woodsworth merely spoke for the "campers." Mostly they advocated for themselves, to the point of rebellion. Refusing to have their dignity trampled, the relief workers organized, published their own newspapers, and formed the backbone of the famous "On-to-Ottawa" Trek of 1935. From Kamloops, British Columbia, to Regina, Saskatchewan, marched about two thousand unemployed workers, mostly from the relief camps. They hoped to converge at Parliament in Ottawa, there to protest the conditions that were destroying their lives and dignity. On July 1, 1935, in Regina, local police and the RCMP crushed the originally peaceful protesters in one of the most repressive government and police actions in Canadian history.[44]

J.S. Woodsworth's description of slum conditions in early twentieth-century Winnipeg poignantly sums up the oppressive conditions faced by the poor in Canada:

> Some of these people may be lazy and shiftless. Small wonder when they are forced into conditions that foster idleness, immorality and crime. And behind all, the fact remains that there is not work for them. Let me tell you of one little foreign girl. She lives in a room in a disreputable old tenement — one of those human warrens which are multiplying with great rapidity in our city. Her father has no work. The men boarders have no work. The place is incredibly filthy. The little girl has been ill for months — all that time living on the bed in which three or four persons must sleep and which also serves the purpose of table and chairs. For weeks this little girl has had itch which has spread to the children of surrounding rooms. She has torn the flesh on her arms and legs into great sores which have become poisoned. The other day I saw the mother dip a horrible dish rag into the potato dish and wash the sores! I took a friend to see the child. The mother started to show us the child's arm. The dirty dress was stuck in the great open sores. As the scabs were pulled away from the quivering flesh the little one writhed and screamed in agony. My friend who has dear little girlies of his own, half gasped, half cried, "My God! This is damnable!" . . . The little one still lives there in her misery. . . . Yes, and many of the well-to-do are drawing large revenues from this same misery.[45]

In what has been called "Canada's Century," those poor remain with us, in their hunger and distorted lives, an ever-present judgement against mass inequities. By 1993, the year the Liberals took power, national poverty stood at a sixteen-year high, embracing 17.4 per cent of the population; since that time that percentage edged up to 17.8 per cent. This translates into over five million people by the end of 1996, or one in six of all Canadians. Income level serves as one major indicator of poverty's presence. Canada remains home for large numbers of poor people precisely because the national wealth is shared with such scandalous inequity. In Ontario alone in 1996 welfare income ranged from between $4,060 to $10,313 below the poverty line, depending on the category of the recipient. Among modern industrial nations only the United States has a worse record than Canada in the category of income distribution.[46]

In the early 1990s Ontario presented a set of statistics that lays out the province's inequity with stark clarity. Between February 1990 and

February 1991, 260,000 jobs disappeared in the province, accounting for 80 per cent of national job loss for that period. In October 1991, 486,000 people were unemployed in Ontario, up 39 per cent in one year. By November 1991 the Toronto welfare rolls had skyrocketed to a record 147,000, a 166 per cent increase in a two-year period. In Montreal in June 1991, 615,000 people lived below the poverty line, over 20,000 people were homeless, and 374 food banks and other aid groups were required to help the poor.[47] The tiny ruling clique seldom if ever rubs shoulders with the poor people whose lives collectively make up these embarrassing statistics. But for those of us in the middle and so-called professional classes, the poor include friends, acquaintances, our own children, and increasingly ourselves as we face the effects of the unemployment that is all around us, that impinges on our own lives.

Over one million Canadians are unable to find adequate and affordable housing, a figure that translates into about one out of eight households. By the 1990s an estimated 250,000 Canadians were homeless and desperately relying on sporadic public charity for an emergency roof over their heads. These crises are exacerbated by sharp increases in housing and rental costs, the disappearances of rooming houses, government cutbacks in public housing and co-operative projects, the lifting of rent controls, and the dominance of profit motivation in the arenas of real estate development. In Toronto alone more than 28,000 homeless citizens used Metro hostels in 1996, up from 25,009 in 1994. When those staying with relatives or friends or those who sleep on the street are added, the total increases to more than 50,000.

One single mother living on social assistance with three children describes her plight: "The welfare housing allowance is not enough to rent a decent house. I have to spend money on rent that I should be spending on food and clothing." In even worse conditions, Bill of Bancroft, Ontario, lived in a bus for two years after being evicted from a cabin. The bus rental cost him $285 a month. Ferencz, a Hungarian refugee from the 1956 uprising, lives among his rags on the concrete ledge of a Montreal parking garage. He has been living like this for nineteen years and finds most of his meals from garbage cans. Suzie and Half-Pint, two teenage street kids in Toronto, hang around warm doughnut shops during the day and sleep on street grates at night. Many of the settlement houses and hostels of the nation's urban centres exist as hotbeds of violence, intimidation, theft, and dehumanization. The plight of the poorly housed and homeless remains an outrage in a land where vast resources are so iniquitously maldistributed.[48]

Children

The tongue of the baby at the breast sticks to his palate for thirst, little children go begging for bread; no one spares a scrap for them.

— *Lamentations 4:4*

Among the poor and the producer classes, children have emerged as the most vulnerable of all. They are the most dependent sector of humanity, and they remain the first victims of oppression. This has long been the case in Canada's urban ghettos. In pre-Depression Montreal, for example, infant mortality in the working-class neighbourhoods was appalling. Wealthier suburbs, such as Outrement and Westmount, registered an infant mortality rate of less than 6 per cent, while older working-class areas reported a rate of around 20 per cent. Poverty, substandard housing, malnutrition, and overcrowding were the key factors leading to these appalling statistics. Children existed as an important source of cheap labour for the factory owners of Montreal and elsewhere. They entered the workforce around the age of twelve, and remained there as long as employment was available.[49]

The Depression brought more pain for children on top of an already impossible situation. Farm youth were not immune to the economic crisis and suffered with all the poor of the land. In rural Saskatchewan official reports described appalling family conditions. Near Shaunovan one family had nine children dressed in gunnysacks, while a tenth had recently died of deprivation. At Bone Creek a family of eleven had been forced to live in a one-room shack.[50] Hunger was a constant reality for the poorer children of the nation. One resident of rural Saskatchewan during the Depression recalls the extreme privation of a number of desperate farm families:

> Those poor bastards couldn't wait until spring to plant, not when they saw their children starving before their eyes and they boiled the seed wheat, they made porridge and gruel and bannock out of it, and this is the way some of those farmers got their families through the winter. That was starvation in one of the greatest and richest nations of earth.[51]

In the 1990s children remain among the most vulnerable people of the world. Infanticide is still a common practice globally, and in many places the children of the poor are denied education and rushed into unhealthy and dangerous work environments even before the age of ten. Children, especially in the developing world, provide a continual supply of cheap labour.[52] Canadian society, while not engaging in direct extermination policies, is hardly a haven of refuge for poor children.

Indeed, a bad situation grows progressively worse year after year. In 1989 Canada had 998,000 children, or 15.2 per cent of the population, defined as poor. By 1996 that figure had risen to 1,500,000, a whopping 50 per cent increase in that seven-year period. Poverty strikes one of six children in two-parent families and a shocking eight out of ten in single-parent homes. Almost all the economic indicators point to a massive increase in suffering for Canada's children based on sheer economics alone.[53]

The voices and experiences of the flesh-and-blood suffering children who make up these cold statistics need to be heard over the cacophony of pious platitudes offered by our political and corporate elites. For instance, one child, Chris, age twelve, drew a picture of her mom for Sheila Baxter, author of *A Child Is Not a Toy*. In the drawing the child's mother is crying as she gazes in despair at her empty refrigerator. Chris described her drawing:

> This picture is when my mom didn't have money and we couldn't afford to buy food, so we had to try to live without much food in the fridge. There was hardly any clothes to wear, and we couldn't buy any and we had to wear the same clothes for a couple of days. I felt so sad and embarrassed when I went to school. I was afraid that kids would make fun of me.... At night I would cry as well because I would be hungry for food.[54]

Adolescents are increasingly caught in such cycles of misery. Tina, age eighteen, describes her life:

> Why am I poor? Because my job doesn't pay me enough to live on. I work at McDonald's, but it's always part time....
>
> I would like to have a full-time job. I have to make my room rent. I don't want welfare. Sometimes I think about becoming a hooker. I think working for companies that keep your hours down makes a woman look for a man to help her. I've got a boyfriend. He helps with the rent. He pushes me around when he's high. He really beat me up last Christmas. If I had a good job with a pay that I could live on, maybe I could leave him. I don't know.
>
> If I could change things I would make it easier to go back to school. I would make these outfits pay a wage that people could live on. I would give every poor person a dentist and medicine.... I would make bus fare cheaper.... I'd make rich people have to give some of their money to the poor.[55]

The malignant priorities of our nation underscore the plight of poor children. The federal government maintains the generosity of "perks" to the wealthy, such as business lunch write-offs, but refuses to fund a broadly based child-care program that would directly confront the growing epidemic of child poverty. Once again our children are a casualty to the greed of the rich.[56]

The Elderly

On the aged you laid your crushing yoke.
— Isaiah 47:6

At the other end of the age chain live the forgotten elderly, most of whom held down jobs in their preretirement days. In a society in which youth, vigour, and productivity are applauded, seniors emerge as especially vulnerable. At best the elderly are patronized and viewed as frail, confused, and constantly in need of help. At worst they are discarded. Consequently seniors are stereotyped to be pitied, ignored, or shunted aside. It is not surprising, then, that the elderly fall victim to both economic and social injustice. Large numbers of the elderly remain among the poorest of our citizens despite having led long, productive lives. The limited pensions and social benefits that accrue to our retired and older citizens often prove so minimal that those people are pushed into poverty. In 1995 60 per cent of unattached elderly women, mostly widows, lived below the poverty line. The corresponding figure for elderly men was 20 per cent. Private pensions, save for the rich, are hopelessly inadequate. Their purpose has been largely to provide a pool of capital for investors, and the benefits paid out are rarely linked to inflation. Government pensions do not fill the gap of need, and even so they are falling under increasing attacks by Tory and Liberal governments bent on cost-cutting. The public pension plans, even with a Guaranteed Income Supplement for the especially needy, still fall below the poverty line. All other pension schemes remain tied to previous employment and the wages made in such jobs. This translates into good pensions for the already well-to-do elderly with tiny or non-existent pensions for the poor. Even more unjust have been the efforts of both the Mulroney government and its Liberal successor to cut back this already threadbare pension system.[57]

Patriarchy

Women

> Yes, I hear screams like those of a woman in labour . . . they are the
> screams of the daughter of Zion, gasping . . . "Ah, I despair!" . . . with
> murderers surrounding.   — *Jeremiah 4:31*

Economic categories alone do not provide sufficient clues as to the pervasive nature of oppression. Beyond and within economic inequities
and the class basis of the capitalist system lie fundamental springs from
which exploitation bubbles and poisons the social fabric. Allied with
class oppression are other forces destructive of a society based upon
shalôm. Chief among these is the deeply rooted system of patriarchy,
which proclaims the superiority of Western male dominance over
women in particular and society in general.

In considering Canada's long history of exploiting its primary producers, workers both of field and factory, what is all too frequently forgotten and repressed is the reality that these labourers were often
women. With astonishing regularity, the oppression that they have
experienced had its own unique twist. On the frontier, newly settled
farm families might have experienced a rough equality of gender, yet
married women were fully expected to follow the ambitions and migra-
tion patterns of their husbands. While farm women worked outside the
household in barns, gardens, and fields, and were expected to take up
the extra chores, the traditional household work — cooking, cleaning,
preserving and making and mending clothes — was still their exclusive
preserve. Women had to develop marketable skills, such as weaving, in
order to survive either economic disaster or the death of a spouse.
Women on farms experienced the same structures of oppression as the
men in their lives, but often their lot was even harder.[58] As Agnes
Macphail pointed out in 1923: "It is true that farmers work hard; it is
true their days are long and their pay is poor. But it is also infinitely
true that the farm woman's day is longer and her pay poorer. . . . One
mistake that I think the men continually make in the House is that of
treating the problem of rural depopulation as a man's problem and a
man's problem only."[59]

Even more tragic was the life of the working-class woman. The
conditions of unsanitary, unsafe, and grim lodgings in the working
ghettos of Canada's industrial centres fell most heavily upon working-
class mothers, who spent so much of their time in such hovels. Their
social life was practically non-existent, whereas the men had the factory and tavern to provide some variety and some escape. Above all,

large numbers of proletarian women worked outside the home in the dirty and dangerous factories of the Industrial Revolution, and their lot proved more difficult than that of their male comrades. Despite the patriarchal ideology of "the weaker sex" and "the mother is queen of the home," the middle classes and the ruling elites had no compunction about proletarian women being herded into the factories of the nation. There these women endured the same injustices as male workers, but their oppression did not stop there. They also experienced sexual harassment by foremen and bosses, against which they had no practical recourse. Work was not a choice for these women, but rather a necessity. They entered the workshops in early adolescence to supplement their families' incomes or to find their own way as single women. As wives they were bounced alternately between home and factory, caught between the exigencies of patriarchal values and economic necessity. They tended to labour in the most dangerous, most poorly paid non-union workshops, and throughout the twentieth century women toiled at factories for wages significantly below that of their male counterparts.

These women did not succumb easily to such rank injustice. They helped to organize unions, and they led strikes, such as the 1907 Bell Telephone Operators work stoppage and the 1924 protest at the Eddy plant in Hull, Quebec. Yet even within the progressive movements of the time women militants were circumscribed in their struggles for equality. To be sure, women exercised both leadership and activism in the Communist Party, the Co-operative Commonwealth Federation, and the labour movement far more extensively than in other arenas of Canadian life, but even in these circles they met resistance and were forced to spend time enlightening and struggling against their male comrades.[60]

Young rural women, pressured by overpopulation and often fuelled by hope, migrated to the urban centres looking for work, and frequently ended up labouring as domestic workers, a life characterized by harassment, drudgery, low wages, and the vulnerability of isolation. A few of them drifted into prostitution. Although frowned on by Victorian society, "sex for sale" existed as a thriving industry throughout our nation's history. Despite pompous moral disclaimers by the elites, prostitution remained a profitable trade largely ignored by the patriarchs who so righteously deplored it. After all, it was men and their economic interests that created this sector of female exploitation.

Gender oppression has continued its relentless pressure to our own day. Globally, the cherishing of infant boys over infant girls remains widespread and often leads to the practice of female infanticide. During the preschool years girl tots receive less care and attention, and in developing countries two-thirds of the one hundred million children not receiving primary education are female. Many countries treat adolescent women as a burden unless they can be married off swiftly for economic gain. In every major area of life — education, literacy, work, professions — women in the poorer nations are undoubtedly more exploited and oppressed than their male counterparts.[61]

Canada, a more prosperous country, does not mirror the same cruel injustice against women shown on the global scene, yet patriarchy thrives here on a number of levels. Income for single-parent families headed by women has fallen in recent years while the numbers of such families has risen. A wage differential between the genders remains endemic. Men making over $50,000 annually represent 17.2 per cent of the total for their gender; for women the figure is only 4.6 per cent. Both men and women come closest to pay equity in the $20,000 to $29,999 range, yet even here the differential to the detriment of women stands at 3.6 per cent. Such anti-woman bias, woven inexorably into the market system, stands out glaringly in actions by the Ontario Conservative government. Its scrapping of employment and pay equity, its abandonment of public child-care, its welfare cuts (which have their hardest impact on sole-support mothers), its cutbacks of women's shelters, and its attempts to use legislation to impose traditional family structures on society all serve to entrench the cruel oppression of patriarchy.[62]

Injustice towards women takes root more deeply than statistics alone can convey. Patriarchy as a word describing the collective oppression of women involves a multitude of factors, including injustices in the workplace. Most low-paying, unhealthy, and stressful employment involves female labour. One example is the increase of women working for the garment industry out of their own homes. This kind of piece work mirrors that of women toilers in the early decades of the Industrial Revolution. For example, one home garment worker, Pik, a thirty-eight-year old immigrant, earns her $12,000 a year livelihood working seventy hours a week at her sewing machine. She gets no overtime, no pension, no vacation pay, no unemployment insurance, no workers' compensation. Pik is only one of around two thousand workers in this home trade who receive less than the minimum wage and remain unprotected by the law, except in theory. Work vulnerability for women also characterizes the fast-food industry, where the young women who are most commonly employed work under constant stress.[63]

More often than not the workplace is hazardous to the worker's health, and women are frequently more vulnerable to such environments than men. Matters like sexual harassment and damage by toxins to women's reproductive systems are borne virtually alone by the female gender. Even labour-market discrimination has put women more at risk than male workers, precisely because, in our society, women tend to toil at the worst jobs, and these are the jobs in which health hazards are proportionately greater.[64]

Finally, given the patriarchal nature of the society women remain a vast sector of unpaid employment in our society — homemakers or domestic proletarians, the so-called "housewife." Even if women toil for pay outside the home, whether single or coupled, they still bear the brunt of home labour. Even among progressive men this reality is addressed only with the utmost reluctance. Miriam Edelson, a trade-union activist, confesses her difficulty in convincing her male co-unionists that family and relationships need not be sacrificed for "the cause."[65]

Few critics have pointed out how essential patriarchy is to the entire market system as well as feminist Marilyn Waring. As a political and social militant for more than two decades, this New Zealand woman has brought into the light of day how the entire capitalist global edifice is built upon the repression of women, particularly through their massive unpaid toil. In her trailblazing *If Women Counted* she shows how the market system, which values only the labour that produces money, depends upon the vast unpaid labour of women across the face of the Earth. In such a sexist structure a young adolescent girl in school is worth less than a street prostitute of the same age who generates financial profit for her male pimp. Waring points out: "The biggest irony is that while the world's accounting system . . . ignores the unpaid work of women, the world's economies would collapse if it were withdrawn."[66] The role of unpaid housework, accomplished mostly by women, amply illustrates capitalism's disregard of a vital segment of our national economy.

In addition to strictly economic exploitation, the image of women promoted in this society remains another major source of oppression. The feminist voice continues to speak mostly from the sidelines and is systematically ignored or scorned. There are few prominent voices for women's issues in the mainstream media. The other side of the coin is the sometimes open, sometimes subtle promotion of women as sex objects. Feminists and alternative media to the contrary, our society sustains an overwhelmingly antiwoman bias. An excellent film, *Killing*

Us Softly, provides a strong commentary on the sexual objectification of women and their body parts in order to sell virtually any product. Such pervasive brutality upholds and feeds the more overt violence against women in our land. Marc Lepine's mass murder of fourteen young women at Montreal's École Polytechnique in December, 1989 stands as perhaps the most dramatic moment of such mayhem. Domestic violence of husbands against wives remains shockingly common, ranging from verbal abuse through rapes and beatings to outright murder. The number of women's shelters is growing, but not fast enough to meet the crisis. A recent federal study showed that one in four women in Canada can expect to be sexually assaulted before the age of seventeen, and that one million Canadian women suffer abuse annually by their husbands or live-in partners. Such overt violence arises from a profit-oriented system that turns women into commodities to be owned and used. This is the society in which our sisters live. So pervasive is this destructive oppression that failure to confront and exorcize it from progressive ranks will guarantee the continuing "divide-and-conquer" rule of the powerful elite.[67]

The Other

The division of the oppressed majority into warring factions remains an intrinsic cause of the continuing control of this vast global population by the wealthy few. By restricting the flow of economic and social goods to the "have-nots" and the "have-a-littles" the tiny elite works to turn one group of oppressed against the other. Varied cultural and social heritages are stirred into this potentially lethal mix, and strategies are employed to turn such differences into division. Racism, hatred of the foreigner, ethnic loyalty, cultural superiority, religious beliefs, patriotism, and heterosexism have a long history that illustrates how oppressed sectors turn upon each other in the name of destructive values.

Persecuted Minorities

> You must not harm the stranger or oppress him, for you lived as strangers in the land of Egypt. — *Exodus 22:20*

Racism and xenophobia (hatred of the stranger or foreigner) stand out as integral components of Canadian history. These especially virulent forms of oppression exist in factory and farm and cut across both age and gender lines, pitting oppressed against oppressed rather than forging solidarity against a common oppressor. These tendencies link up with the most narrow and ugly of patriotisms, and they support capitalism's need for either land-grabbing or a vast pool of cheap labour.

The Aboriginal Peoples

Well before the arrival of white traders and settlers, numerous Native peoples fished, hunted, trapped, gathered, farmed, and lived on the land. For the most part the European newcomers treated these original peoples with arrogance, dishonesty, and often murderous cruelty. The so-called "two founding nations" (French and British) stole their land and oppressed them for the sake of economic power and profit. In early Newfoundland, cultural clashes between the British fishing settlements and the resident Beothuk people were settled largely by armed force with the resultant eradication of the Native population. Although some of the newcomers in New France showed sensitivity towards Aboriginal peoples, the exigencies of the fur trade defined the relationship of Native to European, resulting in the destruction of First Nations' lives and culture.[68]

The pattern of exploitation continued as the European settlers moved across the country. As long as resident tribes were needed as fur trappers or military allies, the new arrivals and the Native peoples maintained a shaky peace. But as the fur trade declined and wars ceased, Aboriginal peoples were expelled from their land and pressured to assimilate into the dominant British culture.

In Manitoba in the 1870s, many resident peoples, called Métis, were the progeny of French trader and Native unions. Living near present-day Winnipeg, they farmed and supplemented their income working for the Hudson Bay Company. Their way of life was threatened immediately after Confederation by a new wave of Canadian imperialism that led to the creation of Manitoba as a province. This prompted the famous uprising led by Louis Riel. The revolt managed to slow down the rate of change, but not halt it. Ultimately the Métis crusades failed, and after a failed uprising in present-day Saskatchewan Riel was executed in 1885. His efforts to save Aboriginal culture and life had failed. Ultimately the economic and political elites used famine and force to undermine and destroy the Aboriginal way of life and reduce it to an oppressed backwater, which it remains to this day.[69]

The ill treatment of Canada's Native population continued unabated into the twentieth century. The Liberal government of Wilfrid Laurier, under the aegis of Clifford Sifton, reduced government benefits to reservation Indians. Rations were slashed, and medical assistance suffered significant cutbacks. As well, Sifton became party to cheating the Assiniboine Indians out of 45,000 acres of prime farmland. Native children were uprooted from their homes and herded into residential schools in a program of forced integration into Western and British values.[70]

Behind much of the oppression against the First Nations' people, even to this day, stands a conflict of fundamental values. Most Aboriginal peoples espouse notions of land ownership and use that conflict radically with the values of white Western capitalism. In the European-based tradition, land is a commodity to be bought, owned, and sold for the purpose of profit or pleasure for "the owner." By contrast, Native peoples feel a deep kinship and communion with the land. It frequently becomes imbued with a sacred character in which private ownership gives way to communal care. Although some Native peoples are caught up in the capitalist system, and some are exploitative and use the land in self-aggrandizing ways, Aboriginal movements and their struggles for justice remain based upon a traditional view of the land that is alien to the profit-making and consumption-oriented society at large. It was this clash of values that led to the Oka Crisis of 1990.[71]

This fundamental opposition of worldviews between the colonial newcomers and the First Nations has been taken to further lengths by more specific forms of oppression: the division of families, the historical reduction of the status of Aboriginal women by forcing them into Western patriarchal models, the ghettoization and poverty experienced by Aboriginal people. Even murder, fuelled by racism, is not unknown to Native communities. The gunning down of Leo LaChance by Aryan Nation white supremacists in Prince Albert, Saskatchewan, in 1991 stands as only one shocking example of racist violence against Canada's First Nations. Statistics demonstrate the continuing marginalization of our Native population: 24 per cent of on-reserve homes do not have drinkable water, and 20 per cent have no toilet or bathroom facilities. In Regina, Saskatoon, and Winnipeg, 60 per cent of Aboriginal families live below the poverty line, and that figure rises to 85 per cent when these families are run by mothers alone. Even people in the dominant culture who might be considered to be "progressives" have difficulty honouring Aboriginal concerns in encounters that bring together Native peoples and others. This is especially true in the environmental movement and in trade unions.[72]

Non-European peoples

Certainly racism was a major ideological weapon used against
Canada's Native people, and it served the cause of injustice against
black and Asian newcomers as well. Although Canada existed as the
terminal point for much of the underground rail system engineered by
U.S. abolitionists, this country did not treat its Afro-American immigrants with dignity or equality. Black slavery existed in both English
and French Canada and was not abolished until the mother country
enacted such legislation in 1833. In the Halifax-Dartmouth area a black
neighbourhood emerged that was scarcely different from the racial
ghettos of the urban United States in the late nineteenth and twentieth
centuries. Between the wars the Ku Klux Klan was imported into
Canada and used its racist values to target blacks, especially in
Ontario.[73]

The large influx of cheap labour from Asia, especially China,
beginning with the nation's great railroad-building venture, provided
the occasion for outbursts of racial hatred. Most early Chinese immigrants lived in the urban centres of British Columbia, but racial prejudice and violence led many of them to migrate eastward into the
Prairies. Discrimination was so pervasive that even advanced social
reformers, such as J.S. Woodsworth, needed years of experience to
exorcise their own anti-Chinese feeling. Behind this rejection of Asians
lay the arrogant imperialism and integrationism of the English-speaking elites.[74]

Perhaps the most shocking example of racism against our Asian
residents involved the government internment of Canada's Japanese
citizens into concentration camps during the Second World War.
Roughly twenty-one thousand Japanese were forced from their homes
during the war.[75] One Japanese citizen, describing this shameful epoch,
placed racism against his people into a broader social context:

> Do you know that [in] the 1930's . . . most of the Japanese in British
> Columbia were Canadian citizens. Born in Canada. Canadian citi-
> zens. But we couldn't do this and we couldn't do that. First, we
> couldn't vote. . . . A Japanese man with a doctor's degree couldn't
> serve in the provincial legislature. . . . No Japanese could. Or be an
> alderman, or a school trustee. . . . You couldn't work for the govern-
> ment either, even with a shovel on the roads. You couldn't serve on a
> jury.[76]

In Canada's urban settings, people of colour have remained targets
of both overt racial hatred and the more subtle cruelty of institutional

racism. In the last decade white supremacist groups, hate organizations such as Aryan Nation and the Heritage Front, have singled out blacks, Asians, and other people of colour for their attacks. Related beatings and confrontations in Toronto and Montreal are on the rise, as well as incidents between the police and non-white sectors of the population. Racism has erupted into overt violence and brutality. In Montreal racist material appears regularly in ad hoc publications that circulate among the police. Although most Canadians disavow racism and express disapproval and dismay at such crude oppression, what is rarely acknowledged is the low-key racism that pervades our culture, giving tacit permission to its more virulent form. In the Reform Party of Canada a not-so-subtle racism lurks behind the political blasts levelled against multiculturalism and immigrants. Preston Manning's quick dismissal of overtly racist candidates, however laudable, leaves open the question of how and why such candidates found themselves on Reform Party tickets in the first place. Finally, racism is "writ large" in the economic hierarchy of our country. "People of colour" remain concentrated in low-paying, temporary, dangerous, and non-union workplaces with few or no benefits. When these people are women their status worsens.[77]

Such racism is exacerbated when the immigrants are poorer, more vulnerable, don't speak English or French, and are not white-skinned. Refugees emerge as the epitome of the dispossessed among the coloured peoples of the world. Habitually they are welcomed only as sources of cheap labour or kept out for economic reasons via the ideologies of hatred and fear. For the most part, Canada too marches to the tune of this rampant injustice. The country tends to hide behind restrictive, self-serving legislation, although more recently the discrimination has taken the form of propaganda linking immigrants of colour with crime, irresponsibility, and family breakdown.[78]

The foreigner and European immigrants

Xenophobia, the hatred of the foreigner or stranger, though older than the Canadian nation, lives among us to this day. Indeed, it has thrived ever since the Plains of Abraham battle against the French. After the Conquest the French-speaking population, concentrated for the most part in what is now Quebec, was forced into a subordinate position both economically and politically. The so-called French-English partnership has necessitated a subordinate position for the francophone population. By the end of the nineteenth century francophone Quebec had political sway in its own land while remaining dependent on anglophone economic overlords, many of whom resided in Montreal.

Anglo dominance took the increasing form of U.S.-based capital in the twentieth century, and only during and after the Quiet Revolution of the 1960s were Quebec governments, either Liberal or Péquiste, able to make liberative strides in taking charge of their own economy. Whether English Canada likes it or not, progress towards justice in Quebec has been intimately linked with Quebec nationalism and the push towards various forms of autonomy. Anglo Quebeckers and Canadians may well point out the excesses and xenophobia in such patriotism, but the refusal to accept the just claims of Quebec nationalism helps to solidify the centuries-long oppression imposed by English-speaking Canadians upon their francophone sisters and brothers. Anti-French feeling survives and propagates itself from coast-to-coast within the anglophone population. Even progressives do not hesitate to add to these deeply rooted prejudices. Until understanding takes the place of ignorance, and solidarity replaces anti-French feeling, such hatreds will continue to divide those forces who struggle for justice and *shalôm* in the lands north of the United States.[79]

Beyond anglophone prejudice aimed at francophones, ethnic hatred has directed itself against virtually every wave of immigration that has settled in this new land. In theory and propaganda Canada was hailed as a new land of opportunity in which immigrants would be welcomed with open arms. As long as workers proved necessary to fuel the economy, immigrants were lured to Canada, but during hard times the immigrant was treated with contempt, violence, and prejudicial legislation. The peoples most harmed by this were those arriving from Eastern Europe. English-speaking Canadians viewed them as dirty, diseased, unlettered, uncultured, and inferior.[80] Despite the myth of the Canadian "mosaic," a more American-style "melting pot" syndrome dominated the economic and political powerbrokers of the land. Above all, these elites were on the lookout for foreign "troublemakers," and any effort on the part of immigrants to organize resistance to injustice was met with the full force of legislative and armed might. The threat of deportation and anti-union aggression by the establishment linked itself inexorably to anti-immigrant sentiment. This tendency reached lethal proportions during the Winnipeg Strike and reemerged within the Bennett government during the Depression.

Jewish immigrants and citizens stand out as special cases in point. Whether the French-speaking Catholics of Quebec or the English-speaking Protestants of the rest of Canada, most established Canadians viewed their land as a Christian domain. This belief involved a continuation of that long history of anti-Semitism so endemic to the Christian tradition. When this is compounded with anti-immigrant sentiment, the mix becomes explosive, and especially so in the 1920s and 1930s with the arrival of organized hate groups in Canada. The Ku Klux Klan became a force throughout Canada in the 1920s. Although it described itself as "anti-Jewish," its hatreds proved more ecumenical. During its heyday it led attacks on French-Canadians, blacks, Asians, and other non-English-speaking immigrants. In Quebec, Adrien Arcand's "Blueshirts" singled out the Jews as the archetypal enemy of Christian humanity.[81] "Now more than ever we have to fight against the Jews," he stated. "[Their] ideas and methods are the cause of an intolerable sickness, and those who believe that our race has a right to peace will not hesitate to battle unceasingly until the Jewish menace is finally stamped out."[82]

While it might be convenient to dismiss the KKK and Arcand as representative of a lunatic fringe that is alien both to Canadian history and life, more accurately they exist as extreme versions of a disease that remains all too prevalent in Canadian history. Anti-Semitism has emerged as well in the mainline press and among members of the elites themselves. Interwar Quebec proved a hotbed of anti-Jewish feeling. The Catholic church there published anti-Semitic notions regularly in its own "respectable" church organs, and Arcand had the tacit support of Duplessis and his government. Matters were not significantly different in English Canada, as witnessed by a speech made by minister of trade and commerce, W.D. Euler, at the pro-Nazi German Unity League (1937). Most appalling was the refusal of the Mackenzie King government to allow Jewish immigrants fleeing Nazi Germany to enter Canada. King himself was attracted to Hitler through much of the 1930s and remained a notorious anti-Semite.[83]

Tragically, Jews are still targeted by hate groups. Organizations like the Heritage Front and Aryan Nation have harassed Jewish communities increasingly over the last decade. The celebrated trials of Ernst Zundel and James Keegstra in the mid-1980s over their Holocaust-denying propaganda campaigns underscore even further the continued virulence of anti-Semitic crusades.[84]

Gays and lesbians

Perhaps no persecuted minority in our nation has been so universally excoriated as gays and lesbians. Fear and revulsion towards homosexuals characterize the entire society, whether overtly or subtly. Even those with progressive credentials balk at such rudimentary goals as fair and equal treatment of gays and lesbians before the law and in the economy. However, leftist trade unionists are increasingly recognizing that worker solidarity must take precedence over sexual orientation. The Canadian Auto Workers' support of socialist gay activist Svend Robinson for the leadership of the NDP in 1995 provides a case in point. Yet progress remains slow and checkered. Even the courageous and costly moves of the United Church of Canada to address this issue contrast sharply with the timidity and denials of other Christian denominations. What remains especially scandalous is the willingness of those who have moral qualms about the homosexual lifestyle to engage in cruel and discriminatory practices. Such oppression is compounded by the fearful spontaneous conspiracy of silence found in much of the population.[85]

The Forgotten Oppressed
Victims of War

> Too long have I lived among people who hate peace, who, when I propose peace, are all for war.   — *Psalm 120:6-7*

Throughout Canadian history patriotism has served to cloud the fundamental reality that war is about victims. Stories of heroism and military valour push to the background the fact that soldiers usually come out of the very classes that are oppressed in their society. They remain the replaceable parts of war, which is both caused by and waged in the interests of the wealthy elite of any given nation. To be sure, on the issues of war and peace Canada has contrasted favourably with the likes of Britain, France, Germany, the United States, and Russia and it has been portrayed on the international stage as a celebrated peacemaker. But a much darker reality challenges such a picture. Capitalist society by its very nature is warlike. Competition and acquisitiveness lead to conflict with inexorable regularity. Historically the struggle for profits, markets, and power has spilled over again and again into outright violence — as witnessed by the devastation of Aboriginal peoples and the brutal crushing of peaceful strikes and protest marches. The nation of Canada itself was born of a military conflict between the British and the French. It is a simple progression from such internal events to military conflicts between nations.

Canada has never been the prime mover in wars between nations. Nor has it hesitated to wave the patriotic banner shrilly when the "mother country" declared war. In the case of the two major global conflicts of the past century, the financial and corporate elites prospered while the masses of the populace suffered. What also proved true was that war meant an end to recession. Profits soared as factories boomed due to the exigencies of war. At the same time, worker gains did not keep pace with such "good" economic times. Labour militancy was curtailed conveniently in the name of patriotism and wartime unity, while xenophobia and "wartime hysteria" ran rampant even among workers themselves. Conscription was forced upon the nation, which produced violent repercussions in Quebec. In Berlin, Ontario (now Kitchener), during the First World War anti-German feeling ran so high that one local Lutheran pastor was forced out of his home by anglophone soldiers and compelled to kiss the Union Jack. Both during and after these global conflicts democracy stood aside while pacifists and critics of the war found their rights of dissent suspended. Nor can it be forgotten that it was overwhelmingly workers and farmers who shed their blood on Vimy Ridge, at Dieppe, and elsewhere.[86]

Even in our own day war continues to be a "growth industry." Mercenary armies dot the global landscape, and national victories in wartime are honoured regularly. War and the mentality that feeds it remain highly complex issues that defy easy analysis, but a focus on one facet of militarism, the arms trade, provides some useful insights. This industry alone creates victims in a twofold way. On the one hand, weapons sold are used to kill, which the proliferation of conflicts amply demonstrates. On the other hand, revenue spent on war means money not utilized for life-giving programs such as health and education.

By the beginning of the 1990s more money worldwide was being spent on weapons than on anything else, and although arms production and even arms sales declined somewhat after the end of the Cold War, the war and munitions industries remain a major facet of global life. Of the six major suppliers of arms in the world today, all but last-place China are part of the "free-enterprise" industrial West. The United States heads the list, with sales in excess of $56 billion, just slightly less than the other five combined.[87]

Canada is not one of the "Big Six" among the arms suppliers, nor is it among the six top purchasers. But this does not mean that our nation is not complicit with the war industries. Since the Second World War Canada has linked itself faithfully to the U.S. war machine and has supported that country in most of its military and imperialistic endeavours, with Canada's participation in the Desert Storm fiasco standing as the most recent example. As of 1990 Canada was still spending 2.2 per cent of its GDP on defence, and the recent exposé of brutality in the nation's Air-Borne Unit in Somalia provides testimony to the continuing spirit of militarism in our land. Canada profits from the arms trade, especially in its Asian markets. Even the celebrated role played by Canadian peacekeepers has proven more mythical than real. Indeed, in 1991-92 only $120 million of a military budget of over $13 billion was committed to the peacekeeping program. The rest was for high-ticket items, such as major war toys and NATO costs, though NATO's *raison d'être,* the Warsaw Pact, is now defunct.[88]

Creation as Victim

> Wail, oaks of Bashan, for the impenetrable forest has been felled! The wailing of the shepherds is heard; their glorious pastures have been ruined, the roaring of the young lions is heard; the thickets of the Jordan have been laid waste.   — *Zechariah 11:2-3*

The ecological crisis and the environmental movement might have a novel quality about them, but they are by no means simply a phenomenon of the 1980s and 1990s. Ever since the Industrial Revolution took hold in Canada there has emerged an at least partial awareness of the cost to creation of the single-minded drive for power and profit. The nation's economy was built upon natural resources from the very beginning. Fish and furs dominated the colonial period, and the early years of the nineteenth century experienced a lumber boom, especially in the Maritimes. With the arrival of the Industrial Revolution came a massive expansion in the extraction of minerals.

In every instance the rush for profits resulted in a ruthless devastation of the environment. The beaver almost perished, and the early lumber business displayed massive waste. Within decades the great forests of the Maritimes were largely denuded. A similar story comes to light through the voracious character of the pulp and paper industry in Quebec and the decline of forests in that province. The "boom and bust" of Canadian mining towns provides one more example of the historical disregard of the surrounding natural environment. Treating creation as a source of profit above all else is nothing new, and such an attitude has led to a perpetual war against the environment.[89]

In more recent times a widespread consciousness has sprung up that recognizes the devastation of the natural order—a devastation characterized by assaults on creation generated by a vast global industrial network that ignores pollution in the name of profit and consumption. Still, in Canada even the limited controls set in place have now been diminished. Deficit reduction provided the excuse for the Chrétien Liberals to slash 1,400 jobs and $235 million from

Environment Canada. Natural Resources cut another 1,500 jobs, and Parks Canada has sustained a budget chop of $98 million. In British Columbia the provincial government wooed Louisiana-Pacific, a lumber conglomerate, to build plants on its territory. Not only is L-P notoriously anti-union, but it also has an abysmal record on environmental concerns. Vancouver Island's Clayoquot Sound and parts of northern Alberta have emerged as two other crisis areas in which lumber barons are moving against the environment and its supporters.[90]

Water, another of Canada's abundant natural resources, is being despoiled by corporate giants without any concern for the natural habitats of this most precious life-giving and life-sustaining liquid. In the case of the Athabaska River in Alberta, the pulp and paper industry has proven to be the culprit. In the corporate rush for profits the surrounding forests are being destroyed and the mills themselves are producing toxins that are dumped into the river. The dumping results in serious oxygen depletion, endangering all life dependent upon the river as well as releasing known carcinogens into the water. Vast hydroelectric projects in the Niagara Basin and in the north have become increasingly common over the last two decades and are viewed as a quick fix for economic woes. Water is being shipped to consumers, mostly industrial, south of the border. Huge megaprojects dump dangerous toxic wastes into our hydro systems and destroy natural habitats for Aboriginal peoples as well as for the flora and fauna of those areas.[91]

Given other additional issues, such as the depletion of the ozone layer, the growing "greenhouse effect," the North American obsession with the private automobile, and the promotion and increase of herbicides and pesticides in agriculture, it is easy to see that we live in the midst of a runaway ecodisaster. The epidemic only compounds itself when our society's elites create divisions among the potential opposition, who should be forming coalitions along lines of common concerns. For example, environmentalists and Native peoples battle each other, and so too, even more severely, do middle-class environmentalists and trade unionists. In that case the issue posits itself as "jobs versus the environment," a polarization that serves only to benefit the profit-makers. As well, environmentalism has become a growth industry in and of itself. Corporations carry on vast programs promoting themselves as "green," a sensitivity that frequently goes no further than packaging their products in green colour.[92]

The Middle Class

I know all about you, how you are neither cold nor hot . . . but only
lukewarm.   — *Revelation 3:15-16*

Certainly, what has been called the "middle class" plays and has played
a critical role in Canadian society, far more so than in the developing
world, where such strata are much smaller. No one doubts this, yet
there remains a nagging question. In the industrialized G-7 countries,
are members of the middle classes *oppressors* or *oppressed*? The answer
to this question is not immediately obvious. A good case can be made
that they are both. For example, teachers in our society reflect such an
ambiguity. Many serve the corporate-government agenda by promoting
its ideology in the classroom on a regular basis, while others teach
their disciplines in ways that encourage critical thinking and participation in just causes.

In fall 1997 Ontario teachers moved in a more militant direction.
In response to the provincial Tories' Draconian legislation (Bill 160),
126,000 teachers walked off the job and set up pickets from October
27 to November 10. Quickly the protesters mounted a campaign to
swing the public to their side. Although Premier Harris took to the air-
waves and John Snobelen was replaced by the supposedly moderate
David Johnson at the education portfolio, the teachers soon moved
ahead of the government in the public relations battle. They demonstrated effectively that the real issues in the dispute were not educational; rather they centred around governmental grabs for power and
money. Soon the polls indicated a public solidly behind the teachers.
Food and snacks were brought to picketers; other unions offered large
loans without interest; church doors opened for picketers; and parents
mounted a green-ribbon support campaign. Tory MPPs were besieged
by mass demonstrations at Queen's Park, at fund-raising banquets, and
in their constituency offices. For only the second time in Ontario history the teachers had hit the picket lines. Their anger and the solidarity
of their rank-and-file were a sight to behold, serving as a reminder that
middle-class Canadians can be radicalized.[93]

But the issue lies far deeper than the individual responses and
motivations of middle-class people. Given the fundamental societal
structures, we can argue that the middle classes are indeed oppressed,
even though the workings of society might send out the opposite message. Despite an ideology that seeks to divide "workers" from "middle-
class professionals," based upon income and the nature of work performed, the middle classes remain workers; that is, they are defined by
the performance of the labour that they sell. Like other workers, their

lives remain determined by their paycheques. If their income is notably higher than this or that other particular worker, they may still be only two or three paycheques away from disaster, and once it is on the way they have little or no control in averting that disaster. They have no more decision-making power over their employment than a miner or autoworker.

It serves the interests of the "shakers and makers" to encourage polarization between these varying sectors of society, so much so that the middle classes are conditioned to forget their oppression and to identify with their oppressors. Such a "divide and conquer" policy proves necessary to the continuing rule of the tiny elitist minority. Showing a keen understanding of this problem, the editor of *The Catholic New Times*, Sister Mary Jo Leddy, wrote a piece challenging the middle class to recognize its chains and link up with the obviously poor and oppressed. More recently, with massive cutbacks in the ranks of middle-management and public-sector professionals, middle-class employees are realizing that they are workers and that they need to organize into unions. A new mood of solidarity is in the air as middle-class people join with traditional workers in the trade-union movement. The recent entry of teachers' associations into the Canadian Labour Congress illustrates this quite well, a move strengthened by the unprecedented solidarity between picketing Ontario teachers and their trade-union allies in October and November 1997.[94]

Christian Reformers and Radicals

Your sword devoured your prophets like a destructive lion.
— *Jeremiah 2:30*

Another clear illustration of middle-class social double-think has emerged through divisions within the ranks of organized Christianity. Although the church has often sided with the wealthy elites throughout Canadian history, it has also produced bold prophets, people who have condemned the oppressors for their injustices. Quite predictably these prophets have suffered persecution at the hands of the powerful. For example, the more radical social gospel advocates, found largely in the Prairies, attacked the plutocrats and began to increasingly side with organized labour. Such positions became subject to concerted counter-attacks by the business interests and their ecclesiastical allies.

One such victim was the Rev. Salem Bland, church history professor at the Methodist Wesley College in Winnipeg. His criticism of the business community and his open advocacy of the cause of the labour and farm movements got him into serious trouble with the elites in the Methodist Church. J.H. Ashdown, "the Merchant Prince," perhaps the city's most celebrated corporate citizen, was chairman of the board at the college. In 1917, in the midst of a financial crisis at Wesley, the board removed Salem Bland and his social gospel colleague A.J. Irwin from their posts in the name of fiscal restraint. Bland's friends and supporters were furious, alleging political motives. Bland concurred and took his case to Methodist adjudicatory bodies. Although these groups gave Bland their vocal support, the dismissal was upheld.[95]

A second social gospel victim of corporate might was the Rev. William Ivens. During his Winnipeg pastorate at McDougall Methodist Church Ivens became active in support of the local labour movement, a move that did not endear him to many of the church's congregation, even though they were largely working-class. Ivens's pacifism in the face of conscription and the Great War also played a part in his dismissal. Prominent church members inaugurated a campaign to remove him, while others within the congregation joined the city's labour movement in a letter-writing campaign to keep him at his post. Despite the strong support for Ivens, the Methodist Conference's stationing committee removed him from the split congregation and offered to send him to another church. Ivens refused and asked the committee to grant him a year's leave so that he might create a church geared towards labouring people. The Methodist Conference granted his request.[96]

Ivens's martyrdom had just begun. As minister of the first labour church, organized in Winnipeg on July 8, 1918, this pioneering pastor plunged fully into social gospel radicalism, a radicalism that led him to a prominent leadership role in the Winnipeg General Strike a year later. At the centre of the strike rallies was his labour church, and Ivens himself edited the strike bulletin, the *Western Labor News*. Because of these activities he was arrested out of his home in the middle of the night. Further, the chair of the national Methodist Department of Evangelism and Social Service, T.A. Moore, was working with the RCMP against the labour churches. Once again Ivens's denomination had turned its back on him, this time to the point that its own social gospel unit was involved actively to destroy the religious movement Ivens had set in motion.[97]

More recently, the lay Catholic activist Tony Clarke has felt the weight of official church disapproval, which has occurred in a church that has produced highly progressive social statements, many of them borrowing heavily from the insights of liberation theology. The Fête du

Travail publications of the Quebec bishops stand as an example of those views. Indeed, Clarke himself proved instrumental in helping the Canadian Catholic bishops draft a collective statement that aligned the church solidly on the side of justice for the oppressed. Called *Ethical Reflections on the Economic Crisis* (1983), this document received wide national coverage, thus giving heart to the marginalized and chagrin to the establishment. The reigning Trudeau government and members of the corporate elite lambasted the bishops and even threatened retaliation. In time such threats, linked with the personal ties of certain corporate magnates with the more conservative bishops, came to fruition. Tony Clarke had taken a leave of absence from his position as social policy advisor to the bishops in order to give more attention to the national campaign against free trade. His high-profile attacks upon the corporate agenda proved embarrassing to the bishops and their big-business friends. Consequently Clarke found that he no longer had a job after his leave of absence had run out. His story exists as a vivid reminder that the persecution of church reformers remains as real today as it was at the time of the Winnipeg General Strike.[98]

Oppression is the shocking underside of Canadian history, a history in which the land's vulnerable and marginalized peoples and environments are plundered by a tiny ruthless band of exploiters. Their control of power, information, and resources has permitted them to devastate the land and its people and, in addition, has enabled them to pit one sector of the oppressed against the other. All told, this proves to be a direct and vicious attack on the Biblical vision of *shalôm*, and these victims stand as the very favoured of the God who embodies radical love and justice. The litany of death and destruction remains vast, a dirge in the face of a global epidemic. Is mourning our only alternative, or perhaps denial? Can something be done in the face of so pandemic a scourge? The Biblical response erupts with a resounding "Yes!" to this last question.

5 Liberating the Oppressed

To ask "What can I do?" in the face of rampant injustice and inequality is both an honest and an appropriate question. It remains the most frequent query directed at me by people confronted with the overwhelming nature of oppression in our society. Probably most of you who read this book would classify yourselves as middle class. I do. Most likely this means that we possess enough of life's basics — food, clothing, shelter, education, mobility, leisure, and economic resources — to enable us to pursue a good number of hopes and dreams. Perhaps this means that it isn't every day that we have to confront the overwhelming reality of injustice in our land.

In answer to the question, "What can I do?" all the major religious and philosophical traditions, including humanism, cry out, "Do Justice!" This would seem to be the answer, put simply. Of course, matters are not that easy. The problems remain overwhelming. The forces for the status quo are always strong; when they are put to the test they can be brutal. Nonetheless, the call for Biblical *shalôm* emerges clearly. We are to "Do Justice."

I have no easy answers; no one does. Yet others who have gone before us have faced these issues, these realities. There are footprints we can follow, and there are those who stand beside us. And I want to emphasize that Christians do not have a monopoly when it comes to justice and solidarity with the oppressed. I don't wish to forget *any* comrades who live and even die that justice may be done. I have walked with too many Jews, Muslims, Hindus, Marxists, atheists, agnostics and others to exclude them from these struggles. Still, I am a Christian, and it is appropriate, on that account, to speak principally here on the basis of beliefs and practices within my faith community.

Especially when asked by decent middle-class people, the question "what can I do?" can be merely rhetorical. The implied answer is, "There's nothing I can do." This reflects a dishonesty, because the answer indicates that the question is merely a dodge. The New Testament's rich young ruler fits such a category. I've also encountered another question that follows the stated question "What can I do?" That is, "What can I do to help out without my own life and lifestyle being threatened?" The honest answer to this question is, "Virtually nothing."

By way of contrast, Jesus promised that those who would follow him in solidarity with the oppressed would pay a cost for their choice: "Beware! They will hand you over to the [religious courts] and scourge you in their [worship centres]. You will be dragged before governors and kings for my sake to bear witness" (Matthew 10:17-18). Put bluntly, being Jesus' disciple brings with it persecution from both religious and civic elites. To those who would walk with him, Jesus said, "If you want to be a follower of mine, renounce yourself and take up the cross and follow me" (Mark 8:34). Ironically, Jesus calls such people happy or blessed: "Happy are those who are persecuted in the cause of right, for theirs is the Reign of God" (Matthew 5:10). He is saying that those who join the ranks of God's reign will find themselves on the side of the poor and marginalized. This will inevitably position them against the powerbrokers of societies, people bent on domination and manipulation. The consequence of such solidarity will be a threat to the lives and well-being of the disciples, and Jesus speaks forthrightly about this danger. There is no masochism in this position. Rather it reflects a direct willingness to pay the cost of solidarity with Jesus and the gospel in doing justice, in embodying *shalôm*.

Yet a single person does not bear this cost alone. There can be no "Lone Ranger" mystique in Biblical faith. Rather, Christ's persistent call to "love one another" highlights solidarity over individual heroism. In light of this fundamental principle, one answer to the question, "What can I do?" is simply: "By all means, do not try to stand alone! Find your sisters and brothers and be with them. You are not alone." The question becomes no longer "What can I do?" but "What must we do, and *how* are we to accomplish justice in the midst of so much oppression?"

For me and other Christians who feel called to such a task, there remain constant and legitimate pleas for direction. We discover these paths by pointing to concrete ways in which we can serve the liberating gospel in Canada and in the stuff of our everyday living. I make no attempt here to be exhaustive, but I suggest that the following categories cover the major arenas in Canada in which a pro-liberationist approach has manifested itself in both the Christian faith and the wider society. There have been liberationists in Canada; there are now liberationists in Canada; and we can find them, search them out. This linking with others contains the answers to the "how" questions that assault us when oppression seems so endemic and intractable. I would suggest that Christians can effectively accomplish solidarity with the poor, marginalized, and oppressed in God's name through two avenues, both of them communal in nature: (1) communities of Christian liberationists; and (2) wider movements of liberation.

Communities of Liberationist Christians

There is no particular order in which neophyte liberationists link up with communities of support. The connections can depend on such random factors as personality, geography, life-shaping events, and the Holy Spirit. Nonetheless, certain arenas of Christian experience have provided the nurturing, training, and opportunity for militant solidarity in the name of the gospel.

Sources of Liberationist Consciousness Raising

Since the emergence of the social gospel movement at the end of the nineteenth century, bodies of conscious Christians have gathered together for the twofold purpose of serious research in the service of justice and mutual support in the struggle for liberation from injustice.

The social gospel

The pioneer work of J.S. Woodsworth in the field of social work serves as one striking example of the social gospel in operation in everyday life. For Woodsworth the amelioration of grim living conditions moved beyond charity into the arena of social analysis and social transformation in the name of the reign of God. In the context of his work in the Winnipeg slums he stated:

> It is right to help the sick; it is right to do away with filth and over crowding and to provide sun-light and good air and good food. We have tried to provide for the poor. Yet have we tried to alter the social conditions that lead to poverty? . . . You can't separate man from his surroundings and deal separately with each.[1]

This kind of insistence that poverty grows out of unjust social conditions in need of amelioration set Woodsworth apart from the charitable mindset of most of the ecclesiastical establishment of his day. He directed Winnipeg's All Peoples' Mission, which reached further than the standard "handouts to the needy" approach. It ran classes designed to assist people in day-to-day living, and it became a centre of political action and social analysis. From this settlement house Woodsworth agitated for broader organs of reflection and transformation both in the church and in society at large. He organized social service workers into a broader organization, and his efforts led to the famous Social Service Congress of March 1914. This event marked the birth of modern social work in Canada. As well, his two books *Strangers within Our Gates* (1909) and *My Neighbour* (1911) were profound analyses of the oppression of workers, the poor, and immigrants, with the express purpose of organizing society along what today would be called liberationist lines.[2]

Woodsworth was joined by such colleagues as A.E. Smith, Beatrice Brigden, William Ivens, William Irvine, and Salem Bland. All participated in grass-roots consciousness raising both within and outside of the church. Irvine, for one, operated a number of newspapers in Alberta that espoused radical farm and labour causes. The Methodist Brigden was a much sought-after public speaker as well as a teaching leader in the labour churches.[3]

Salem Bland was the only professional theologian, and in this respect he represents the model of what it means to be a Canadian liberation theologian in the strictest and narrowest sense of that term. From his arrival as church history professor at Wesley College in 1903 until his dismissal in 1917 he mentored such radical social gospel students as J.S. Woodsworth, A.E. Smith, and William Ivens. Bland was no "ivory-tower" academic. He had ties with the local labour unions and wrote regularly for the farm movement's *Grain Growers' Guide*. Within his own church he locked horns with business and political elites who had massive influence within ecclesiastical circles, a conflict that led to his dismissal from the College.[4]

Bland refused to be silent. In 1920, shortly after the Winnipeg General Strike, he published *The New Christianity*, a small book that could justifiably be called Canada's first "liberation theology" text. Bland saw Canada at a crossroads in a world fraught with turmoil: a crossroads of choice between the forces of wrong and "the two great Christian principles of democracy and brotherhood."[5] In the book he outlined the march of democracy throughout history to the point at which private control of industry remained the last bastion of elitist control to be replaced.

A check must be placed on the fatal fashion money has of breeding money. Wages of labor, wages of invention, wages of superinten-dence, are just; profits of capital must grow less and less to the van-ishing point.

The bitter conflict between capital and labor over the division of the profits will never be settled. . . . It will cease to be. Capital will cease to be a factor; only labor in the broadly inclusive sense of the term will remain.

The onward march of democracy, then, cannot be staid. . . . Democracy is nothing but the social expression of the fundamental Christian doctrine of the worth of the human soul. . . . A share in the control of church, community, industry is the Divine right of every normal man and woman.[6]

Bland's words echo what Biblical material describes as oppression and liberation. Indeed, with some frequency Bland used many of the same Biblical texts employed by more current liberationists. In the name of equality he promoted an economy based on "co-operative pro-duction for human needs" manifested by the transfer of the economy from private to public hands.[7] Thus, for Bland, God worked in the wider world, bringing in the Divine Reign through the growth of democracy and solidarity. In this context the Christian church was urged to join with the labour movement, which exemplified those val-ues broadly conceived as Christian. Although Bland saw failings in both the church and labour, he was convinced that their conscious alliance remained the modern world's chief manifestation of God's con-crete historical work.[8]

Not surprisingly, the grim years of the Depression spawned Chris-tian groups involved in both militant justice causes and consciousness-raising. Committed Christian academics, like Bland, moved beyond university security into the troubled waters of radical analysis and social transformation.

The SCM

From the early years of the 1920s the Student Christian Movement (SCM) in Canada came to embody a preliberationist theology and praxis. The organization itself grew out of the social gospel. Certainly many, if not most, of the students came from the middle classes, but their involvement in the burgeoning SCM brought them into contact with social gospel leaders such as Bland and the pro-labour Ernest Thomas.[9]

From that time until well into the 1950s SCM militants adopted Christian socialist positions embodied by the adult-led Fellowship for a Christian Social Order. To give more life to these convictions, the SCM began a series of workcamps that lasted well into the 1970s. This experience helped its members in the practice of a primitive communism similar to the type of church described in the Biblical Book of Acts, and it enhanced their sympathy for the labour movement. In the Welland, Ontario, area, the campers laboured full-time in some of the nearby factories. On the shop floor these youth encountered labour militants and were drawn into solidarity with the union movement. This combined camp and factory experience brought middle-class youth into a base-Christian community that radicalized them profoundly.[10]

The FCSO

The adult Fellowship for a Christian Social Order (FCSO) emerged from the Depression itself. Created in 1934 in Kingston, Ontario, it brought together existing fellowships located largely in Toronto and Montreal. Soon its influence reached across the country, and the national body that emerged was patterned after the organizational structure of the United Church of Canada. The values that prompted the Fellowship echoed the turn-of-the-century social gospel through the assertion, "The teachings of Jesus Christ, applied in an age of machine production and financial control, mean Christian Socialism." Like their predecessors the FCSO organizers blended the principles of the left social gospel with social-scientific tools in order to transform society along just lines.[11]

The FCSO found its leadership among academics, but these men had received their baptism of fire in the SCM movement or in the social gospel tradition of the United Church of Canada and its predecessor bodies. In fact, J. King Gordon of the United Church College in Montreal was the son of the social gospel Presbyterian minister C.W. Gordon, better known under his pen name Ralph Connor. The FCSO resolutely opposed the current political-economic order: "This Fellowship is an association of Christians whose religious convictions have led them to the belief that the Capitalist economic system is fundamentally at variance with Christian principles; and who regard the creation of a new social order to be essential to the realization of the Kingdom of God."[12]

Attacking conservative or corporatist solutions, it called upon Christians "to recognize the fact of the class struggle and to interpret the mind of Christ to their day and generation by identifying themselves actively with the cause of the exploited and dispossessed in the effort to build a classless society."[13]

The presence of Gordon and other high-powered academics gave credence to the FCSO in important church and middle-class circles. In 1936 two of its leaders, Biblical scholar R.B.Y. Scott and philosophy professor Gregory Vlastos, edited a trailblazing book called *Towards the Christian Revolution*. These men and their cowriters created a veritable theology of liberation for the Depression-ridden 1930s in Canada. Vlastos underscored Jesus' complete identity "with the hungry, the thirsty, the stranger, the naked, the sick, the prisoner."[14]

Not surprisingly these Christian radicals came under fire within both the churches and the universities where they were employed. Vested interests in the business community used their financial muscle during a moment of fiscal crisis at Montreal's United Theological College to rid themselves of King Gordon. After his position had been terminated, Gordon toiled as travelling secretary of the FCSO, although for a brief period he considered working for Canada's new socialist party, the CCF. King Gordon, the ex-academic, had brought his theological skills into the arena of active combat, thus demonstrating, as Salem Bland had before him, that Christian scholars can and do join the ranks of liberation militants.[15] He summarized that position well in a CCF journal in 1934: "Christianity has a profound contribution to make to the movement for a reconstructed social order. . . . While it cannot identify itself with a political party it must be prepared to identify itself with the cause of the oppressed. . . . Its goal . . . will, in the main, include the goal of Socialism but will go beyond."[16]

The Antigonish Movement

Perhaps the most significant example of consciousness-raising groups was the Antigonish Movement of Nova Scotia. Gregory Baum, a current proponent of liberationist Christianity, described it as "the most original and the most daring response of Canadian Catholics to the social injustices during the Depression."[17] It was "a cooperative movement, based on a special kind of adult education, that sought to enlighten farmers and fishermen in regard to their economic helplessness and organize them as co-owners of new enterprises for the distribution and, in some cases, the production of goods."[18]

This Antigonish spirit and the subsequent movement originated at Saint Francis Xavier University with the arrival of Father J.J. ("Jimmy") Tompkins in 1902. Coming from a long line of activist Maritime priests, Father Jimmy opted for social transformation through education. He encouraged his students to resist siding with the "bigwigs" who oppress the "little people" and developed a style of pedagogy that presaged the work of Paulo Freire in Latin America. In 1921 he published this approach in a booklet called *Knowledge for the People—A Call to Saint Francis Xavier College.* He appealed to that school to create a popularly based adult extension program linked effectively to the co-operative movements of the Maritime Provinces. Sadly, Tompkins's crusty personality alienated some of the bigwigs and others, which led to his dismissal from the university and his posting at an impoverished church in the fishing village of Canso. There he and the fishers got some roads built, raised some foundation money for his educational agenda, and pressured the creation of the governmental MacLean Commission on the Maritime Fisheries.[19]

By the end of the 1920s Father M.M. ("Moses") Coady had been called to Saint Francis Xavier to direct the new extension program. From then until his death in 1959 Coady embodied the Antigonish Movement. For him "the great work of adult education" had to be geared towards "participation by the masses of the people in the economic processes."[20] He was as good as his word. He led discussion and learning groups in schools, churches, and kitchens throughout the towns and villages of Nova Scotia, and by the outbreak of the Second World War the results spoke for themselves. The Maritime provinces had 2,265 study clubs containing 19,600 people in the program. Some 342 credit unions had been established, as well as 162 other co-op organizations. Annual conferences were held at the university. In 1930 the United Maritime Fishermen Limited was formed as a federation linking together local fishing co-ops, and overtures were made to integrate working-class issues and the unions into the program. Father Coady used the printed page, newspapers, and radio to reach more people and extend the influence of the movement.[21]

Coady and his movement had their contradictions. As a traditional Catholic, Coady repudiated socialism, yet many of his ideas fell easily into the socialist camp. He had no desire to transform Canadian society radically; at many levels, he was a social reformer. At the same time his language, classes, and organizing work among the marginalized earned him those avant-garde credentials that made him so uneasy.[22] That more radical side of Coady emerged in his public speeches. In one 1952 address he stated: "The feudal lords who run our society are not going to change their minds in the direction of a more democratic society because educational leaders say it's the right thing to do. . . . To persuasion and education we must add force, that gentle yet all-powerful force of economic, social and political action sponsored by a majority of the people, by the masses."[23]

For Coady the tyranny of the wealthy and powerful needed to be replaced by a more regulated economy with natural monopolies socialized into governmental bodies, with a large co-operative sector working alongside small private industries. Coady called this mixed system "economic democracy."[24] His legacy survives to this day at Saint Francis Xavier University. The Extension Department continues the work, and added to it has been the Coady International Institute, which educates Canadians for work among marginalized populations overseas. The Institute also trains leaders from developing countries in both organizing and technical skills as part of its goal to work towards social justice and transformation.[25]

Some current teams

Other consciousness-raising groups dot today's landscape. In my own area of Kitchener-Waterloo, Ontario, at least five such groups exist, and I have worked with three of them. In downtown Waterloo, the Global Community Centre has as its mandate "to raise public awareness of, and foster action on, international development and social justice issues." Acting on the slogan "think globally and act locally," the centre has mobilized efforts on behalf of immigrants and refugees and other marginalized groups both in our society and around the globe.[26] In the seminary building where I teach is the office of the Institute for Christian Ethics, a social justice "think-tank" and advocacy body jointly sponsored by the Eastern Synod of the Evangelical Lutheran Church in Canada and the Waterloo Lutheran Seminary. Directed by the Rev. David Pfrimmer, it conducts research on justice issues and advocates before public and government bodies.[27] In Kitchener an organization called the Working Centre, directed by Joseph and Stephanie Mancini, arose in response to recent economic downturns and massive unemployment. It provides support and counselling for people who are out of work and looking for jobs.[28]

In Toronto, at least until its shutdown in 1997, the Jesuit Centre for Social Faith and Justice on Queen Street was one of the nation's most highly respected clearing houses for information and advocacy for liberation both globally and nationally. It engaged in overseas development work, social analysis and research on human rights issues, and public education. Perhaps the best-known of such organizations are Canada's interchurch coalitions, including the Aboriginal Rights Coalition, the Inter-Church Coalition on Africa, the Taskforce on the Churches and Corporate Responsibility, the Canada-Asia Working Group, the Canada China Program, PLURA, Ten Days for Global Justice, the Inter-Church Committee on Human Rights, Project Ploughshares, the Inter-Church Committee for Refugees, the Interchurch Fund for International Development, and the Ecumenical Coalition for Economic Justice. These groups concentrate on the specific concerns indicated by their names, and produce for church bodies and public groups excellent resources on pertinent issues.[29]

GATT-Fly and ECEJ

The Ecumenical Coalition for Economic Justice (ECEJ) originated in 1973 with the name GATT-Fly and committed itself to "be a gadfly, pestering the government on trade and economic justice issues." Three full-time staffers, John Dillon, Dennis Howlett, and Reg McQuaid, embraced the mandate "to do research, education and action on trade and economic issues affecting the Third World." GATT-Fly immediately adopted the liberationist model of education (praxis-reflection-praxis) as its own and took up the issues called for by its mandate. Within its first years it used its research to lobby governments, provide data for progressive MPs, and organize public support campaigns for just causes.[30]

One of GATT-Fly's most creative methods has been its "Ah-hah" seminars or workshops. These grew out of the experiential struggles of the GATT-Fly team's attempts to convert complex issues into the passion and commitment generated from people's own lives, awareness, and struggle. The approach gave grist to the research mill of GATT-Fly itself and helped that team retain its focus on "grass-roots" activities.[31] Its work among the poor and marginalized has shaped GATT-Fly markedly over the years. By the mid-1980s the team, or "collective," as its members called themselves, was passionately engaged in the anti-free-trade coalition. Its full-time staff works co-operatively in a strictly team approach, and members share menial chores equally. They work out salaries on the basis of Biblical justice, equity, and need, and reach decisions on such matters collectively.[32]

In 1990 GATT-Fly changed its name to the Ecumenical Coalition for Economic Justice (ECEJ). The change grew out of debate and dialogue between GATT-Fly and the churches. Some church activists felt that the churches' class-mixed constituency would remain a brake on social progress and that the GATT-Fly team's future lay with popular, "grass-roots" movements. Other church members felt that GATT-Fly remained too independent and troublesome. The upshot of the conflict strengthened the new ECEJ's ties with the church, and the mandate adopted included a frankly liberationist agenda

> to strengthen the churches' ability: 1) to maintain an active Christian presence among the poor and marginalized groups involved in struggles for economic justice; 2) to develop positions that both criticize and advocate alternatives to major issues of economic and social policy in Canada and their relations to the Third World; 3) to participate in building coalitions with a variety of popular groups struggling for economic justice.[33]

In the last few years ECEJ has held to this mandate, providing resources for both popular coalitions and church-based groups dedicated to social justice and transformation.[34] ECEJ interprets its vocation according to the "prophetic tradition which understands that people come to know God by participating in the struggles for justice for the poor, the marginalized and the oppressed." As ECEJ activist Dennis Howlett affirms, "Underlying [our] whole approach has been a theology strongly influenced by Latin American liberation theologians."[35]

Quebec Équipes

Teams of Christians geared to providing resources and commitment for social justice have historical roots in Quebec, although earlier bodies there proved right-wing and corporatist with the exception of groups under the inspiration of Father Georges-Henri Lévesque.[36] But not until after the Quiet Revolution and Vatican II did distinctly liberationist consciousness-raising groups emerge in Quebec. Independent of the church was the ecumenical and markedly socialist Politisés Chrétiens. Containing from three hundred to four hundred Christian radicals throughout Quebec, the Politisés Chrétiens formed in 1974 and lasted for eight years. This network (*reseau*) defined itself as "an ensemble of persons *linked to the interests of those workers involved* in the struggle for their own liberation and who *gather together as 'believers'* in a common witness to the gospel of Jesus Christ." As well the *reseau* pledged "to restore the popular character of the church . . . *in solidarity with the truly militant workers* and on the side of the 'little ones' and the 'oppressed.'"[37]

The network itself was not involved in direct action but consisted of militants who worked within specialized Catholic Action, *groupes populaires*, trade unions, and other progressive organizations. Much like GATT-Fly, the Politisés Chrétiens was research-based and prepared materials to aid militants in their activism. For its values, it utilized

"Marxist analysis in light of the Gospel" and endorsed what it called the "option for class consciousness" based on "a Christian socialist perspective." Overt militancy and the open critique of the church, as well as a movement towards the right in Quebec society, undermined the *reseau* in the early 1980s and led to its demise.[38]

More acceptable to the church and more long-lived are the less obviously radical "think-tanks"—the Centre de Pastorale en Milieu Ouvrier (CPMO), based in Montreal, and Quebec City's Carrefour de Pastorale en Monde Ouvrier (CAPMO). In their structures and values these bodies resemble the Politisés Chrétiens. All three engage in consciousness-raising and research for social transformation, and all three adopt frankly liberationist values. Nonetheless, CPMO and CAPMO connect with official church bodies and embody less blatant socialist convictions. Founded by Father Claude Lefebvre with episcopal support in 1970, the CPMO had by the end of the decade evolved in its self-definition. It called itself "a centre of formation for popular organizations and trade unions," with a fourfold mandate: (1) as a "resource bank" of people, (2) as a place for militant training, (3) as a crossroads (*carrefour*) of debate for justice advocates, and (4) as a locus for the publication of practical resources for activists.[39] For twenty years the CPMO has kept faith with this mandate. In 1974 it joined with Politisés Chrétiens, *groupes populaires*, a team from the left-wing Catholic journal *Vie Ouvrière*, and the specialized working-class Catholic Action at Cap Rouge, Quebec, to challenge the church's bishops to join in the creating of a renovated and radical "church on the move" as opposed to a "church with its brakes on."[40]

CAPMO in Quebec City, is a more regional example of the larger CPMO. It calls itself "a voluntary town meeting place" of unity and solidarity for those militants and groups engaged in activism for and with the working class and the poor. It strives "to render the church in greater solidarity with the labouring world." Although CAPMO softens its socialistic predilections, it does embrace most of the city's left-wing Catholic militants within its ranks. In the early 1980s it published an extensive manifesto entitled *Pour une pastorale ouvrière* (*Towards a Working Class Ministry*), which criticized a church which "no longer walks the way of the worker."[41]

Current liberation theologians

Today in Canada Christian militants and liberationists can come into contact with or find resources from a handful of professional theologians. Some of them have sympathized with liberation theology and others fall squarely into the liberationist camp. Gregory Baum, a transplant to Quebec and a theologian of international repute, forms a bridge across both camps. He greets liberation theology with affection and solidarity. Although much of his writing has been leftist commentary on recent social encyclicals, he has strong links with Quebec's Catholic liberationists and gives them voice in his publications.[42]

A more openly Canadian liberationist perspective can be found in Ben Smillie's *Beyond the Social Gospel: Church Protest on the Prairies* (1991). Smillie, a retired professor and minister at the University of Saskatchewan's United Church College, lives in Saskatoon, Saskatchewan. In an earlier article, "An Update on Liberation Theology in the Canadian Context," Smillie stated his liberationist premise in unequivocal terms:

> If Liberation Theology in the Canadian context is to be different from [the] liberal optimistic idealism of the Social Gospel and if it is to have any impact on the life of Canada, it must do a class analysis of Canadian society. Specifically, it must expose the rich with economic power who control the political machinery of this country and whose wealth increases in direct proportion to the shrinking resources of the poor. The major task of Liberation Theology is to cut through the mystification which suggests that we live in a democratic, free and open society with equal opportunity for all.[43]

Smillie has called for a "historical materialist perspective," a social analysis from the standpoint of faith, because he feels that this approach "is the only method which clearly exposes those whom the Bible calls 'the rich' and 'the poor'!"[44]

His *Beyond the Social Gospel* stands out as a clear theology of liberation for the Canadian scene. The phrase Smillie uses is "hinterland theology," an appropriate term for the context of the Canadian Prairies in relation to the rest of Canada. In this work his class understanding remains as trenchant as ever: "Without class analysis to assist in identifying who is responsible for the oppression of the poor, the problem of poverty tends to be reduced from a problem of structures to one of individuals. . . . To universalize sin is to trivialize it. To avoid class analysis is to universalize sin and to guarantee that nothing will be done about oppression."[45]

Smillie's theology demands a praxis of protest against racism, sexism, and class discrimination. In this context the church's mandate calls upon us to "take on [the] power brokers" and "de-legitimize their public image." This necessitates, he believes, an "ecumenical boldness and insurrection" as "the church's road to resurrection."[46] Smillie is no "ivory tower" intellectual. He remains active in grass-roots protest groups and was one of the few academic theologians to march against the War Measures Act of 1970. He calls himself a "theologian of the streets."[47]

Christian feminists provide central insights for a developing Canadian liberation theology that focuses on patriarchal as well as class elements. For instance, Marilyn J. Legge's *The Grace of Difference: A Canadian Feminist Theological Ethic* (1992) makes a significant contribution towards the articulation of a liberation theology for our land. Teaching at the same institution where Smillie worked, Legge offers a critique of the radical Christian legacy in Canada, with its tendency to pursue exclusively economic or class analysis. Nonetheless, she identifies with this tradition's "rejection of capitalism" and its utopian struggles for justice. At the same time she calls for a clear articulation of the more sustained economic oppression that has been women's experience in Canadian life. "Without awareness of women's work, the types, causes, and pervasiveness of human alienation and oppression can neither be named or challenged. . . . The dehumanization of labour that women's lives reveal deepens our understanding of economic ethics." Legge advocates a more holistic praxis that embodies the entire narrative of women's experience, not in opposition to Canada's radical Christian tradition but rather a new creative and cultural depth that gives it fullness and life.[48] She puts it this way:

> The import of this approach to culture is that it enables us to engage cultural resources in a way that discloses the problematic of women's everyday social contexts and to approach culture as a generative context of concrete transformation. A critical hermeneutics of women's experience will attend to the dynamic connections between social-cultural orders, and the subjective forms by which we live and create meaning, such as consciousness, emotions, memories, and the sense of oneself, others, and God.[49]

Mary Jo Leddy, a former nun in the Sisters of Our Lady of Sion, has militated in a wide range of justice causes for many years. Her order is committed to challenging actively the anti-Semitism so deeply embedded in the Christian tradition. She represents that brand of feminist spirituality that is both vulnerable and strong. For years she was editor of the left-leaning *Catholic New Times*, and in this context she promulgated the necessity of developing a relevant theology of liberation for the middle class. Towards that end she calls upon Canadian progressives to concentrate on liberating Canada with its middle-class consumer culture and its middle-class churches. Our churches, she says, are also "in the captivity of the middle class" and cannot engage in liberation unless they become aware of that fact and cast aside those invisible chains by dispensing with the idols of a culture that values only marketability and things. Her own life has exemplified these principles, whether in direct justice struggles or in her work with refugees at Romero House in Toronto.[50]

United Church minister Robert Haverluck, through his "liberationist" cartoons, has contributed effectively to the cause of justice in our world. One of his cartoons shows a grotesque figure holding a bunch of nails; the caption reads: "Political? Worldly nonsense! These nails are spiritual, the cross is just a cloud and Pilate is your Aunt Sally." In another particularly blunt cartoon, published in the socialist journal *Canadian Dimension*, Haverluck portrays a hardnosed capitalist responding to Jesus' injunctions versus the idolatry of money: "It's not *money* that's the problem. It's the *love* of money. Me, I don't love money. I just fool around with it. Have a good time. Money talks and I get a hard-on. But, it's not really love."[51] Over the years this theological jester of justice and joy has gravitated to art over mere words as his means of proclamation. He loves the church but is not hopeful that it can be an engine of transformation. "One doesn't go to church for liberation theology," although one might find there "a space or crack from within one might work."[52] Haverluck is outrageous, a joyous clown, a prophet of liberation, a crazy God's crazy and loving tool. He has prophetic words for middle-class Christians:

> Only those who cry deeply can laugh deeply. Deep weeping and laughter are both ways of engaging boundaries and limits to well-being. Those whose security is chained to injustice, to false limits, will experience much of what the prophets find laughable as "not funny. . . ." It is important for us as middle-class Canadians (who are as safe as houses . . . built on sand) to be open to laughter which is directed at us. But if we will not be corrected by laughter, we will be awakened by much harsher things.[53]

Christ's Little Flocks

The small groups of radical Christians who gather together regularly for worship, study, mutual support, and action provide a contrast to the consciousness-raising groups. It is primarily a question of emphasis. The latter concern themselves primarily with building Christian community through a combination of nurture and activities aimed at social justice. The oldest instance of these "little flocks" in Christian history appears in axiomatic fashion in the Book of Acts (2:42-47; 4:32-35). The members prayed and worshipped together, shared meals, practised the egalitarian distribution of earthly goods, and lived in relative gender equality.[54] Small intentional "house" communities have continued throughout Christian history, consisting of believers committed to a more intense living of the Christian life. The Anabaptists are one such group from the distant past. Today such communities exist as well, including, among the most well-known in North America, Koinonia and Jubilee, both in Georgia, and Sojourners in Washington, D.C. They live simply, hold their goods in common, and, in Christ's name, militate actively among the oppressed in the name of peace, justice, and solidarity.[55]

L'Arche

Examples of such groups exist in Canada as well. One among several that concentrate on specific groups of society's marginalized is the L'Arche community founded by Jean Vanier, the son of George Vanier, governor-general of Canada (1959-67). In 1964 Vanier and two men with physical disabilities moved into a small home in Trosly-Breuil, France, and L'Arche (the ark) was born. Since then over ninety-five such communities for men and women who are physically and mentally challenged have sprung up in twenty-four countries around the world. These "little flocks" are based rigorously on the gospel solidarity of radical, transforming love.[56]

Vanier has based his convictions on Jesus' inaugural sermon to preach "good news to the poor" (Luke 4:18). He has stated:

> The struggle of L'Arche is a struggle for liberation, the liberation on the one hand of handicapped people who are oppressed by the rejection of society and, on the other, of those who live with them. . . .
>
> L'Arche wants to take its small place, working with many others in this larger struggle for peace and justice; seeking for new ways of living universal brotherhood where all people, and especially the poor and weak, are held in honor, respected and received.[57]

Vanier understands that a truly Christian liberationist community must be based upon a radical egalitarian love, and that based on this love those whom society rejects and those whom society values must decide to live and work together in a profound and daily solidarity. Vanier offers the "bright, beautiful and successful" people of our society an alternative liberation. "What characterizes assistants who come to L'Arche," he says, "is that they accept to share their lives with devalued people, to establish real bonds with them. This choice goes against the current values of society."[58]

One could hastily conclude that L'Arche is chiefly an institution of charity. Instead, L'Arche's spirituality and values stand as a blatant repudiation of the current dehumanized profit-oriented society geared towards marketing and consuming products irrespective of the human cost. In contrast L'Arche exists as a community that values and cherishes people discarded by society. Indeed, L'Arche and its people find transformation and nourishment from the very people who seem most needy and helpless.[59]

Henri Nouwen experienced this reality when he entered the L'Arche community Daybreak north of Toronto. There he formed a friendship with twenty-five-year-old Adam, a man who could not dress himself, eat, or walk without the help of others. In coming to know Adam and forming bonds with him, Nouwen found himself transformed.

> Most of my life I have tried to show the world that I could do it on my own. . . . But as I sit beside the slow and heavy-breathing Adam, I start seeing how that journey was marked by rivalry and competition, and spotted with moments of suspicion, jealousy, resentment and revenge. The great paradox is that in his complete emptiness of all human pride, Adam is giving me a whole new understanding of God's love.[60]

Radical Monasticism in Quebec

Initially the thought that Catholic monastic orders provide useful examples for Christians seeking to live a liberationist faith might seem ludicrous. After all, such communities have often represented an elitist, clerical, and minority expression from within the Christian community. Yet at their best such orders have generated a living critique of wealth and an expression of direct compassion by their living with and support of oppressed sectors in their society.

That has certainly been the case with many religious communities working in the urban ghettos of Quebec since the Quiet Revolution of the 1960s. In Montreal and its environs are teams (*équipes*) of religious defined by the spiritual values of Charles de Foucauld—a spirituality of identity and living with the discarded of society. Included in these orders are the Petites Soeurs de l'Assomption, the Petites Soeurs de

Jésus, and the Petits Frères de l'Évangile. These nuns and lay brothers live in small groups of roughly five religious to a house in the midst of the poorer working-class neighbourhoods of the metropole. They practise participation and solidarity with those around them. Their homes provide hospitality to their neighbours, and their kitchen tables are an endless source of coffee-drinking and sharing of each other's lives. Brother Paul-André Goffart repairs and renovates the modest dwellings of his neighbours, and some of the sisters are trained social workers. In a number of cases members of these orders have performed factory toil as an act of solidarity, and they have militated within the trade union movement.[61]

In the shadow of Montreal's Olympic Stadium resides the Mission Saints Pierre et Paul, a neighbourhood-based community dedicated to identity with "the least of these." This worldwide network originated with the Dominican Jacques Loew, who was one of France's pioneer worker-priests. In Montreal the community is directed by Father Georges Convert and Brother André Choquette. Both of them did labouring stints after the "worker-priest" model. Their multipurpose building in a working-class sector of Montreal serves as a residence for their team and a drop-in centre for the entire community living around them. It also provides a worship space and a locus for education and consciousness-raising after the fashion of the Brazilian liberationist Paulo Freire. On a daily basis members of the order serve their neighbours in practical and mundane ways. For example, Brother Choquette does electrical and television repair work for those who need it. In addition the members of the mission work in concert with grass-roots groups created to bring justice and transformation in municipal life and neighbourhoods.[62]

Capuchin *équipes*, inspired by the radical Christianity of Francis of Assisi, live and work among the poor and marginalized in Montreal, Quebec City, and Hull. Specifically, Bishop Paul-Émile Charbonneau sought to organize a more grass-roots church in Hull. Towards that end he recruited Capuchin activists to aid in both church renewal and community organizing. An *équipe* arrived in 1967 and installed itself in a modest home in working-class Hull, where the team remains to this day. Throughout the years Father Isidore Ostiguy has worked with the poor in his neighbourhood for clean and sanitary low-cost housing. The work placed him in direct conflict with the realtors and government officials (federal, provincial, and municipal) who had joined together to cash in on a real estate boom generated by Hull's role as a "bedroom" community for federal government workers. Fathers Claude

Hardy and Pierre Viau collaborated with the city's militant citizens' committees (*groupes populaires*) in issues involving justice at the workplace, affordable housing, the creation of co-operatives and day-care centres, assistance to young working-class organizations, inauguration of alternative schools, and participation in popular culture festivals. Two younger Capuchin brothers, Michel Plamandon and Gaëtan Oulette, undertook full-time labour in low-paying demeaning jobs as a means of demonstrating solidarity with their oppressed neighbours.[63]

In Montreal the Fils de la Charité order has sent a number of its priests into the urban ghettos as an expression of solidarity. Two of them, Ugo Benfante and Guy Cousin, settled in the working-class quarter of Pointe-Saint-Charles. Father Benfante, a parish vicar in Pointe-Saint-Charles, consciously chose "to have a lifestyle nearer to the life and lifestyle of the labourers" who lived there. He accomplished this by leaving the rectory and living in the poor rental accommodations so characteristic of the *quartier*. Père Guy Cousin followed Benfante's lead. This solidarity of dwelling led both men into militant activism for and with the poor. They joined the *groupes populaires* and later undertook full-time toil as worker-priests. As well, they linked up with neighbourhood base-Christian communities, a form of "house church" modelled after the Latin American experience. In Quebec the base-Christian community was called the *église populaire*.[64]

House Churches

One reason why these religious orders provide such a profound Christian model for liberation *praxis* is to be found in the networks they establish with lay Christian and non-Christian activists. For example, Fathers Benfante and Cousin are not just active militants for social change and justice but also play a role in Quebec's urban house churches called the *églises populaires*. These small groups of practising Christians model themselves consciously on the Latin American experience. Although base-Christian communities in this Third World setting are frequently more radical than their North American counterparts, there remain important overlaps. Both define themselves as communities "formed of a majority of people from the popular strata and controlled by them, who identify with the exploited and oppressed and who endorse the option for their collective liberation."[65] Although all these house churches have in common a small size, which supports intimacy, as well as a direct solidarity with the marginalized of their society, their form varies from group to group. Some gather around the pastoral leadership of priests such as Ugo Benfante, Guy Cousin, and the worker-priest Jean-Pierre Roch of Saint-Hyacinthe. Others forge intimate links with their neighbourhood parishes and assist in that work — as exemplified by Petite Soeur Stephanie's community in central Montreal. Still others have no links either with the clergy or the institutional church, as in Marcel Lebel's Montreal *équipe*.[66]

A particularly instructive example is a base-Christian community that originated at Quebec City in 1973. Inspired by a priest from Brazil, a group of laity organized a small community that agreed to meet weekly, share a meal together, and discuss the juncture of their faith and their militancy. "We share the same kind of faith and involvement," member Vivian Labrie says, pointing to a simple and community-oriented lifestyle of relative egalitarianism. Most of the members live in a housing co-operative. They identify with "the poorest and those treated most unjustly." Indeed, they are themselves among the marginalized. They belong to radical Catholic groups, left-wing municipal campaign movements, and various co-operatives and *groupes populaires* in the city.[67]

Various groups of the *église populaire* attempted to form a Quebec-wide network. The Centre de Pastorale en Milieu Ouvrier sought to coordinate and expand these initiatives. Raymond Levac, its director, published a CPMO study guide called *L'Église populaire en Amérique Latine et au Québec* (1981), in which he made international connections between the Quebec examples and the liberationist communities of Latin America. The CPMO used its *Bulletin de Liaison* to promote the *église populaire*. Finally, for a brief period of time these communities published their own periodical to strengthen the network they were building. They remain an expression of solidarity "with the life conditions of the workers," and they are "with them in their struggles."[68]

I have participated within a house church network in the Kitchener-Waterloo area since 1983. By the time I entered one of five small groups, the K-W house churches had been in existence for well over a decade. Drawing inspiration from Mennonite traditions of community, a number of young couples had purchased a home in downtown Kitchener and decided to live under the same roof as families practising Christian discipleship. Two Mennonite academics, Walter Klaassen and John Miller, brought ideological and practical leadership to the growing movement. At its height in the mid-1980s the K-W house churches totalled six small groups. These, in turn, formed a larger incorporated network, which included Sunday school for the children, an annual retreat, a pastoral care committee, and a newsletter named *Oikos*. Recently the original house was converted to a centre to aid refugees integrating into Canadian society.

The heart of this house church movement remains the small group. Much like the others, our "little flock" meets weekly in one of our homes for a period of two to three hours. During that time we have a brief worship, discuss topical matters, and share our intimate concerns. The fruits of these meetings have combined nurture and challenge. My debt to the house church is enormous; these followers of Christ embody for me the presence of a radical God of love and justice.

In our own particular community the justice component emerges as fundamental. One member, Margaret, worked with the Global Community Centre, where she designed and participated in workshops at schools and churches to combat racism and other ills of our society. Stephen and Gloria served a stint in Africa, and Jonathan and Alice work among El Salvador's peasants. The poor among us have challenged our middle-class securities, and those in our membership who struggle with mental illness lead the rest of us by their courage and fidelity to Christ's gospel. One of them lives an economically simple life in response to Christ and refuses to accept any interest on his account at the Mennonite Credit Union. Still others provide support for teenagers from broken families, build homes for Habitat for Humanity, work with the handicapped, and struggle to develop a more egalitarian pedagogy with Native people and the university community. Indeed, my brothers and sisters have assisted me by studying and discussing this book in manuscript form as a community.

Our house cell has been called the social justice group among the remaining Kitchener-Waterloo house churches. We advocate, we march, we picket, we petition, and two of us have spent brief periods in jail. For years Lorrie and Fred have refused to pay taxes used for military purposes. Their presence and leadership in the house church were precipitated by a visit to the Koinonia community in Americus, Georgia. Since then they have modelled justice within our community. They have openly shared the conflicts in their own marriage and family and have enriched us all by their very human presence. Lorrie and Fred, and those like them, represent the force that stands as liberative within Christ's "Little Flocks."[69]

Parishes and the Institutional Church

It is not at all surprising that radical Christians gather themselves into small groups, what the Scriptures call "the leaven in the lump" or "the remnant." This has always been the case, and the approach logically leads liberationist disciples into consciousness-raising and supportive communities. Still, this is by no means reason to abandon the institutional church, though it is easy to recite a litany of its failures and betrayals. Institutional Christianity remains ambiguous, often torn between its status quo desire to survive and the radical mandate that Christ gave to it. The liberationist light does continue to shine here and there in the churches.

The social gospel and the labour churches

During the period of the Protestant social gospel, a number of preliberationist ecclesiastical institutions saw the light of day. In the aftermath of the Great War, towards the end of 1918, the Methodist General Conference meeting at Hamilton, Ontario, promulgated what historian Richard Allen calls "the most radical statement of social objectives ever delivered by a national church body in Canada." In spite of vociferous opposition and pressure from the corporate elite, the Conference declared that "all special privilege not based on useful service to the community" was "a violation of the principle of justice." It made sharp indictments of the capitalist system, which gives profit priority over the needs of labour, and called for fair wages and public control of "mines, waterpower, fisheries, forests, and means of communication, transportation and public utilities." It demanded an end to the capitalist system "as one of the roots of war," and in its place asserted the necessity for "an industrial system" that would give labour "a voice in the management and a share in the profits and risks of business."[70]

Signs of hope emerged in parishes here and there in the country with the labour church standing out as perhaps the most dramatic example. Its founder William Ivens, the pacifist and pro-working-class radical who served as pastor at Winnipeg's McDougall Methodist Church, was active in his city's labour politics and an open opponent of the First World War. After sectors of the congregational establishment sought to remove him, his case went before a regional Methodist body for adjudication. The committee recommended that he leave without blame, and he was offered another Winnipeg post. Instead Ivens bargained for the freedom not to be stationed for a year so that he could work to create a labour church in the city.[71]

That church came about in the summer of 1918. "I am willing," he stated, "to support an independent and creedless church that will be placed on the Fatherhood of God and the Brotherhood of man. Its aim shall be the establishment of justice and righteousness on earth."[72] Not surprisingly, workers and their families constituted most of the members of the labour church, but people from other classes collected there as well. They met in the local Labour Temple until rising membership required the rental of local theatres. Soon structures and practices developed that melded together elements from both Methodism and labour traditions. Statements of principle, hymns, and sermons reflected a broad liberal Christianity committed to an alliance with labour in order to overturn the capitalist system.[73]

Such convictions boiled over into direct involvement in the Winnipeg Strike of 1919. Ivens ran *The Western Labor News*, the strike's newspaper, and his church served as a central rallying point for the strikers. Radical Christians, lay and ordained, joined other labour leaders at the church's open-air mass meetings to inspire those who had laid down their tools in the name of a better tomorrow. One of them, F.J. Dixon, stated: "Jesus was a carpenter's son, not a lawyer, financier or iron-master. It is easy to guess which side he would be on in this struggle. He was on the side of the poor."[74] Soon the forces of order entered to crush the strike. Ivens himself was arrested in the dead of night from his home. So too was J.S. Woodsworth, who came to Winnipeg to pick up the reins left by Ivens.[75]

Although the strike was crushed and its leaders imprisoned, labour churches continued to thrive for another five years. They expanded in Winnipeg, and the Methodist leader and radical Rev. A.E. Smith of Brandon, Manitoba, took up the cause with the assistance of Beatrice Brigden. Like Ivens, Smith was pressured out of his Methodist parish and in response set up a local labour congregation in Brandon. In addition to his pastoral work at this "People's Church," Smith gave extensive support to the Great Strike and the cause of labour. He made a whirlwind lecture tour in the spring of 1920 throughout the Western provinces, organizing labour churches wherever he went. As a result of this radical evangelism such bodies took root in Vancouver, Victoria, and Calgary. As Smith put it, the churches were committed to "the abolition of the profit system." A Methodist labour church under the pastorate of Rev. G.L. Ritchie originated in Edmonton as well.

By the mid-1920s the labour churches had disintegrated, for a number of reasons. Internal divisions emerged, as well as the drainage of their leaders into labour politics. In addition, they faced the entire organized hostility of the ruling elites—economic, political, military, police, and ecclesiastical. Yet their vision, their egalitarian practice, and their prophetic challenge survive as an inspiration to those Christians seeking to embody liberation praxis in ecclesiastical institutions.[76]

Liberation and church parishes

As in the past, today's parishes are under pressure to survive and maintain the status quo. Budget needs, the mix of class, and leadership residing in professionals or wealthy members militate against a liberating praxis. Despite such formidable obstacles, the liberating gospel erupts here and there throughout our land.

Again taking my home base of Kitchener-Waterloo as an example, I am familiar with some ecclesiastical institutions involved with projects having liberationist components. For a number of years the churches of Kitchener's downtown core have participated in an ecumenical effort to address poverty and related issues in the city. The most enduring legacy of this network has been the "Soup Kitchen" located at St. John's Anglican Church. Another example is the Olive Branch Mennonite Church, organized by progressive Christians from the Anabaptist tradition who were not satisfied with any of the traditional congregations of the area. Their concern is to be part of a community committed to mutuality and participation by all. Recently they have emerged from a struggle over the inclusion of gays and lesbians as full-time members in their fellowship. They reached consensus on this matter, with the help of those gays and lesbians worshipping there, and now they are one of the few Mennonite congregations that practises such a welcoming policy. The progressive character of Olive Branch is enhanced by a membership that commits itself to the peace movement, aid to refugees, and Third World concerns.[77]

An influx of people fleeing life-threatening situations in El Salvador, Nicaragua, and Guatemala came to the Kitchener-Waterloo area, where they struggled to support each other and find a new and safer life. Their needs included the creation of a faith community. Nancy Kelly, a Lutheran activist in the area, was just one Canadian resident who assisted them in the founding of the Hispanic Lutheran Ministry. Housed at the existing parish of St. Stephen's Lutheran Church, this congregation of Spanish-speaking refugees worships regularly in their own language, celebrates their chief cultural festivals, and helps members to integrate into Canadian society.[78]

These creative expressions of parish ministry with liberationist components can be seen across the national landscape, and their solidarity with the poor and marginalized covers the gamut from nurturing to activism. Three Toronto examples from different Protestant denominations illustrate this variety.

~ ~ ~

St. John's Evangelical Lutheran Church, from the more conservative Missouri Synod of Lutheranism, remains a paradigm of ministry in a pluralistic setting. Today its directory lists ten nations representing various ethnic, racial, and linguistic backgrounds: Canada, Germany, Eritrea, Ghana, Guatemala, Guyana, India, Persia, South Africa, Tamil, and Zaire. Originally a typical, Eurocentric Lutheran parish, St. John's decided to confront its dwindling membership by turning to a more neighbourhood-centred ministry. Michael Drews arrived as pastor in 1987, and through many ups-and-downs he has provided a ministry in support of a church committed to solidarity with the multicultural neighbourhood. Refugee sponsorship gave way to a grand variety of worship experiences in many tongues, and although the church experiences language difficulties and different cultural values, its congregation struggles to participate in the joint activities designed for all the parish's multifaceted membership. In the wider community the church works with a co-operative and a thrift store and for years supported the South African struggle for liberation.[79]

~ ~ ~

Trinity Anglican Church at Toronto's Eaton Centre is best known for the "hands-on" palliative care it offers to the dying, but this is just one example of the radical love that emanates from that church. Its Sunday morning worship services exemplify a radical inclusiveness of society's marginalized. The worshippers sit in chairs arranged in a circle, and the variety of membership is striking: blacks, Asians, and East Indians, as well as white people. There are the rather well-to-do, and there are the very poor. There are a few academics. Bag-ladies frequent the church either to escape the cold or to participate actively in the congregation's worship and life. During announcement time a cacophony of voices can be heard. For about fifteen minutes members stand up one by one like a human billboard of activities that include anything and everything from potluck suppers to marches on City Hall. They highlight issues of peace, rent control, low-cost housing, and violence against women. Laity often preach the sermons, and the character of mutual sharing marks Holy Communion itself. The spirit of hospitality dominates both the worship and the socialization that follows it.[80]

~ ~ ~

Trinity-St. Paul's United Church sits on Bloor Street near Spadina in downtown Toronto. I became aware of its existence through a poster on a telephone pole advertising it to the neighbourhood. The placard showed the face of a laughing Jesus and welcomed all — poor, "street people," gays and lesbians — to come to the church in whatever clothing was comfortable. I was intrigued and contacted Frank Hamper, the church's pastoral intern. We arranged for a visit on Pentecost Sunday, June 4, 1995. When I arrived at the church I was heartened by a sign outside that read "Seeking to serve the love, justice and freedom of Christ." As I searched for the door to the sanctuary I was assisted by a street person who assured me that I was about to attend "a great place." He said to me: "Where else in the city can you go to Mass and get a great meal? You get both — the physical and the spiritual."

Frank spotted me when I entered the narthex of the church, and he invited me to join the people for worship. It was delightful, a tribute to the diversity of the Pentecost Spirit and the gospel itself. I saw Asians, Africans, people of East Indian and Spanish backgrounds, as well as the expected assortment of Anglo-Saxon types. The community spirit emerged strongly throughout the worship. The language was gloriously inclusive (the pastor is a woman), and the storytelling was funny, poignant, and always moving. Announcements, given by pastor and congregation alike, involved numerous social justice and neighbourhood concerns. The passing of the peace among the members was a rollicking, joyous affair and went on and on. Especially moving was the reading and enactment of the Pentecost story in Acts 2. Pastor Joan Wyatt began to tell the story and in the process introduced roughly fifteen people who read together from the language of each one's cultural and ethnic heritage. Amazingly, we heard Portuguese, Spanish, Dutch, Bemba, Greek, Korean, Japanese, Nepali, French, Latvian, Cantonese, German, and Syriac, and perhaps a few I've missed. In that babble of reading I was moved to tears; the winds of the Spirit blew there in exuberant diversity.[81]

After the service I met with Frank and a group of members from the Welcoming Diversity and Mission Action and Service Committees, a group in the congregation dedicated to creating an atmosphere of Biblical hospitality that glories in human variety and reaches out to the immediate neighbourhood. I heard the insights and reflections of Jim, Ron, Chiyeko, Margaret, Lynn, and Frank, and I was struck by their honesty and openness. Concerned that I might view them as liberationist, one of them, Ron, said they were only "on the road" towards a liberation gospel. As a person economically marginalized, Ron realized how difficult it is to belong to a congregation that remains fundamentally middle class. For him the alternative evening service, with its influx of poor artists and some street people, approximated more closely the gospel of liberation. Lynn praised the "storytelling" reality of Trinity-St. Paul's, but he lamented how slowly the congregation was becoming a part of its urban core neighbourhood. Chiyeko was saddened by what she felt was the "subtle" survival of racism and added that the racial mix on a Toronto subway was not replicated in her church. She wondered if the motives behind good programs might be more a response of charity than justice. Margaret, often echoing this sentiment, added that she and others, who are middle class, needed to seriously reflect upon their own involvement in oppression. Jim said that he and other members ought to wrestle with two concerns: whether street people would be comfortable in the church, and whether the church people would be comfortable out on the street. His summary of Trinity-St. Paul's was basically the consensus of the group: "We are a liberal congregation with a slight twinge of radicality."[82]

The group was unanimous on one other facet of the congregation — its openness to diversity, its welcoming spirit. This radical inclusivity drives the congregation and its activists. This is the essence of its self-definition, which emerged about fifteen years ago when its pastor announced publicly that she was a lesbian. Thus began a difficult period in the congregation's life, but in this particular area of sexual orientation the people of God at Trinity-St. Paul's have responded with radical love and acceptance, despite some pain and strife. It is an "Affirming Congregation," one that welcomes gays, lesbians, and bisexuals as full and equal participants in its church life.[83]

Trinity-St. Paul's has broadened its inclusive mandate by reaching out to other marginalized people and is working to live this out. Like most parishes, which struggle to embody the gospel, it sustains an ambivalent and stressful existence, often torn between its traditionalists, liberals, and radicals. Still, as I heard in what can be described as a "praxis-reflection" session, it is a congregation on the road towards liberation.

A Liberation Diocese

Quebec has its share of parishes that endorse the gospel of radical justice. One of them is located in Quebec City's Saint Roch district, where its curé Paul-André Fournier has organized the parish in service to the neighbourhood in such issues as employment, lodging, and leisure, through links with working-class Catholic Action and CAPMO.[84]

But what stands out most among francophone Catholics in Quebec is the existence of a liberationist diocese. The diocese of Gatineau-Hull was created out of the spirit of Vatican II. Its first bishop, Paul-Émile Charbonneau, found his inspiration from John XXIII's notion of "the servant church of the poor." Charbonneau consciously chose to shape the new diocese with that principle in mind. His headquarters was constructed as a modest all-purpose building in the midst of Hull's working-class neighbourhoods. He began his ministry by consulting with progressive lay leaders in the area and created a committee on pastoral and social action that included social service people, militant clergy, and community activists. This group set about the task of creating a ministry that concentrated upon a mission of presence within the city's ghettos.[85]

To ensure this the bishop imported seasoned activists from religious orders committed to solidarity with the working class and the poor. Chief among these were the Capuchins and the Oblates. The Capuchins were active in campaigns for low-cost housing, and the Oblates, led by Father Roger Poirier, helped to meld into working units the various leaders and committees embodied in this newly emerging visionary diocese. From 1968 until Charbonneau's retirement in 1973, Poirier united the disparate radicals and reformers into an efficient fighting force for religious renewal and social transformation. By that point Gatineau-Hull stood ready to receive its most liberationist bishop.[86]

Adolphe Proulx arrived at his see in 1974 and remained there until his death in 1987. He was committed to continuing and expanding the communitarian efforts of his predecessor, and he was a bulwark of defence for radical Catholics, lay and clerical, throughout Quebec. Proulx's ministry breathed both dialogue and action. Though liberationist in theology and committed to solidarity with the poor and exploited in Hull, the bishop produced no detailed agenda. He was responsive to his diocesan council and endorsed its commitment to social radicalism even when he came under fire. He raised his prophetic voice publicly for concrete social transformation, and he stood as an ally of the trade union movement, the unemployed, the physically handicapped, seniors, women, welfare clients, the homeless, and peace activists. He upheld his militants in their strike actions, their housing protests, and community organizing, and he sponsored a diocesan study on the 1980s economic crisis and poverty in the Hull area. Proulx recognized that the poor exemplified a fundamental source of Christian faith. "I dare to say that the poor evangelize us who are bourgeoisie," he affirmed. "My contact with them has caused me to discover certain dimensions of the Gospel. . . . The poor have given us a real sense of the words sharing, fraternity, solidarity."[87]

Spirituality and Christian Liberation

Spirituality and the struggle against oppression belong together. Liberation praxis is not simply "doing." It is also "being" — "being" in intimate relation with God, "being" in solidarity with the oppressed. For a militant liberationist to lose touch with God's intimate presence ensures burnout, cynicism, a loss of joy, and self-righteousness. Yet liberation spirituality is not just any spirituality. Its fundamental reality is not individualistic, nor is its purpose to make us feel good about ourselves. Rather it puts us in the presence of the God who liberates the oppressed, and it aligns us in our faith and life with the rejected of our society. The following examples portray the shape that liberation spirituality might take.

Aboriginal Spirituality

Canada's First Nations have much to teach us about a spirituality of solidarity. The United Church of Canada recognized this at Sudbury, Ontario, in 1986 by its public apology to Aboriginal peoples. This collective act of repentance highlights both the colonizers' sins and the debt the faith owes to Aboriginal spirituality:

> Long before my people journeyed to this land, your people were here, and you received from your elders an understanding of creation, and of the mystery that surrounds us all that was deep and rich and to be treasured. We did not hear you when you shared your vision. In our zeal to tell you of the good news of Jesus Christ we were closed to the value of your spirituality. We confused western ways and culture with the depth and breadth and length and height of the gospel of Christ. We imposed our civilization as a condition of accepting the gospel. . . . We ask you to forgive us and to walk together with us in the spirit of Christ so that our peoples may be blessed and God's creation healed.[88]

Instrumental in the drafting of this "apology" was the Rev. Stanley McKay, himself a Native and director of the United Church's Dr. Jessie Saulteaux Resource Centre in Beausejour, Manitoba, which trains Aboriginal people for ministry in the church. Speaking of the contributions of his people to the entire church, Rev. McKay said, "The image of living on the earth in harmony with creation and therefore with the creator is a helpful one for me," because it means "moving in the rhythm of the creation," "vibrating to the pulse of life in a natural way without having to 'own' the source of the music." McKay speaks of the Native "myths and rituals which remind us of the centrality of the earth in our experience of truth about the creator." He says: "We seek to integrate life so that there will not be boundaries between the secular and religious. . . . There is a word that is central to the movement into harmony with other communities and that is *respect*. It allows for diversity within the unity of the creator." For McKay, such mutuality and dialogue does not involve "dogmatic statements." Rather, it employs the Native style of "sharing stories" and "listening as well as talking."[89]

Like so many of his Aboriginal sisters and brothers, Stan McKay practises this spirituality of radical solidarity in a gentle and inclusive way. When he delivered a paper on caring for creation among Brazilian liberation theologians, he encountered anger and righteous indignation that called his views "romantic and poetic." McKay did not respond in kind. He listened and waited. Slowly people, including a number of Brazilian Aboriginal people, began to share stories with him individually. By the end of the session group members concluded that at all future conferences they should have representatives from Brazilian indigenous communities. McKay reflected on this experience: "By sharing the teachings of the elders, by being patient rather than aggressive and argumentative about the teachings, those at the meeting began to see the need to be more gentle, even as liberation theologians. The meeting moved towards an understanding that not only must people be liberated from their poverty, but the earth must be healed."[90]

Aboriginal spiritual values add dimensions to liberation that have been largely ignored by Euro-American radicals — respect for the elders, solidarity with all creation, unity, and harmony. These are foundational values vital to justice among peoples and the very survival of the Earth itself. They embody the prayer dimension of respect for all, mutuality, and love of the land, and they stand in radical opposition to the individualism, competitiveness, and consumerism of our society. McKay states:

"Because of our understanding of the gift of creation we are called to share in life. It is difficult to express individual ownership within the native spiritual understanding. It follows that if the creatures and creation are interdependent, then it is not faithful to speak of ownership. Life is understood as a gift."[91]

Feminist Spirituality

The women's movement and the Christians within it stand as yet another divine dimension within liberation. Feminist spirituality directly challenges the patriarchal values of hierarchy, competition, aggression, rationality, and violence. At the Waterloo Lutheran Seminary, where I teach, the student female population stands at roughly 50 per, and in many classes women are in the majority. Our seminary faculty had two women members, one in New Testament and the other in Liturgics and Spirituality. Along with many of the female students, Carol Schlueter has been instrumental in leading the struggle for more inclusive God-language in the classroom and chapel. In her Biblical courses she draws attention to the more feminine images of God and Christ. For her part, Donna Seamone intensifies the presence of feminist symbols and actions in the worship life of our community. Although such approaches have been resisted by some men among us, these liturgies generate a spirit of repentance and solidarity that inspires all of us to strengthen our community. Not only does this practice encourage male growth, but it also helps build a more intimate and radical community.[92]

My wife Bonnie, a United Church minister and feminist, presented me with a gift that has enhanced my own spiritual life. It is called *Exploring the Feminine Face of God* and organizes itself around artistic images, Biblical passages, and reflections for prayer and meditation that draw from the well-springs of feminist spirituality. Its purpose is stated with utmost clarity:

"This book is intended for women and men who are open to a new encounter with God and are prepared to journey into what will be for some uncharted waters, to plumb the depth of God's infinite love revealed in feminine images of God. . . . It presents a creative approach to discovering the transforming power of women's spirituality through this reflection."[93]

One section of the book calls for meditating upon God as "a Comforting Mother." Based upon the Biblical text of Isaiah 66:11-12, the "Prayer Reflection" section asks of us to "Allow God to caress you . . . hold you in her lap . . . play with you . . . delight in you . . . nurture you . . . marvel with you over the splendors of creation . . . comfort you in your losses and pain." In this context we are requested to respond to a number of questions, including: "How does God as comforting mother challenge you to minister to the needs of family, friends, the poor, the world?"[94]

The book describes another facet of feminist spirituality that both threatens men and stands as essential to the liberationist gospel. That is the element of righteous rage and empowerment that remains so intrinsic to women's liberationist spirituality. These characteristics explain the Christ-like image of crucified women — women crucified by demeaning labour, marginalization, verbal and physical violence in the home, and sexual and physical mayhem in society and the market-place. The well-known and controversial "Crucified Woman" statue on the campus of the United Church's Emmanuel College in Toronto illustrates these points.[95]

The blend of righteous indignation and self-esteem leads to the individual and collective empowerment of oppression's victims. Feminist spirituality contributes mightily in this direction, while its sense of empowerment remains healing rather than oppressive. In this respect feminist spirituality highlights a dimension frequently lacking on the part of male liberationists. Mary Jo Leddy captures this element in her journal *Say to the Darkness, We Beg to Differ*:

> We are beginning to have a sense that power is not "power over" but "power with". . . .
>
> We do not possess such power, nor does it possess us; such power liberates all. This is the kind of power which is the stronger for being shared. This power creates equals and allies, not opponents and enemies. . . . The dream becomes not that of being president of the corporation but of changing the corporation so that there are no more presidents![96]

Sister Leddy speaks of the feminine prophets within the church, who, with their subterranean "nagging" and persistent voices, shake our institutions towards liberation. Her model is the Canaanite woman who called and instructed Jesus "to a transformation of consciousness about his own vocation."[97]

A spirituality of the feet

Another possible shape of liberation spirituality embodies solidarity, a "walking with." This direction is reflected most consciously by the radical Capuchins, who pursue a spiritual life based upon the life and work of Francis of Assisi. His was "a life of fraternity and a life of poverty . . . rooted in the working class and popular movements," asserts Benoît Fortin, one of Quebec's more militant Capuchins. In Hull the *équipes* of about five members each deem it "important to reflect upon their faith" collectively. They celebrate the Eucharist and meet weekly for a *revision de vie*, a liberationist model of praxis and reflection that they have adopted from working-class Catholic Action. The Hull *équipe* exists as part of a wider Capuchin network, the *reseau,* which, along with some contemplative nuns, identifies with a liberationist way of life.[98]

This lifestyle, both incarnate and participatory, emerges consciously as a "spirituality of the feet." Father Fortin speaks of his "conversion of the feet," and Father Claude Hardy calls his solidarity with the oppressed "turning his feet around." Brother Gaëtan Ouellete describes his hospital orderly work as an incarnation in which "he planted himself in the values of a social milieu within which he travelled by foot." According to him, "We must abandon thinking with our head in order to reflect with our feet, breathe with our feet, and sense the deep pain of those feet that labour. We must live as the working class lives. That is our spirituality." For the Capuchins, this identity is the means by which they encounter Christ. "We have been evangelized and supported by the poor," insists Benoît Fortin. "Their life and their action have trained us."[99]

A spirituality of imperfection

It is the rare Christian who cannot identify with a "spirituality of imperfection." Such a spirituality emerges as especially precious to liberationists, chiefly as an antidote to those sins that dog the steps of Christian radicals: the "Lone Ranger" instinct, self-righteousness, despair, and burn-out. A spirituality of imperfection stands as a constant reminder that a loving and compassionate God is in charge and that we are called to be faithful and not perfect.

Henri Nouwen's *The Wounded Healer* remains a classic example of such a spirituality. Using the language of liberation and community, Nouwen describes a spirituality of solidarity that can empower those who align themselves with the forgotten and marginalized of our society:

> No [one of us] can save anyone. . . . This is so because a shared pain is no longer paralyzing but mobilizing, when understood as a way to liberation. When we become aware that we do not have to escape our pains, but that we can mobilize them into a common search for life, those very pains are transformed from expressions of despair into signs of hope.
>
> Through this common search, hospitality becomes community. Hospitality becomes community as it creates a unity based on the shared confession of our basic brokenness and on a shared hope.[100]

Although Nouwen concentrates on personal struggles, such as loneliness, his *Wounded Healer* has also a powerful collective and liberationist dimension. What Nouwen and those like him give to us is a spirituality that can sustain us in dark times. Wounds and failure are inevitable, and liberationists need a spirituality to sustain their hope. J.S. Woodsworth stands as a profound model of this approach. So often his life was scarred with failure and disappointment, yet he held firmly to the visions that drove him onward. William Irvine, a friend and brother in the struggle, described such a spirituality for dark times, at Woodsworth's graveside. Woodsworth, Irvine said, "not only had courage of a physical kind, the courage to face a hostile crowd, to become a longshoreman, to go to prison. But he had that courage expressed in lines which he himself quoted, the courage 'to go on forever and fail, and go on again'—the courage which enabled him to rest 'with the half of a broken hope for a pillow at night.'"[101]

God's Wider Work of Liberation

Given the Biblical basis of liberation theology, as well as its long journey through the history of the Christian movement, one would expect to find it expressed and lived among followers of Jesus of Nazareth. The examples we've seen earlier in this chapter will, I hope, provide inspiration and havens for those Christians already committed to the liberation of the oppressed and for those who feel compelled to embark on such a journey. But it would be both limiting and arrogant to assume that a life of liberation is found only among Christians. To the contrary, it exists among people of all the major religious faiths, and it lives among humanitarians who describe themselves as agnostic or atheistic. In short, God's work of liberation also takes place beyond the Christian community, in the wider world wherever justice is done, wherever radical compassion prevails, and wherever the oppressed are set free.

The Scriptures testify to this. Cyrus, a pagan king, freed God's special people from their Babylonian captivity and allowed them to return to their own land. For that action, the ancient Hebrew text describes God as calling him "Messiah" (Isaiah 45:1,4). In the Greek New Testament the more narrow-minded Peter needs his bigotry corrected through a dream indicating that God and the Christian gospel were already working among certain pagans well before Christians arrived to do their baptizing (Acts 10). Canadian liberationists have understood this for some time. Social gospeller Salem Bland was aware of this broader work of God. For him, wider movements for justice, compassion, and solidarity were not secular as such. Rather, they embodied "the overflow of Christianity from the conventionally religious into the economic realm." Indeed, he insisted that Christianity's "divine claim" rested upon "this irrepressible impulse to overflow."[102] Bland's insights remind liberationists that God's transforming work emerges outside the walls of distinctly Christian manifestations. Hence the followers of Jesus of Nazareth are called to insert themselves in those wider movements for liberation in the land.

Canadian Movements for Liberation

In Canada liberation movements abound, and some Christians work actively within their ranks. Increasingly gay and lesbian rights groups press for equality under the law, and the United Church of Canada continues to open its structures and institutions to ministry by people without regard to sexual orientation. The environmentalist movement has grown in size and sophistication and includes among its activists and organizers progressive Christians. For example, in British Columbia the United Fishermen and Allied Workers' Union (UFAWU) took on the Alcan Corporation, which had received massive water rights to the Nechako River from earlier Social Credit governments. When the successor NDP government came to power in 1991 it backed off an earlier promise to hold a full environmental assessment. Mae Burrows, the UFAWU's environmental director, led her union into a confrontation with the government. She and others helped form a coalition to prevent the expansion of Alcan in its use of the river. Included in the coalition were Native, youth, anti-free trade, and church groups. Such environmental efforts have emerged across Canada.[103]

Antiracist coalitions exist in most of our cities. In Kitchener, Ontario, the Holocaust Education Committee brings together Jewish and Gentile human rights activists. They concentrate on educating school children and the wider community around the dangers of racism in general and of anti-Semitism in particular. In addition, the Committee has sponsored school and broader public events, and some of its members have picketed local Heritage Front activities.[104] Antiracist protests have also had national exposure, including efforts directed against ending apartheid in South Africa. The Inter-Church Coalition on Africa was involved in these struggles.[105]

People who fight racism and work on environmental issues often overlap on questions of Aboriginal rights and land claims. Liberationist elements among First Nations people grow out of the wisdom and insights found in Native spirituality. Aggressive struggles to retain their lands and a more holistic way of life have existed throughout recent Aboriginal history, from the Métis uprisings led by Louis Riel to the more current events at Oka and Ipperwash. Indeed, the last two decades have witnessed protracted efforts by Native people to stop corporate and neo-colonialist projects that would diminish or destroy Native life and land in the name of resource development and profit. Native peoples have resisted megaprojects and continuing land claims as part of this ongoing struggle. Progressive people in the mainline churches have formed alliances with Aboriginal sisters and brothers, many of whom are Christians themselves. The clearest example of recent Christian involvement has been the ecumenical coalition Project North, associated with Hugh and Karmel Taylor McCullum. Over the years that grouping evolved into the Aboriginal Rights Coalition.[106] Such specific justice movements reflective of Biblical *shalôm* are legion, but the following few examples, I hope, are representative.

The Farm Movement

During much of the early decades of Confederation, agriculture reflected the economic base of the new nation. Not surprisingly farmers were among the first citizens to organize against unjust oppressive conditions. This happened across the land, from the co-operatives of the Maritime provinces to similar efforts in British Columbia. In Quebec this work took the form of the *caisse populaire* movement. An aggressive farm activism arose in Ontario as well. By the end of the nineteenth century both the Grange and the Patrons of Industry had built up an extensive following, and out of their ashes emerged the United Farmers of Ontario (UFO) in 1914. By 1919 the UFO had elected forty-four MPPs and, with Labour's twelve members, formed the first Farmer government in Canada, led by the moderate E.C. Drury. The UFO had a radical wing, exemplified by W.C. Good and J.J. Morrison, one of Agnes Macphail's mentors. Macphail's role in the federal parliament made her the recognized spokesperson of the UFO, and given her membership in Woodsworth's "Ginger Group" and the later CCF, hers was a strong voice on the left.[107]

The farm movement was most effective on the Prairies, where a radical response to the oppressive alliance of banks, railroads, and government emerged. The movement erupted in the rural town of Indian Head, Saskatchewan, on December 18, 1901. Its initial meeting led to the founding of the Territorial Grain Growers' Association (TGGA). Immediately the militant group advocated for laws to protect the farmers at the rail lines and grain elevators. Within a few years all three Prairie provinces had similar organizations, and they were quick to perceive that the entire global marketing system, owned by financiers and railroad barons and abetted by governments, was the fundamental cause of their grievances. In response they created their own Grain Growers' Grain Company (GGGC) under the leadership of the radical E.A. (Ed) Partridge of Sintaluta, Saskatchewan. Partridge led this co-op company through its first years and then moved on to become the editorial voice of the movement's newspaper, the *Grain Growers' Guide*. He was a leading advocate in the Wheat Pool movement of the 1920s and ended his career as one of the founding members of the CCF.[108] His philosophy emerged from the humanitarian socialism so prominent in Great Britain at the time.

With the success of the Wheat Pool the Prairie farm movement was well on its way towards developing an agrarian infrastructure that could stand up against capitalist marketing. The Depression and crop failures undermined this movement and drove the farmers towards populist parties that provided alternatives to the "old-line" Liberals and Conservatives. In the 1920s the United Farmers of Alberta represented this different option, and during the 1930s the Co-operative Commonwealth Federation upheld that mandate. But it would take more than a decade for the "socialistic" CCF to come to power in Canada. Not surprisingly the locus was Saskatchewan. In 1944 the province's CCF, under the leadership of ex-Baptist minister T.C. (Tommy) Douglas, formed the first socialist government in North America. This victory underscored four decades of farm struggle, often against incredible odds.[109]

Woven throughout Prairie farm radicalism was the ideology of the Protestant social gospel. Ed Partridge affirmed that "true cooperation has its final goal in socialism, which is the continual observance of the Golden Rule." Rev. Salem Bland wrote a regular column in the *Grain Growers' Guide*, and the same paper stood by Bland when he was sacked at Wesley College.[110] Such a social gospel-farm movement connection was graphically illustrated in the speeches of farm militants. For example, W.C. Good stated:

> We are, I think, on the eve of a great forward movement. The giant of special Privilege, who has enslaved and degraded this nation for so long, is beginning to tremble in his castle. It is our duty to press forward in the fight for justice. . . . The tide of commercialism and greed has well nigh overwhelmed us; and has ready brought in its train desolate and wasted fields and a discouraged and demoralized people. We need a new ideal, a new vision of our privilege in being called to become God's partners in the creation of a new earth wherein dwelleth righteousness.[111]

Although the farm movement sustained grievous losses in the following decades, it by no means died. In the late 1970s and early 1980s, for instance, independent Ontario farmers fell heavily under the weight of debts they had incurred at the advice of the major banking chains that serviced rural towns. In the midst of this crisis the banks organized to call in their loans by foreclosing on farm mortgages. In response to this crisis, the militant Canadian Farmers Survival Association formed in 1981 in Grey and Bruce Counties. It called for more just arrangements between governments, banks, and the farmers and demanded an "immediate one-year moratorium on bank payments to avoid further farm bankruptcies and receiverships." To achieve these ends the organization held meetings and rallies and petitioned banks and government departments for support. When this failed the farmers led demonstrations in the towns, including Toronto, and gathered en masse to prevent the physical shutdown of farms. At sheriff auctions they organized to buy the advertised goods cheaply and then gave them back to the original owners. Within a brief period of time the Farm Survivalists formed coalitions across regional and national boundaries.[112]

As another example, activist Brewster Kneen has used the printed medium to advocate a socioeconomic system that would be the antithesis of agrarian capitalism. His books *From Land to Mouth* (1989) and *The Rape of Canola* (1992) unequivocally condemn the corporate globalization of agriculture. Kneen's newsletter *The Ram's Horn* offers a continuing update on farm issues and alerts readers to the changing intricacies of the issues covered in his books. His is a voice akin to the prophets of old. He brings a fierce condemnation of the "food bank" industry; he warns of petrochemicals polluting our food and soil; he condemns the alliance of national governments and global transnationals.[113]

The Opérations Dignité in Quebec is another example of a recent farmer alternative to capital control of the land. In 1970 various citizen groups in eastern Quebec began to organize against those elites who, in the name of profit, were undermining the lives and livelihoods of rural people of the area. The initial protest came in the form of a manifesto by "19 angry priests," who couched their dissent in the liberationist language of Paul VI's *Populorum Progressio*. The nearby archbishop of Rimouski lent his support, and developments gave way to the "grass-roots" expansion of citizens' groups, which utilized the existing parish structures so characteristic of this part of rural Quebec. Soon the protests involved regional coalitions. The Opérations Dignité were able to halt the destructive advance of the elites and to provide some alternative and co-operative models of development for their area. As those activities declined, other citizens' groups took up the cause, which continues to this day.[114]

A healthy survival of Biblical values and respect for creation can be found within the current farm moment. This survival is apparent in the role the church played in Opérations Dignité and in the conscious Scriptural language of Brewster Kneen. The Jesuit Farm Project near Guelph, Ontario, reflects similar views.[115]

The Women's Movement

Unless women participate fully and as equals in Canadian life, full liberation will elude us. The toil that has built the nation in both farm and factory included women, while the recognition of that contribution has been submerged. It is thus not surprising that the profound, collective voice of women has arisen from the fields and shop floors of our land.

In the farm movement women initially found themselves relegated to female auxiliaries, a position challenged with some success almost from the outset. By 1912 Frances M. Beynon was writing editorials for the *Grain Growers' Guide*, and a year later she was instrumental in organizing a convention for farm women sponsored by the Saskatchewan Grain Growers' Association (SGGA). Out of this grew a fully autonomous women's section of the SGGA. In 1915 the United Farm Women of Alberta emerged under the leadership of Irene Parlby, and within five years the group had roughly two hundred locals, with about three thousand members. Parlby herself was elected to Alberta's legislature in 1921, and she was appointed minister without portfolio in the United Farmers' government. In 1918 Violet McNaughton organized the Interprovincial Council of Farm Women from her Saskatchewan base.[116]

Most recognized among women farm leaders was Canada's first female member of parliament, Agnes Macphail. Her role in prison reform was second to none. She spoke out against war and tax injustice. She railed against sweated labour and called for an overhaul of the capitalist system.[117] She was one of the honoured charter members of the CCF and was instrumental in bringing Ontario farm organizations into the new party.

Macphail lifted up her voice in the women's movement. The equality she championed for farmers and workers was something that she advocated for Canadian women as well. "I am a feminist," she told a

Toronto rally in 1927, "and I want for women the thing men are not willing to give them — absolute equality." For her, the advent of women into political life was crucial in order "to push human values to the forefront of politics." She concluded, "I believe this to be the fundamental effect of the political enfranchisement of women." In parliament she challenged the oft-repeated notion of woman as "the queen of home and hearth." In one speech she argued: "When I hear men talk about women being the angel of the home I always, mentally at least, shrug my shoulders in doubt. I do not want to be the angel of any home; I want for myself what I want for other women, absolute equality. After that is secured then men and women can take turns at being angels."[118]

Women have remained active in farm struggles to this day, adding their distinct and valuable emphases to the broader movement. In fall 1981, for instance, Beth Slumskie and Doris Sweiger called a meeting of the local Bruce County, Ontario, farm women. Out of the 250 who attended, the Concerned Farm Women organization (CFW) "was formed in response to the needs created by extreme financial pressures on farm families." The CFW held public meetings, lobbied politicians and marched in demonstrations. They also worked in tandem with existing organizations, such as the Ontario Federation of Agriculture.[119]

For decades women engaged themselves actively in labour politics and the union movement. In Valleyfield, Quebec, women represented large numbers among the toilers in the textile trades, and in the early years of this century, women accounted for two-thirds of the membership in the Federation of Textile Workers in Canada. In Valleyfield these female toilers had their own local, the Dames et Demoiselles de Valleyfield. Some were militant enough to walk off the job in 1900 in what became known as *la grève des jeunes filles* (the strike of the young women). Immediately after the Second World War, the heirs of these activists immersed themselves deeply in the United Textile Workers of America. One of them was Madeleine Parent, the famous organizer and secretary-treasurer of her union's National Council. The Bell Telephone Strike of 1907 emerged as just one other example in which exploited female labour decided to resist. These instances, along with many others, provide ample proof of the capacity of oppressed female toilers to fight back against their oppressors.[120]

Women were also active organizers and labour leaders. One such example, Teklia Hryciw Chaban, arose out of the Ukrainian community in Alberta. Much of her adult life was spent as a grass-roots left-wing labour organizer. She helped create a labour temple in the mining town of Cardiff and was instrumental in many of its educational and cultural programs. As a member of the One Big Union movement, she became involved in general strike activities and in urging the miners to join the United Mine Workers of America. She was at the heart of the Edmonton organizing drive, where she fought hand-to-hand against the scabs brought in by the owners. More than once in her career she suffered wounds in such battles, and numerous times she was arrested because of union activities. Communist women leaders formed vital links with women in both the paid and unpaid workforces. Above all, they embodied the work of the Women's Labor League (WLL), a group organized by Florence Custace. Especially creative were their efforts to raise the consciousness of housewives and bring them as militants into the public arena.[121]

Female leaders in the CCF emerged also in labour politics. In addition to Agnes Macphail, two well-known women socialists were elected to British Columbia's parliament. There Dorothy Gretchen Steeves was a firm proponent of birth control and sex education. Steeves, a fiery orator and uncompromising socialist, advocated firmly for women's rights. Her companion in parliament was Grace MacInnis, wife of labour MP Angus MacInnis and daughter of Lucy and J.S. Woodsworth. MacInnis proved a sharp contrast to the more flamboyant Steeves. MacInnis was more pragmatic and methodical in her work, while Steeves was the more dramatic presence.[122]

A militant social gospel existed within this arena of labour politics, a tendency no less true with women than with men. Grace MacInnis and her mother Lucy are examples. Another was the Methodist leader Beatrice Brigden, who actively supported the Winnipeg General Strike and succeeded A.E. Smith as pastor of the People's Church in Brandon. From that point she became active in her province's Independent Labor Party (ILP) and was one of the founding members of the CCF. Although she left the Methodist church for partisan labour politics, she did not leave her faith behind. "People often set politics up in opposition to religion," she asserted, "but that was hardly the case for me. Politics is working together to fulfill the needs of others as you would have them fulfill yours. Put that way, it describes my religion as much as it does my politics."[123] By the mid-1920s Brigden had integrated her faith with a growing consciousness that could be called a "socialist-feminism." She was acutely aware of the vast systems of inequity that repressed women, but she was convinced as well that full gender equality demanded the replacement of capitalism by a democratic socialist order.[124]

Whether in the farm movement, in labour militancy or in left-wing politics, women were involved at both the grass-roots and the leadership levels. The female activists managed to act upon these issues because of their very specific concerns as women. The causes they served went beyond what has been narrowly called feminist. At the same time, distinctly feminist organizations and movements emerged that centred directly around women's rights. Most well-known of these was the collective struggle of Canadian women to achieve the right to vote. Most of the women involved in this battle came from the middle-class and had learned their leadership skills as active members of social gospel churches. One arena of such on-the-job training for women involved the temperance movement, which became a critical launching pad for the female suffrage campaign.[125]

Thérèse Casgrain and Nellie L. McClung achieved national prominence in that cause. Casgrain, one of Quebec's great social reformers, mounted the hustings for women's votes at the age of seventeen, when she joined the Montreal Suffrage Association. Later, as president of the Women's Rights League, she pressured Quebec's National Assembly to legislate the vote for women, an achievement not on the books until 1941. After the Second World War Casgrain joined the CCF and soon became its Quebec leader. She ended her long career in antinuclear activities and in the nation's Senate. Casgrain and other middle-class feminists in Quebec formed links with progressive nuns prepared to advocate for women's rights. Marie Gérin-Lajoie, the daughter of one such feminist, organized the Institut Notre-Dame du Bon-Conseil, a progressive order of nuns. Over the years these sisters have positioned themselves at the avant-garde of social justice for women and the poor within Quebec's Catholic church. One member of this order, Sister Dolorès Léger, has worked actively among the poor for almost two decades. Her efforts proved to be a labour of love that led her to a full-time working-class ministry ("worker-nun") and from there into feminist politics.[126]

In English Canada Nellie McClung remains the most noted figure of the historic women's movement. Like so many others she was impelled into action by her religious principles and by the Women's Christian Temperance Union (WCTU). Soon she took up writing as well and became a best-selling author of essays, short stories, and novels. McClung entered the political arena, where she advocated directly for female suffrage and the full equality of rights for women. Throughout the years her strong advocacy for her sisters was consistent. In describing the women's movement, McClung said: "Investigation is taking the place of resignation. For too long we have believed it our duty to sit down and be resigned. Now we know it is our duty to rise up and be indignant. . . . This is the meaning of the woman's movement, and we need not apologize for it."[127]

Gaining the right to vote was not sufficient to obliterate other political and legal inequities, let alone economic and social oppressions. In one of the great ironies of Canadian history, Edmonton's Judge Emily Murphy, the first woman magistrate in the British Empire, was told that women could not be senators because by law they were not "persons." Judge Murphy's position was upheld by the Alberta Supreme Court, but the federal government continued its refusal to appoint women as senators. For a decade campaigns were organized against this injustice by women's groups across the land, culminating in an appeal made to the Supreme Court of Canada by Emily Murphy, Nellie McClung, Louise McKinney, Irene Parlby, and Henrietta Muir Edwards. Finally, on October 18, 1929, the British Privy Council declared that "women were deemed to be 'persons' and could therefore be appointed to the senate."[128]

The Contemporary Scene

However long the battles have been fought, the oppression of women has not faded into history, nor have women ceased to struggle against the unjust chains that bind them. Virtually all Protestant denominations now ordain women, and women clergy are slowly but surely winning their place in stubbornly patriarchal ecclesiastical institutions. The United Church of Canada (UCC) remains the most progressive of the major churches in the nation. In 1936 Lydia Gruchy was ordained as the first woman minister in the United Church. Since that time her denomination has emerged as a role model for Christians in the arena of gender equality under the gospel. To be sure, much remains to be done, even in the United Church, but this denomination has large numbers of female clergy not only in parish ministries but also at the highest levels of church leadership.[129]

Indeed, a number of women, lay and clerical, have been moderators of the UCC. The first of these was the Rev. Lois Wilson, appointed in August, 1980. Throughout her years of ministry Rev. Wilson has lifted up her voice for her unorganized and organized sisters in their long struggle for justice. In fact, Rev. Wilson embodies liberationism in the deepest and broadest sense of that word. She cries out against sexism, militarism, racism, and assaults on the environment. She challenges colonialism both political and economic and remains profoundly ecumenical. She has appealed for a broader, more gentle language of God that includes "Isaiah's image of God as nursing mother."[130]

Beyond the Christian family are wider and effective women's movements. Perhaps the largest and most far-reaching is the National Action Committee on the Status of Women (NAC), with its five-hundred-plus membership groups. An important lobby group, it provides consciousness-raising and educational activities and serves as an effective mobilizing force at the annual International Women's Day. It continues to press for a pro-choice mandate, an intensified campaign against domestic violence, and stronger workplace equity laws. It promotes antimilitary campaigns and defends Canada's social safety net. Under the presidency of Judy Rebick in the early 1990s, NAC came to emphasize increasingly grass-roots activities, incorporation of minority movements, and conscious networking with other movements, such as labour and poverty organizations. After all, Rebick said, "We are up against formidable opponents who are ruthlessly driving to improve the corporate bottom line with no concern whatsoever for the human bottom line."[131]

Women activists are not just found in strictly feminist organizations. They are militants in other progressive groups as well, as we have seen in the farm movement, and it is no less true in Aboriginal, gay rights, and other minority organizations.[132] They are in the union movement, where increasingly unions are tackling the issues of sexual harassment and violence at the workplace — which is, in no small measure, due to the female leadership in these organizations. One finds an increasing number of high-profile women at the leadership level of trade unionism: Monique Simard, formerly first vice-president of the Confédération des Syndicats Nationaux; Shirley Carr, a recent president of the Canadian Labour Congress, and Judy Darcy, the national president of the Canadian Union of Public Employees (CUPE).[133]

The Labour Movement

For well over a century the working women and men of Canada have been active in organizing against the nation's elites and the capitalist system. Without denying labour's failures and even some betrayals, the union movement has left and continues to leave a legacy of justice and struggle that does it honour in the deepest sense of Biblical *shalôm*. There were the great moments of struggle, and there was the mighty effort of the Knights of Labor to organize all workers in one union. The toiling classes remember as well the One Big Union movement out of the West, and dear to labour's memory are the origins of the CIO and autoworker militancy before and after World War II. The examples are legion in labour's historic honour role and need to be cherished by all who walk the road of liberation.[134] We've already touched on the active participation of Christians in the nation's historic labour movements, such as the Protestant social gospel and the labour churches. Many of these social gospellers became active in labour politics, and a number of them were elected to national and provincial parliaments.

An active Christian presence in the labour movement, both clerical and lay, also characterized Quebec history, especially in the Catholic federations. To be sure, this early presence tended to be conservative and paternalistic, but the Asbestos Strike of 1949 provided the critical watershed for the Confédération des Travailleurs Catholiques du Canada (CTCC). During this conflict priests and workers joined hands to resist the oppressor coalition of government and "big business," and left-wing social Catholic doctrine gave this resistance its ideological underpinnings. From that moment until it dropped its Catholic identification in 1960 the CTCC represented the most militant sector of Quebec's labour movement.[135]

Today in Canada the trade union movement remains one of the most critical sources of liberationist strength. To abandon solidarity with it and its struggles would mean crippling the liberation movement fatally. Within labour's ranks are links with vital related causes: youth issues, gay and lesbian rights, Aboriginal claims, gender equality, popular culture, and international solidarity. CUPE's partnership with Mexican grass-roots unions stands as a case in point.[136]

As well, the union movement continues to fight labour's traditional struggles. Nowhere has this emerged with greater clarity than in the recent strikes in the Canadian auto industry. Mid-October 1996 witnessed an aggressive Canadian Auto Workers (CAW) strike against the corporate agenda in the form of General Motors and its lesser twins. Led by Buzz Hargrove, the union won a victory for jobs and against "out-sourcing." An Oshawa local occupied one plant, and the entire union rallied in unprecedented solidarity to win the victory. Hargrove's stand during the "hard-ball" negotiations with Canadian Airlines saved jobs that were on the chopping block, as well as forcing the federal government to help resolve this privatization-generated crisis. During these same struggles, the CAW demonstrated its broader radicalism by negotiating for "same-sex" benefits and by pressuring for an increasingly democratic workplace.[137]

However, most intrinsic to labour's *raison d'être* stands the mandate to organize the unorganized, the most vulnerable and exploited of all the toilers. Despite the current media and elitist assault on trade unions, the workers' movement remains as creative as ever in this fundamental task. One finds successes in such difficult arenas as immigrant farm labour, the retail sales trade, taxi driving, and the fast-food chains.[138] One recent example of labour heroism embodied the effort of the Portuguese Lake Erie fishers to organize and win recognition for their union. After extensive exploitation these workers and their families called in Michael Darnell, an organizer for the United Fishermen and Allied Workers Union (UFAWU). Company reprisals came rapidly on the heels of the initial organizing efforts. Within two weeks of the first sign-ups, the company fired 57 of the 376 union applicants. The tactic backfired. Instead of feeling intimidated the entire community rallied in support of the fledgling union. Militants agreed to block the boats, and the police were called in to break the picket lines at the docks. Eight-month pregnant Cristina Copa, a fish filleter and union activist, stood firm under police threats, so the line held. In time, the union won its battles, ending up as Local 444 of the CAW.[139]

Historically, in Canada and elsewhere, labour has understood the need for a political arm. It has sought either to make its concerns known through traditional parties (as done, or at least tried, in the United States) or to form parties of its own (the continental European model). Canada has often been caught between the two approaches. To be sure, efforts have been undertaken to form working-class parties. The Parti Ouvrier was established in Quebec, and after the First World War some candidates from independent labour parties were elected federally and provincially. The CCF and its successor body the NDP have been most successful in making the labour-political connection.[140]

The marriage between the union movement and the NDP has been a stormy one. Most recently matters came to a head over the social contract legislation forced upon public-sector workers by the Ontario NDP government. Labour was uniformly incensed over this violation of contracts and the process of collective bargaining, but was divided over how exactly to respond. Most private-sector unions (the CAW being the notable exception) continued to urge support for Bob Rae and Ontario's NDP. Leo Gerard of the Steelworkers insisted that the NDP, like all our institutions, was also a victim of globalization and that its approach in power should not be rejected out of hand.[141] Buzz Hargrove of the Canadian Autoworkers had a different opinion. He was convinced that the NDP, especially in Ontario, had become so committed to reforming and softening the capitalist system that it had lost its radical historic vision. Further, he argued, it had become a party like other parties and refused to maintain democratic links with the radical social movements prepared to fight for change.[142] As a result, the future of the labour-NDP connection hung in limbo and demanded a critical reshaping, especially when peace and reconciliation subsequently took priority in the face of the right-wing assault and the strong NDP showing in the 1997 federal election. Nonetheless, labour remained acutely aware of the need either to maintain or to create a new political arm.

The workers' movement understands, as well, that political involvement goes deeper than links to particular political parties. Through its own research and educational facilities labour puts forward and mobilizes for its own type of government that would oppose the corporate agendas of the ruling parties. In addition to these efforts, labour is active in coalition-building. Joining with antipoverty groups, women's organizations, the unemployed and the Action Canada Network, labour galvanized its grass-roots to meet in front of the federal parliament building en masse on May 15, 1993, to protest the NAFTA deal. Although many movements travelled to this demonstration, the backbone of the effort came from trade union militants. The event serves as a profound reminder to liberationists to be wary of the rather fashionable practice of taking critical shots at organized labour. We expect attacks from the corporate and political elite; it is their way. But it is tragic when allies engage in such self-defeating rhetoric.[143]

With few exceptions, today's unions are non-sectarian, and well they should be. Although the earlier Catholic trades in Quebec have undoubtedly aided the mighty work of liberation, the narrow denomi-nationalism of those unions contributed as well to the repression of militancy, division among workers, and naive and destructive forms of class collaborationism. Christians can rightly honour elements in this religious past, but we also need to rejoice in the pluralism and non-sectarian character of today's unions. This does not mean that there is no Christian presence in the labour movement. There is, and there ought to be — not to make converts but to demonstrate solidarity and a commitment to the liberation of the oppressed. Two especially creative examples of this work in the current epoch emerge from Quebec. The oldest of the two, the specialized Catholic Action movement, dates from the early 1930s. The working-class forms of this broader movement were called the Jeunesse Ouvrière Catholique (JOC), for proletarian Catholic youth, and the Ligue Ouvrière Catholique (LOC), the adult counterpart. The premise for these working-class Catholic Action organizations demanded that they be a Christian presence within the surrounding milieus. They adopted the principle of Pope Pius XI that the apostles to workers would be workers themselves. Initially the organizations, derived from episcopal power and control, were designed to serve institutional goals as much as worker needs, but the very presence of labourers throughout these grass-roots organizations shifted the balance of power over the years.[144]

In the mid-1960s a specialized Catholic Action forced the bishops to grant its forces increasing autonomy. Since then, both the JOC (now called the Jeunesse Ouvrière Chrétienne) and the Mouvement des Travailleurs Chrétien (MTC, once the LOC) have moved further towards a liberationist position. Both join coalitions with unions, immigrant organizations, and *groupes populaires*, and both support a new Quebec radically different from the current capitalist model that drives it. Both endorse solidarity with workers. The JOC defines itself as "a movement of young workers who assume their responsibility in the struggle for the liberation of the oppressed, taking as their point of departure the class struggle perpetrated by the ruling class."[145]

Another creative model of Christian presence found here and there in the nation's workplaces is that of the "worker-priest/nun." Retired NDP MP Dan Heap of Toronto was an Anglican worker-priest in the 1960s, and the Windsor Catholic priest René Giroux experimented with this approach in the early 1970s.[146] But this form of solidarity took most effective root in Quebec. The combination of the Quiet Revolution and the Second Vatican Council provided a context for the emergence of the experiment in the Archdiocese of Montreal. The Jesuit André Pellerin and the Fils de la Charité priest Ugo Benfante were authorized to take up full-time jobs as examples of the church's solidarity with the working class. Soon others followed, and by the 1980s between twenty and thirty priests and nuns had taken up the challenge.[147]

The plunge into working-class life, toil, and struggle created a conversion experience for most of these clerics. They experienced the poverty of the proletarian ghetto, the dangers to health and safety in the workplace, the nature of tedious and exploitative labour, and the solidarity of trade union life. They were radicalized by the experience, transformed into avowed liberationists. Over the years they learned also to be in touch with each other, both in regional networks and a larger provincial body. At their regular meetings they reflected on their lives and struggles with their labouring sisters and brothers.[148]

Most dramatic were those few instances when they were called upon to organize unions that would confront both the bosses and company unions. The secular priest Jacques Tanguay helped create a militant CSN local at a BFG Admiral Plant near Montreal. Tanguay himself was arrested in the midst of these battles. Fils de la Charité Guy Cousin joined his comrades at the Zeller's chain to replace a corrupt Teamsters' local with a CSN union. Cousin was harassed and fired — and his life was threatened — but he refused to back down until his cause was vindicated. Benoît Fortin, a Capuchin priest, led the battle to replace a company union at Quebec City's Hilton Hotel with a militant CSN union. For six years he and his comrades fought, and even after being fired for these activities he persisted. He finally won his case in the Supreme Court of Canada, and his union of hotel employees grew to about twelve thousand members.[149]

Benoît Fortin summarizes the values of the liberationist consciousness that springs from these kinds of militant actions:

> We must rejoin the real world of people who struggle day after day for a more just world. We must also live the incarnation, our hiddenness, the return to our roots for a long time. . . . We must be reborn from among the poor, near to their cries, in solidarity with their struggles. Jesus has taken up the human condition, he has taken the way of the stable. We will recognize nothing of human distress if we do not live in our own flesh solidarity with the most oppressed.[150]

Broader coalitions — The Council of Canadians

It becomes increasingly important for all progressive movements to join together in a common united struggle against the forces of oppression. A recent example of such an effort has been the Council of Canadians, a coalition of reformists and radicals from other movements who have banded together to resist the encroachment of the corporate agenda in Canadian life. Born in 1985, the Council defines itself as "an independent, non-partisan, public interest organization" of over ninety thousand members committed to "the protection of Canada's sovereignty, culture and environment and for the right and responsibility of all citizens to participate in the decisions that affect them and their country." Its prominence grew out of the free-trade debates of the late 1980s and early 1990s, and its leadership came and continues to come from the ranks of other movements. Maude Barlow, its current chairperson, is an active feminist and social critic who, along with Catholic liberationist Tony Clarke of the Action Canada Network, was instrumental in a cross-country tour that rallied people for the anti-NAFTA mass protest in Ottawa in spring 1993, and is currently mobilizing against the Multilateral Agreement on Investment (MAI).[151]

The Council of Canadians provides information on the issues facing Canadians today through its periodical *Canadian Perspectives.* The magazine highlights corporate aggression and seeks to inspire Canadians in large counterattacking campaigns, whether against the dismantling of the social safety net or in preparing voters for upcoming elections. The Council also provides a resource network geared to creating immediate mass action usually against particular government-corporate offences. Mailings of "Action Link," called "the Grassroots Action Network of the Council of Canadians," are part of this work. For example, the Council sends out petitions and postcards to be filled out by members, their friends, and sympathizers, including addresses and phone numbers of where to register the protests. Although its vision may be critiqued as being not particularly radical, the Council of Canadians is committed to mobilizing all progressive groups into a common voice of outrage against oppression, especially in its opposition to government cuts to social programs. Despite the fact that the Council operates with more traditional forms of protest and seems to have no fundamental vision of social transformation, nonetheless it exemplifies a left-of-centre, reforming strategy for the future and deserves large-scale support.[152]

Liberation and Politics: Movement or Party?

A Quebec Example

Liberationist forces in Canadian history have long struggled with the issue of whether they should work within a movement or a party. There has always been a legitimate fear that corruption and oppression will result when the idealism and grass-roots integrity of a movement becomes a political party committed to itself and its own survival. History has only reinforced this concern. That has certainly been the experience of numerous Quebec worker-nuns and worker-priests. Many not only welcomed the arrival of René Lévesque's Parti Québécois (PQ) to power in 1976, but also battled within that party in the name of liberation. Sister Dolorès Léger worked actively for women's issues in a PQ committee. Ugo Benfante laboured locally for the PQ, and Sister Marie-Paule Lebrun welcomed its electoral victory as a blow against U.S. capitalism. Most striking was the example of the Jesuit worker-priest Jacques Couture. In the mid-1970s he received a leave of absence from his order to run in the 1976 election that brought the PQ to power. He held two portfolios in Lévesque's government and sought to promulgate his liberationist values as a governmental minister. Nonetheless, disillusionment quickly set in, and most of these committed radicals broke with partisan activism. Couture returned to his order and was sent to Madagascar to work among the poor. By the time of the second Lévesque government the worker-priest Benoît Fortin was saying: "With my working-class experience I made my final judgement that this was also a capitalist government . . . in the service of the bourgeoisie." Tragically the PQ government of Lucien Bouchard offers more of the same.[153]

The CCF-NDP Connection

The Co-operative Commonwealth Federation (CCF) was born in 1932-33, constituting itself at a convention held in Regina, Saskatchewan. Its existence culminated from almost thirty years of struggles by Canadian radicals representing a wide variety of ideological positions. At Regina they fought and squabbled and dug in their heels, yet in the face of the Depression and their powerful oppressors they forged a political movement exemplified by the Regina Manifesto.[154] The heart of this founding document captured the principles of CCF socialism: "We aim to replace the present capitalist system, with its inherent injustice and inhumanity, by a social order from which the exploitation of one class by another will be eliminated, in which economic planning will supersede unregulated private enterprise, and in which genuine democratic self-government, based on economic equality, will be possible."[155]

Throughout the 1930s the CCF struggled for a place in the hearts and minds of Canadians. Its handful of MPs spoke out courageously for the poor and marginalized, and CCF organizers and grass-roots leaders took to the streets and public arenas to mobilize the populace. Tenaciously it held its own while growing slowly, but its major successes emerged only towards the end of World War II. Although the Cape Breton mineworkers supported the CCF as early as 1938, it was not until 1943 that the Canadian Congress of Labour (CCL) endorsed the left-wing party as "the political arm of labour." Thus began the labour-CCF/NDP connection, which has since grown in strength. During the war the popularity of the CCF and its platform of social programs rose markedly, so much so that Prime Minister Mackenzie King led his Liberal Party on a massive campaign using "Red Scare" tactics against this increasingly viable left-wing alternative. To ensure its defeat in the federal election of 1945 King had his party adopt social welfare legislation, which turned out to be a remarkably successful strategy. The

Liberals won a resounding victory, and the CCF went down to defeat without changing its fringe third-party status. Yet the very threat of the CCF had forced the Liberals to adopt progressive legislation that they had refused to consider during the dark days of the Depression.[156]

Without a doubt the greatest victory of the young CCF was its electoral breakthrough in the Saskatchewan provincial election of 1944. Ex-Baptist minister Tommy Douglas led his party to power as the first democratically elected socialist government in North America. Although the Douglas governments were not socialist as such, his team promulgated legislation which was the envy of progressives throughout North America. From 1944 until 1961, when Douglas accepted the federal leadership of the NDP, he was premier of a government dedicated to the most vulnerable sectors of Saskatchewan's populace. A few measures adopted by the Douglas team included: equalization of educational costs and opportunities, higher minimum wages for teachers and others, the right to vote for eighteen-year-olds, a provincial bill of rights, low-cost provincial automobile insurance, government support for cultural programs, collective bargaining for public employees as well as their right to participate in politics, an eight-hour workday legislation, paid holidays, advanced trade union legislation, government support for co-operative economic enterprises, and electrification and running water for farm communities.[157] The crowning achievement of the Douglas years was the passing of the Medical Care Insurance Act (1961), the closest thing to socialized medicine in North American history and the precipitating cause for all subsequent provincial and federal health legislation designed to provide quality and equal health care for all citizens.[158]

Tragically, the transformation of the CCF into the New Democratic Party in 1961, with Douglas as federal leader, has never achieved its potential. Its inception was the beginning of a gradual evolution that has sacrificed principles for the goal of electoral success. At the very beginning the NDP dropped the term socialism from its official platforms and constitution, and the party then spent the next three decades abandoning its substance as well. The NDP became, in essence, a left-centre party of social reform prepared to support the existing socioeconomic regime in exchange for progressive social legislation.[159] Still, socialists and radicals did not abandon the party en masse, as the Waffle revolt of the late 1960s made clear. Led by two academics, Mel Watkins and James Laxer, the left-wing Waffle faction, working within the party, sought to link together nationalism (versus economic continentalism) and socialism in its program. As Laxer put it, "For

Canadians who wish to pursue the elusive goal of an egalitarian socialist society, American imperialism is the major enemy." As long as this
leftist faction remained an intellectual "ginger group" in the party, it
could be tolerated. The Waffle reached its peak when Laxer ran for the
leadership of the federal party at the 1971 Ottawa convention. It took
the eventual winner, David Lewis, four ballots to defeat Laxer by a vote
of 1,046 to 612. This humiliating victory for Lewis and, later, the continuing Waffle interventions into party affairs — and particularly its
attacks on top-level union brass — ensured that the leftist faction
would no longer be tolerated. It was expelled from the Ontario party in
June 1972 at an Orillia meeting.[160]

Since the destruction of the Waffle, the NDP has pursued an
increasingly moderate strategy designed to expand the party's voting
base and bring it to power. In this it has achieved modest success, at
least at the provincial level. Since the Tommy Douglas days in
Saskatchewan, the NDP has been the governing party in that province
for most of the last thirty years. NDP governments have also been
elected in British Columbia, Manitoba, and Ontario.[161] But despite
important social reforms, the ruling social-democratic parties' over-all
strategy has been to be "voter friendly" and this approach has cost the
NDP much of its integrity. It grapples for a vision, yet adopts parts of
the corporate agenda's "deficitophobia" and accepts the strategy of
government cutbacks — even though it might scramble to give these
same measures a more compassionate and friendly face. The Ontario
Rae government, elected in 1990, pursued such a strategy and cyni-
cally called its attacks on the public-sector unions a "social contract."
The plan proved disastrous both at the polls and in terms of
integrity.[162]

To be sure, there is no current electoral alternative for liberationists. Until the NDP renews itself or until a new party emerges on the
left, the best partisan vote must remain with the NDP. The success of
the party in the June 1997 federal election and the "gutsy" leadership
of Alexa McDonough offer some ground for hope along these lines.
Still, for those of us within the party who are fighting for a strong leftist renewal, there ring before our faces the prophetic words of Tommy
Douglas, from 1983:

> The growth and development of the New Democratic Party must
> never allow us to forget our roots. Don't sacrifice conviction for suc-
> cess. Don't ever give up quality for quantity.
>
> In a movement like ours, as socialist movements around the
> world have demonstrated, we're not just interested in getting

votes. . . . We are seeking to get people who are willing to dedicate their lives to building a different kind of society . . . a society founded on the principles of concern for human well being and human welfare.[163]

The Neo-Liberal Parties

In 1987 Preston Manning, son of former Social Credit premier of Alberta Ernest Manning, announced the formation of a new party that he claimed to be "grass-roots," a party of the people. And, to be sure, popular and democratic rhetoric has been used to create a mass constituency for the party. Reform militants called for an elected, equal, and effective (Triple E) Senate, which has great appeal to their Western electoral base, and they advocated for political reforms rooted in earlier populist prairie movements — reforms such as recall, referenda, free parliamentary votes, and a simplified tax system. All of these proposals have an almost instant appeal to frightened and discontented voters, which are often people who have jobs, small homes, and modest (not always secure) incomes.

These people represent easy targets for the scapegoating and fear-mongering of the Reform Party and its clones in British Columbia, Alberta, and Ontario. Manning led his party in the 1993 federal election to a smashing success, electing more MPs to the House of Commons than any other anglophone party but the Liberals. In Alberta Ralph Klein captured the leadership of the Progressive Conservatives in 1992 and went on to win the provincial election of 1993. Mike Harris, Klein's counterpart in Ontario, won a smashing victory in the provincial election of June 1995. Although bearing the Conservative label, both of these governments reflect populist elements similar to those of the national Reform Party.[164]

Despite democratic rhetoric and the folksy "plain talk" of Klein, Harris, and Manning, these parties are no friends of the marginalized citizenry of this country. In fact, they represent the most ruthless form of political oppression that Canada has witnessed since the Duplessis era in Quebec and the Social Credit years of Alberta. This oppression comes to light in their basis of support, their ideology, and their practice. Fundamentally Reformers constitute a party of the right advocating for the most strident agendas of corporate Canada. Their financial resources come fundamentally from the coffers of big business, especially from the petroleum barons of Calgary. Reform's main leadership, Manning included, has strong business ties, and the party is linked to those organizations, such as the Fraser Institute, which have high-profile big business connections. The rhetoric may be populist, at times even deceptively democratic, but Reform's best friends exist among the business elites of the nation. To discover whether a party is truly "grass-roots" means moving beyond its rhetoric to see exactly who funds it. In this respect, the parties of Manning, Klein, and Harris fail to meet the litmus test.[165]

The parties also fail in the rhetoric department. A closer look at their principles reveals that Reformers' values undergird the agendas of the ruling elite, even when it might appear otherwise. One such example of this "doublespeak" emerges in their tax reform agenda. They speak of simplifying the tax system, certainly a principle that would warm the heart of any liberationist. But Reform and its allies of the Canadian Taxpayers Federation do not base their so-called "reform" on tax fairness. Following their U.S. counterparts, Reformers and taxpayer protests are not demanding that corporations pay the billions of back taxes they owe, nor do they support a system in which those most able to pay are expected to carry their proportion of the load. Instead they want an end to corporation taxation and a general rollback of taxes, to be balanced by sharp reductions in those very governmental services designed to cushion the pain for our most vulnerable citizens[166]

This agenda promises a bonanza for the worst kind of capitalism, a phenomenon that goes back to the "robber baron" epochs of the early Industrial Revolution. The agenda is blatantly antiunion, designed to undermine what labour has fought to gain for more than a century. Its desire to free the rich from regulation and dismantle humane programs for the poor and marginalized will reduce these people to a vast, desperate army of cheap labour prepared to accept any kind of employment, however exploitative. In addition to being a voice for economic elites, this political program seeks to raise its grass-roots troops on the basis of their fears and prejudices. Reform and its provincial clones play to racist, anti-French, anti-immigrant, and anti-welfare feelings as if those vulnerable sectors of our population bear the blame for Canada's fiscal woes. Reform, its leaders, and its predecessors have had links with pro-apartheid groups in South Africa in the years before independence there. They have been connected to neo-Nazi outfits like the Heritage Front, extreme right-wing groups from the West, lobbies against gun control, pro-English language organizations in Quebec, anti-feminist outfits, and extreme fundamentalist Christian bodies.[167]

Since 1995 two provincial governments, one in Alberta and one in Ontario, have put Reform ideology into practice. These governments have implemented massive social cutbacks in the name of deficit reduction, and sold public services to private vendors. Both provinces are creating the kind of economic climate near and dear to major corporations and large investors. In reality, Reform and its allies remain the most ruthless forms of big business politics that now dot the national landscape. As such they are part and parcel of the oppressive forces within the land and stand in frank opposition to the gospel of liberation.[168]

When it comes to the question, then, of what can I do? — what can we do to serve the liberating gospel in the Canada of the new millennium? — I would argue that we follow, where appropriate, the example of those who have gone before us in the past. They have shown us creativity and courage. They leave us with a powerful and useful legacy. But we should also remember that we are not alone today. Despite the difficult road ahead, we do not stand by ourselves. Christian and non-Christian groups are still struggling valiantly in the camp of liberation. These include many among the severely oppressed and marginalized, as well as middle-class, relatively prosperous people. New militants are always welcome. Now is the time to either join up or renew our commitments. Christ's call is clear: *"Follow me!"*

6

Towards Liberation and the Millennium

DURING EVERY EPOCH, THE DIFFICULT YET EXHILARATING CALL TO follow Christ on the road to liberation has presented specific challenges and visions, and the present time is no different in that regard. The oppression-liberation struggle has a tenacious continuity in Canada that provides us with resources of knowledge, analysis, and inspiration. The unique challenges of today grow out of that past, and our faith calls us to confront these issues with wisdom and courage. In light of past struggles and current commitments, we must consider the most effective strategies that would move us towards a world of justice and *shalôm*.

Let me begin with personal disclaimers. First of all, no one person, not even a liberationist, can unilaterally provide "THE" blueprint. The Christian liberationist walks as a pilgrim, always on the road, always learning. Finding the right direction is ever the work of God and a community endeavour. We need always to include mistakes in the process and changes in direction. Recently, for instance, I committed myself to pacifism, and this shift in my personal journey was prompted by Biblical study, the witness of friends, and the influence of Walter Wink's profound trilogy on "the Powers." Nonetheless, I cannot write off the convictions of sisters and brothers who believe that there are rare instances in which armed resistance to tyranny might be necessary. Continued dialogue on this issue remains a mandate for liberationists.[1] Nonetheless, in spite of mistakes and the fact that "walking the talk" is the deed of God within a faithful community, I offer some thoughts on possible directions for a liberationist strategy for Canada. These ruminations emerge in general from material and people outlined in the previous chapters. Initially we must examine the landscape around us — globally, nationally, and locally — to assess the current powers of oppression. Then we must link up with those organized forces of liberation so that we can confront those evils.

Numerous writers have described the chilling reality that characterizes the current global situation, and it remains a veritable mandate
for liberationists to keep abreast of developments through regular
reading as well as the support of alternative resources.[2] The post-World
War II epoch of economic expansion in which capital and labour
embraced a historic compromise has ground to a halt. In its place the
corporate elites have inaugurated a global war of transnationals and
their allies against the workers and the poor of our planet. This war
goes by the term "globalization." Transnational financial institutions,
such as the International Monetary Fund and the World Bank, along
with national governments and their corporate backers, repeat the
mantra of "the debt crisis" and "deficit reduction" ad nauseam in order
to divert money from social spending into corporate-driven programs.
In the area of policy this approach takes the form of intervention in
developing countries by the imposition of the "Structural Adjustment
Plans" (SAPs), which force social policies upon the debt-ridden
countries—policies that fall with unprecedented brutality upon the
poor. Foreign aid has more strings attached to it than ever before, and
invariably such "tied aid" carries demands that the debtor countries
intensify the wishes of the First World elites for a market-driven economy. Events in debt-ridden Mexico to prop up the peso underscore this
oppressive reality. Even more chilling is the Multilateral Agreement on
Investment (MAI), a deal hammered out between the transnationals
and the richer nations of the Organization for Economic Cooperation
and Development (OCED). The treaty involves a sellout of national
sovereignty and a carte blanche for the global business elites to run
roughshod over democracy, workers, and the environment. The MAI
will serve as a virtually unlimited Bill of Rights for capital.[3]

The assault of globalization takes its own peculiar forms within
the G-7 countries, which are characterized by Western-style democracies and large and reasonably prosperous middle classes. Nonetheless,
the agenda of the corporate elite is the same—to transfer wealth and
power into fewer and fewer hands by increasing the freedom of the
corporate elites to pursue the maximization of profits and control
within the society and around the globe. The nature and identity of the
oppressors in Canada have remained strikingly constant in the years
since Confederation, but what stands out as different in our day is the
ruthlessness and co-ordination of the elites' assault on the poor and
vulnerable. And the assault now comes down with increasing brutality
upon the middle class as well. The deficit mantra, along with the claim
of "needing to be competitive" on "a level playing field," emerges with

relentless regularity from our reigning politicians, their corporate backers, and the media, to the point that such ideologies become conventional wisdom or "common sense." What the Council of Canadians calls "the corporate takeover of a nation" and other social critics describe as "the corporate agenda" has gone over to the offensive in the form of a brutal juggernaut. Profits of the banks and transnationals are higher than ever, CEO salaries have skyrocketed, while right-wing governments, federally and provincially, weep over deficits and leave corporation taxes uncollected. Instead they blame debt on government in the form of social payments to the poor, unemployment compensation, pensions, and health care. They decry the public sector, including teachers and nurses, as bureaucratic, inefficient, and costly. Based on this faulty logic, they wield the deficit axe against the public sector and the social safety net rather than addressing the problem where it resides — namely with the corporate sector and its privatization agenda. Policies like the FTA and NAFTA reflect this agenda, along with the federal Liberals' gallop to the political right. Many provincial governments embody this "corporate agenda" even more so than the Chrétien and Paul Martin Liberals. Ralph Klein in Alberta and the Mike Harris Tories in Ontario promote this agenda in its most unsubtle form.[4]

Recently I attended a Saturday conference in Guelph, Ontario, called "Taking Back Democracy: Tackling Corporate Rule," which was sponsored by the Guelph-Wellington Coalition for Social Justice. One of the invited guest speakers, Tony Clarke, presented us with a ringing mandate to roll back the "corporate agenda" and build alternatives of our own from the grass-roots forces being pummelled so relentlessly by the economic and political elites. He replicates such mobilizing events through his Polaris Institute, and his book *Silent Coup: Confronting the Big Business Takeover of Canada* remains a must for liberationist militants. This double strategy of resistance and creation fits quite well into the ongoing struggle between the opposing forces of oppression and liberation, a struggle that builds upon the existing communities of liberation in Canada — both Christian manifestations dedicated to the dream of *shalôm* and wider movements of liberation. Because liberation is the goal that drives us, we must count on these people, God's most fundamental resource, at our disposal. Coalitions, embodied and emboldened by consciousness-raising and mobilization, must claim our time and energy. This means taking up the liberationist "praxis-reflection-praxis" and/or the specialized Catholic Action model of "see-assess-take action" (*"voir-juger-agir"*).[5]

Christians and Faith Coalitions

First of all, it is vital that Christian consciousness-raising groups intensify their own internal growth through a combination of spiritual nurturing along liberationist lines and mutual reflection upon the militant actions of members in their wider communities. Part of such self-reflection includes helping each other discover elements of the corporate agenda that live within us. After all, no matter how much we repudiate and challenge corporate values, they reside within us as well. That is the nature of ideological hegemony. Deeper than intellectual awareness, consciousness-raising must probe the subterranean, more visceral presence of the oppressive agenda that dwells within. The ancient practice of exorcism, exemplified by Jesus' "casting out of demons," provides an appropriate Biblical metaphor for such reflections.

Quebec's adult specialized Catholic Action, known as the Mouvement des Travailleurs (euses) Chrétiens (nes) (MTC), provides a Canadian model. Members are required to be militants in working-class or progressive movements, most of which are not specifically Christian. As well, they belong to the MTC, which defines itself with reference to the Christian faith. Its militants meet regularly to reflect upon their lives of activism in light of their Christian faith. These periodic encounters include worship, study, and personal sharing, realities I experience through the house church. However, unlike the house church, the MTC understands its *raison d'être* in terms of a liberationist gospel, and its communities are organized with that focus in mind.

In his book *Behind the Mitre,* Tony Clarke advocates for a broader coalition of the prophetic elements within the Christian ecumenical movement. He is convinced that the corporate agenda reflects a corresponding "moral crisis" that is sowing "the seeds of a prophetic revival" within the ranks of faith communities. Clarke recognizes that many within institutionalized religion have acquiesced to the status quo in what he calls "a covenant of silence," but his hope is grounded in a "prophetic alliance" that crosses denominational lines. In this scenario progressive Christians of all stripes are challenged to commit themselves to the liberationist cause by setting a course as radical as their Master, in going "to the backwaters, the homeland of the poor and marginalized," there to forge an alliance cemented by justice and *shalôm*. For me, the MTC model provides a structure for Clarke's vision, as long as it moves towards an alliance of all faith progressives, marginalized and middle class. Given the middle-class nature of our religious bodies, given the large middle class reality within our society, and given the corporate assault on the middle class as well as the poor, it is both wise and just to solidify and expand such an alliance.[6]

It seems to me that expansion of such MTC-type bodies must involve reaching beyond Christianity to other faith communities. Given the history of religious crusades and oppressive imperialism in the name of religion past and present, movement towards such a broader alliance presents difficult challenges. Nonetheless, there exist significant hopeful signs. Proclamations of public repentance to First Nations' people by the United Church of Canada and the Anglicans bode well for increasing solidarity. Recent gestures by Lutherans along similar lines to Canada's Jewish community add to this growing spirit of reconciliation. In my own Waterloo Region (Ontario) we formed the Interfaith Movement for Social Justice (IMSJ) in January 1996 to challenge the corporate agenda in the form of the Harris government in Ontario. Since then we have produced brochures that quote justice-oriented passages from the sacred scriptures of the major world religions, and during the massive Community Day of Action in Waterloo Region our movement conducted an outdoor religious service that included Jewish, Muslim, First Nations, and Christian (Protestant and Catholic) participation. David Pfrimmer of the Waterloo Lutheran Seminary-based Institute for Christian Ethics, also a member of our interfaith coalition, exercises leadership in the Ontario-wide Interfaith Social Assistance Reform Coalition (ISARC). As part of its mandate, members of the various religious communities monitor government behaviour and challenge our politicians to reflect the broad religious values of justice and *shalôm*. Although navigating through religious differences proves difficult from time to time, the rewards of a growing understanding of each other and the strengthening of the religious voice for liberation make such a pilgrimage both joyous and necessary.[7]

People within faith communities are also obliged to undertake the difficult and often unrewarding task of consciousness-raising among the more uncommitted, the more conservative and the more cautious within their own institutions. This is an issue that our local interfaith movement wrestles with day after day. To be sure, there are those among our co-believers who will remain solidly within the corporate camp. However, most church members remain among the confused and undecided, and they are the people with whom we must connect. Within our IMSJ, one young couple has been trained to lead workshops in congregations with the purpose of raising and discussing social issues with church members. As well, a number of others within the group have committed themselves to a training program run by the

Ecumenical Coalition for Economic Justice (ECEJ), which culminated, in May 1997, in an intensive workshop lasting several days, held at our seminary. Several of us within the IMSJ participated, and our follow-up will involve training other trainers within local congregations. Further efforts are emerging within the IMSJ to galvanize a wider public. More specifically, we are preparing public teach-ins to analyse our current health-care system in order to mobilize an effective citizen response to the corporate effort to dismantle and privatize our provincial system.

These particular illustrations arise from my own local experience and do not preclude in any way parallel mobilizations that crisscross the country. Our IMSJ encountered similar groups through the Community Days of Action held in city after city in Ontario, and that experience has generated mutual learning and inspiration. Parallel campaigns are arising throughout Canada, which is cause for rejoicing. ECEJ's Web networks are forming links that will enhance mutual enrichment between such groups.[8]

Indeed, organizations such as ECEJ and similar bodies in Quebec demonstrate existing links between grass-roots ecumenical bodies and the institutional church. Such ties provide legitimization both within the church, where they engage in training and consciousness-raising activities, and in the wider world, where the organizations can use the media to proclaim the more progressive positions of the major Canadian churches. In this way and through direct delegations, the groups of Christian activists engage the prophetic task of "speaking the truth to power." Church statements on justice issues, whether they come from the Canadian Council of Churches, the World Council of Churches, the Catholic bishops, or other denominational proclamations, remain stillborn unless there are intermediate organizations between the institutional church and the grass-roots that are prepared to implement social justice policies. ECEJ and those bodies similar to it fill such a gap.[9]

The Broader Coalitions

Based upon the realization that God's work of liberation encompasses wider activities outside of ecclesiastical spheres, Christians are compelled to join hands and hearts with justice and *shalôm* movements beyond their own boundaries. Given the power and aggressiveness of oppression today, in the form of the corporate agenda, all progressive forces locally and globally must be united in their opposition. Solidarity, in addition to its effectiveness as an approach, can be an antidote against pride and sectarianism. The MTC mandate requires its members to link up with wider movements, and the challenge now is for all such networks to move beyond individual issues into a broad-based collective solidarity. In Kitchener-Waterloo, the Global Community Centre's mandate, "think globally, act locally," articulates a commission for such wider action.

The Kitchener-Waterloo Experience: Making Links

During the free trade debates in the late 1980s, the Waterloo Regional Labour Council, the Global Community Centre, and other local groups created the Waterloo Regional Coalition for Social Justice (WRCSJ) to combat the legislation. Fresh from these earlier struggles, the coalition increased its breadth and strength with the arrival at Queen's Park of the pro-corporation government of Mike Harris in June 1995. Within a few months protests began to emerge locally. Carol Schlueter, a professor at Waterloo Lutheran Seminary, organized a quiet vigil at Kitchener City Hall to protest provincial welfare cuts. Her collection of friends was joined by members of the regional social justice coalition, thus aiding the birth of street actions by the broader coalition. Around the same time the house church I belong to was finishing a collective study of the manuscript that would lead to this book, which prompted the question, "Where do we go from here?" Our answer drove us to organize the Interfaith Movement for Social Justice, which held its inaugural meeting in January 1996. Meanwhile the protest vigil had continued on a weekly basis, with broader public demonstrations organized by the regional coalition. A mass and raucous protest greeted Harris and Labour Minister Elizabeth Witmer at the opening of the area's annual 1995 Octoberfest activities. A number of people from local faith communities began to participate in coalition meetings, and once the IMSJ held its first meeting, it too joined the wider body and sent official representatives to its meetings.

At that point outside action by both the provincial government and justice coalitions helped shape our local agenda. In the winter of 1996 the antiunion thrust of the Conservative government kicked in with an attack upon public-sector workers belonging to the Ontario Public Service Employees Union (OPSEU), led by Leah Casselman. Rather than capitulating to governmental pressure to "downsize," OPSEU voted to hit the picket lines for the first time in its history. Supporters and detractors alike expected the union protest to buckle. It did not. Solidarity within the union held, in spite of some defections, and seasoned members of the Canadian Auto Workers (CAW) along with militants from other unions and the wider coalitions joined their OPSEU sisters and brothers on the line. The union won some gains by forcing the Harris government to back down on key issues. This victory served to intensify militancy locally and provincially and to cement protesting coalitions all across Ontario. This set in motion a growing preparation for the Community Days of Action planned for mid-April in our tri-city area.[10]

After aggressive protests at Queen's Park during the summer and early autumn of 1995, the labour movement brought its organizational skills to bear in order to construct broad-based street actions across the province — actions designed to bring non-labour progressives into an effective alliance with the trade union movement. The Community Days of Action emerged from this. The first, held in London, Ontario in December 1995, was followed by an unprecedented rally and march in Hamilton in February 1996. In Hamilton about 125,000 protesters confronted a Tory convention non-violently, while the Harris forces displayed a bunker mentality from behind the walls of their convention site. The Kitchener-Waterloo area, the home of Labour Minister Witmer, was designated as Target Number 3 for a series of concentrated actions.

The Ontario Federation of Labour (OFL) sent us superb assistance in the persons of Jim Turk and Paul Forder, and the Waterloo Region Committee for April 19 was born under the leadership of Lucy Harrison of the WRCSJ and Bob Cruickshank, president of the Waterloo Region Labour Council. From the beginning the planning committee embodied a wide base, including school teachers, high school and university students, members of the Ontario Coalition Against Poverty (OCAP), co-op housing people, and our own interfaith movement. Solidarity and enthusiasm characterized the preparations, and the work bore fruit on the Days of Action themselves. Work stoppages were effective, and Friday, April 19, 1996, saw 30,000 to 40,000 people converging on City Hall to hear union leaders, community activists, teenagers, clergy, single mothers on welfare, Aboriginal leaders, and others lift up their voices in defiance against the provincial corporate-political alliance and in hope for a better tomorrow. This was no narrow labour-NDP protest, but rather a broad popular outcry. Our own interfaith community felt honoured to be a part of it all.[11]

Similar Days of Action followed, at Peterborough in June and Toronto in October. In Toronto a highly effective general strike occurred on Friday, the 25th, followed by a massive march on Queen's

Park on Saturday, the 26th, with upwards of 250,000 people. Again, my IMSJ friends and I were struck by the broad-based popular character of the marchers. Labour was there — which in itself should be celebrated — but even more than in the Waterloo Region, the Toronto rally brought together a clear representation of every element of Ontario society save the corporate elite, who remained hidden, both physically and metaphorically, behind the protective walls of the Toronto Stock Exchange or a conference building.[12]

The Community Days of Action stand as a tangible embodiment of that *shalôm* community portrayed in the sacred texts of those of us who claim the name of Christian. They are part of that new world of liberation arising from the oppressive shell of the old, and they represent our connection to the even wider work of God's liberation both nationally and globally. Nonetheless, they are not without their difficulties, characterized by division and distance. It seems to me that division emerges as the more serious of these two problems. The only way a tiny corporate elite can effectively control and take advantage of the vast majority of citizens is through a "divide-and-conquer" policy. The approach usually includes injecting into the oppressed themselves the very ideology and values of the oppressors. The corporate-owned media and the elite's increasing control of the educational apparatus are mechanisms in the "divide-and-conquer" policy. But we also see the problems, to our own sorrow, among ourselves and our coalition partners. We are encouraged to "compete" with our sisters and brothers for "the crumbs" that the elite throws in our direction. Workers are pitted against farmers, and loggers and environmentalists waste energy struggling against each other. Middle-class people are encouraged to view themselves as "educated professionals," at least one cut above factory workers. Unionized private-sector workers are described as overpaid and thus non-competitive, and public-sector workers are castigated as part of a bloated, inefficient bureaucracy. Feminists are painted in ludicrous colours that wash out their necessary struggles against patriarchy, even within progressive ranks. Anti-immigration sentiment hides the pervasive presence of racism, which continues to victimize minorities and First Nations' peoples. And within all these oppressed groups reside deep pernicious contempt and rejection of gays, lesbians, and welfare recipients. Add to all this the narrow focus of insularity, which threatens any just cause, and we can see that much remains to be done within progressive ranks to exorcize our internal evils, which serve the corporate cause so well.

We always have to remember that we have made important gains, however small. Although the provincial NDP government of Bob Rae backed down on same-sex legislation, in fall 1996 the CAW gained such rights for its own constituency in its recent hard-won contracts with the three major automobile corporations. As well, the CAW and some public-sector unions endorsed the openly gay Svend Robinson in the federal NDP leadership race in fall 1995. In British Columbia, Mae Burrows of the United Fishermen and Allied Workers' Union (UFAWU) undertakes environmentalist action as part of both her union mandate and her membership in the T. Buck Suzuki Environmental Foundation. CAW president Buzz Hargrove works actively with Maude Barlow and others in the Council of Canadians, and in small-town Essex County, Ontario, union activists, students, small-business people, environmentalists, ordinary citizens, and NDP politicians and activists formed the Essex County Citizens Against Fermi II, a coalition directed at the megapower industry (Detroit Edison Company). Finally, from May 14 to June 15, 1996, women from across Canada in three caravans converged on Ottawa via a series of marches, teach-ins, demonstrations, and rallies. This "Women's March Against Poverty" crossed class, racial, and ethnic lines and included the participation of male supporters at special junctures. The effort was sponsored by the National Action Committee on the Status of Women (NAC) and the Canadian Labour Congress. This cross-country mobilization received its inspiration from a 1995 March against Poverty led by our sisters in francophone Quebec (the Fédération des Femmes du Québec).[13]

Honesty demands both openness and an acknowledgement of the divisions that exist within the labour movement itself. Most of the private-sector unions place their hopes for the future in the traditional labour-NDP alliance, while the Canadian Auto Workers and most public-sector unions have turned to broad grass-roots social alliances as a priority. Within the NDP itself a malaise reigns as party militants vacillate between serious renewal and a political reformism with its energy directed towards getting elected. These tensions have been acted out in party leadership conventions, elections, and riding associations, and they were apparent in the organizing for the Community Days of Action. Resolution of these difficulties is imperative, and I am convinced that the grass-roots model remains the necessary and most healthy option, yet without a summary cutting of ties with the NDP. At the same time a win-lose battle between factions serves only the corporate elite. Effective and fair compromises must be worked out, and they can be. The gains of the NDP in the June 1997 federal election stand as a hopeful sign in the healing of divisions within labour and

the party. Alexa McDonough's courage and integrity during the campaign, as well as labour's growing unity, speak well of the progressive
capacity for solidarity. As well, the Community Days of Action and the
general support for the teachers' protest in fall 1997 have manifested
an unprecedented unity in Canada's most populous province.[14]

Division, of course, is enhanced with distance, and distance can be
both psychological and geographical. Most of the examples of activism
I've drawn on here emerge from my own personal and geographical
limits. I am a white, male, middle-class, Christian, Ontarian anglophone, new Canadian, and ex-American. I make no apologies for these
characteristics, which embody both gifts and limits. My hope is that
readers of this book from here and there in Canada will be able to
draw from and build parallel experiences out of their own lives and
history. But my personal background and positioning do not mean that
I have no opinions or suggestions on matters more distant from my
experience. That projection remains part of a healthy and continuing
dialogue among progressive forces. Take, for instance, the seemingly
intractable issue of Quebec's national identity. At a deep personal level,
"My Canada includes Quebec." I am a committed and visceral fran-
cophile, and yet it would be a continuation of colonialism to offer Quebeckers suggestions as to what they should do. For that reason I felt
very uneasy about the massive love-in that English Canada held in
Montreal just before the referendum on sovereignty in 1995. The task
of progressive anglophones, it seems to me, begins with anglophones.
We must educate ourselves and each other about Quebec and about
our own vestiges of imperialism vis-à-vis our francophone sisters and
brothers. In addition, wisdom and humility demand that we make serious contact with progressive counterparts in Quebec for the purpose of
building justice alliances, as well as for our own learning. Our most
fundamental task in this process is to listen, and to do so properly
means learning to be reasonably fluent in French. Finally, we must be
prepared to honour the choices of our francophone allies, even if they
should choose a separatist option. Certainly, the taking of that decision
does not eliminate the possibility of co-operation and solidarity
between anglophones and francophones. Rather, it demands that
efforts at co-operation and solidarity be undertaken in the face of different realities. A similar stance is called for in dealing with First
Nations people.[15]

Finally, our faith demands of us that we overcome the distance of
barriers both nationally and globally. Some movement in that direction
has already taken place. Aboriginal peoples and refugees live within

our neighbourhoods and communities, and programs within the churches bring us together in intentional ways. The work of the Toronto congregations, mentioned in chapter 5, exemplify this. Specific ecumenical coalitions organize around such concerns; and the Kitchener-Waterloo Global Community Centre continues its creative work in this context. After all, the corporate agenda is global, and our faith mandate to build a world of justice and *shalôm* can be effective only in those places and efforts where global solidarity unfolds. After all, the Mike Harris program has its clones in the Alberta Tories, the federal Liberals, the U.S. Democrats and Republicans, the current Mexican regime, the New Zealand Labourites — the list could go on and on. Alternative media, such as *The New Internationalist, Our Times*, and *Canadian Dimension*, keep us informed and provide us with contacts of international progressive groups. Churches and other bodies work in the developing world in ways that link justice militants with one another. Resistance against NAFTA crossed national boundaries and included labour organizations from Canada, the United States, and Mexico. The Zapatista uprising in Chiapas inspired international support. In short, we are not called upon to create an international network from nothing. Rather, our mandate is to tap in, to build, and to get on with the task.

Clearly the struggle ahead will be long and arduous. This realistic assessment mirrors the way of the cross. Yet resurrection seeds sprout within and around us. Christ's call to follow him on the road of liberation blends struggle with hope. We march towards a New Jerusalem where peace (*shalôm*) and righteousness dwell. American Socialist leader Eugene V. Debs put it so very well minutes before his jail sentencing in 1918: "Let the people take heart and hope everywhere, for the cross is bending, the midnight is passing, and joy cometh with the morning."[16]

Notes

Chapter 1: Setting the Stage

1 There is much literature on the subject, which I will use and cite in chapters 3 and 4. For now, this is summarized exceedingly well in John Dillon, *Turning the Tide* (Ottawa: Canadian Centre for Policy Alternatives, 1997).

2 For some examples, see Gregory Baum, "The Christian Left at Detroit, 1975," 3-38, in *The Social Imperative* (New York: Paulist Press, 1979), as well as sections of his more recent Massey Lectures in *Compassion and Solidarity* (Montreal and Toronto: CBC Enterprises, 1987).

3 Robert McAfee Brown, *Theology in a New Key* (Philadelphia: Westminster Press, 1973), 60- 62; Leonardo Boff and Clodovis Boff, *Introducing Liberation Theology* (Maryknoll, N.Y.: Orbis Books, 1986), 2-3.

4 Brown, *Theology in a New Key*, 70-72; Boff and Boff, *Introducing Liberation Theology*, 4-9.

5 Brown, *Theology in a New Key*, 67-70.

6 Boff and Boff, *Introducing Liberation Theology*, 27-28; Brown, *Theology in a New Key*, 64-67. The work of the lay liberationist Otto Maduro provides a case of the extensive use of Marxist categories and analysis for Christian purposes. By way of example, see "Labour and Religion according to Karl Marx," 12-20 in Gregory Baum, ed., "Work and Religion," *Concilium* (New York: Seabury Press, 1980).

7 Linda McQuaig's recent *Shooting the Hippo: Death by Deficit and Other Canadian Myths* (Toronto: Viking, 1995) is a scathing and convincing attack on the lies behind the "politically correct" agenda of the elites.

8 Brown, *Theology in a New Key*, 77-85 (this section is well worth reading with infinite care and openness). An excellent example of how liberationists use and understand the Bible is Ernesto Cardenal, *The Gospel in Solentiname* (Maryknoll, N.Y.: Orbis Books, 1978). See also 98-100 in Brown, *Theology in a New Key*.

9 Carol J. Schlueter has edited an excellent little book of sermons by women and about women disciples of Jesus: *The Forgotten Followers* (Winfield, B.C.: Wood Lake Books, 1992). This book contains a sermon by Susan Snelling, the pastor of Six Nations Parish in Ohsweken, Ontario, about the Canaanite woman; it is worth consulting (41-46). Since the sacred Scriptures of Christianity are translations largely from Hebrew and Greek, no English Bible follows the originals word for word. Even the originals we have are not *the* best originals. Hence I have taken some liberty to get at the best translations. Mostly I use the New Revised Standard Version of the Bible because of its attempts to be more inclusive, but I also compare it with the excellent Jerusalem Bible. I have also examined the Hebrew and Greek texts to see if the translations could be enhanced by further clarity. Although the term "kingdom of God" remains exceedingly popular, the more inclusive "Reign of God" is an appropriate translation of the original Greek. Hence I use that more inclusive term.

10 Halford E. Luccock, exposition on Mark 10:21, found in *The Interpreter's Bible*, vol.7 (New York: Abingdon Press, 1951), 804.

Chapter 2: The Liberation-Oppression Struggle in the Christian Tradition

1 For an excellent study of these matters, see Norman K. Gottwald, *The Tribes of Yah-weh: A Sociology of the Religion of Liberated Israel, 1250-1050 B.C.E.* (Maryknoll, N.Y.: Orbis Books, 1979).

2 The history and conflict surrounding the formation of the monarchy are described ably in the classic work by Gerhard von Rad, *Old Testament Theology*, vol. I, trans. D.M.G. Stalker (New York: Harper & Brothers, 1962), 36-68.

3 For a liberation perspective on this gospel, see José Miranda's *The Message of St. John*, trans. by John Eagleson (Maryknoll, N.Y.: Orbis Books, 1977). Meanwhile Walter Wink demonstrates clearly that the term "world" in John ("kosmos" in Greek) does not mean "world, earth or globe" primarily. Rather, for the Gospel writer, the word "kosmos" means chiefly "the human sociological realm that exists in estrangement from God," 51. For details, see his superb *Engaging the Powers* (Minneapolis: Fortress Press, 1992), especially 51-59.

4 New Testament scholar Krister Stendahl writes of "the introspective conscience of the west" in *Paul Among Jews and Gentiles* (Philadelphia: Fortress Press, 1976), 78-96. In this section he describes the way in which a more collective Paul was reframed into the later context of an introspective struggle of sin and grace.

5 Elisabeth Schüssler Fiorenza, "A Discipleship of Equals," 17-33 in Eugene Bianchi and Rosemary Radford Ruether, eds. *A Democratic Catholic Church* (New York: Crossroad, 1992).

6 For details, see Luise Schottroff, *Lydia's Impatient Sisters* (Louisville, Ky.: Westminster/John Knox Press, 1995).

7 The translation of II Corinthians 8:13-14 is my own from the original Greek. Too many recent translators soften the Greek word for equality and thus transform a radical statement into safe charity. The Greek of the text does not support such a softening.

8 Since the eighteenth century scholars have tried to discover the authentic message of Jesus that lies behind the theology of the Gospel writings which appeared from one to three generations after Jesus' death. The famous New Testament scholar Albert Schweitzer summed up their work at the beginning of this century in his "trail-blazing" *The Quest of the Historical Jesus*, trans. by W. Montgomery (New York: Macmillan, 1964 [1906]). Since then the "Quest" has gone on apace. More recently, studies have been more insistent on paying serious attention to the socioeconomic and political context out of which Jesus operated. Some examples are Gerd Theissen, *The Gospels in Context* (Minneapolis: Fortress, 1991); the liberationist Fernando Belo, *A Materialist Reading of the Gospel of Mark*, trans. by Matthew J. O'Connell (Maryknoll, N.Y.: Orbis Books, 1975); and the recent well-received *The Historical Jesus: The Life of a Mediterranean Peasant* (San Francisco: Harper, 1991) by John D. Crossan. My book is cognizant of and welcomes this scholarship, but it is far beyond the scope of my efforts to enter into the academic debate.

9 A number of Christian writers and groups in the United States and Canada make much of this "jubilee" notion. For a brief summary of the meaning of "jubilee," see Robert McAfee Brown, *Unexpected News* (Philadelphia: Westminster Press, 1984), 95-96.

10 Some have pointed out that the "eye of the needle" was a narrow Jerusalem gate that was just wide enough for a camel to squeeze through only if its cargo were unloaded. The message is the same — only divestment of wealth in the service of others is acceptable.

11 Pierre Berton, *The Comfortable Pew* (Toronto: McClelland and Stewart Limited, 1965), 90.

12 This outlaw character of the early Christians is described in detail in the seminal work *The Rise of Christianity* by W.H.C. Frend (Philadelphia: Fortress Press, 1984). See especially 147-51, 162-84, 274-75, 318-28.

13 *The True Word of Celsus*, c. C.E. 177-180, 111 in Roland H. Bainton, *Early Christianity* (New York: D. Van Nostrand Company, 1960).

14 Lucian quote from Anne Fremantle, ed., *A Treasury of Early Christianity* (New York: New American Library, 1953), 218.

15 Pliny and Trajan material from Bainton, *Early Christianity*, 88-89.

16 Ibid., 151.

17 Ibid., 152-53.

18 Ibid., 156.

19 For the full extent of this betrayal, see Alistair Kee *Constantine Versus Christ* (London: SCM Press, 1982).

20 Freemantle, *Early Christianity*, 207.

21 Ibid., 404.

22 John C. Cort, *Christian Socialism* (Maryknoll, N.Y.: Orbis Books, 1988), 44.

23 Ibid., 45, 47.

24 For a superb overview of this entire period after Constantine, consult Frend, *The Rise of Christianity* (especially 473-906).

25 "The Rule of St. Francis," 141 in Norton Downs, *Basic Documents in Medieval History* (Princeton, N.J.: Van Nostrand, 1959).

26 Leonardo Boff, *Saint Francis: A Model for Human Liberation*, trans. John W. Diercksmeier (New York: Crossroad, 1985), 76.

27 Sue Woodruff, *Meditations with Mechtild of Magdeburg* (Santa Fe, N.M.: Bear and Company, 1982), 116.

28 Ibid. 109.

29 Julian of Norwich, *Revelations of Divine Love* (New York: Penguin, 1985 [1966]), 165-66.

30 Brendan Doyle, *Meditations with Julian of Norwich* (Santa Fe, N.M.: Bear and Company, 1983), 101.

31 Dorothee Soelle, *The Strength of the Weak*, trans. Robert Kimber and Rita Kimber (Philadelphia: Westminster Press, 1984), 45-46. For an excellent overview of commoner oppression and revolt, see F. Graus, "The Late Medieval Poor in Town and Countryside" in Sylvia L. Thrupp, *Change in Medieval Society* (New York: Appleton-Century-Croft, 1964).

32 For a thorough examination of the British revolt of the 1380s, see the extensive collection of primary documents with analysis by R.B. Dobson, ed., *The Peasants' Revolt of 1381*, 2nd ed. (London: Macmillan Press, 1983).

33 Ibid., 371.

34 Hans J. Hillerbrand, ed., *The Protestant Reformation* (New York: Harper and Row, 1968), 64-65. An excellent study with primary documents is Tom Scott and Bob Scribner, eds., *The German Peasants' War* (Atlantic Highlands, N.J.: Humanities Press, 1994 [1991]).

35 Ibid.

36 The song has been sung by well-known folk singer and protester Pete Seeger. The translated text was given to me by a colleague. A translation of the phrase "*Die Gedanken sind frei*" would be "thoughts are free."

37 A superb study of grass-roots Protestantism in the towns is Henry Heller, *The Conquest of Poverty* (Leiden, The Netherlands: E.J. Brill, 1986).

38 Perhaps the most significant Anabaptist creedal document of the period was the "Schleitheim Confession" (1527). It can be found in Hillerbrand, *Protestant*, 129-36. Samples from the *Martyrs Mirror* are also in Hillerbrand's book (see 137-42, 146-52).

39 A fine study of Hutterite history and life is John A. Hostetler, *Hutterite Society* (Baltimore: Johns Hopkins University Press, 1974).

40 For superb analyses of Levellers, Diggers, and the entire civil war period in England, examine any book on these by Christopher Hill, especially *The World Turned Upside Down* (London: Penguin, 1975 [1972]).

41 It is personally gratifying to report that my denomination, the Evangelical Lutheran Church in Canada (ELCIC), in convention (1995), passed a document that acknowledges with sorrow the anti-Semitism of Luther. "ELCIC confronts anti-Semitism," *Canada Lutheran* 10, 7 [August, 1995], 13.

42 To see the liberationist side of Luther, consult Walter Altmann, *Luther and Liberation:*

A Latin American Perspective, trans. Mary M. Solberg (Minneapolis: Fortress Press, 1992) and Richard Shaull, *The Reformation and Liberation Theology: Insights for the Challenges of Today* (Louisville, Ky.: Westminster/John Knox Press, 1991), 25-62.

43 Shaull's book points out Calvin's contributions to liberation. However, it is the excellent work by Marxist historian Henry Heller which describes in great detail the liberationist activities of French Calvinists. See *The Conquest of Poverty* and *Iron and Blood: Civil Wars in Sixteenth-Century France* (Montreal and Kingston: McGill-Queen's University Press, 1991).

44 Once again, the works of Christopher Hill paint detailed pictures of this turbulent period in British life. Especially consult *Puritanism and Revolution* (New York: Schocken Books, 1964 [1958]). Another excellent work, which concentrates on the British Puritan rebels, is Michael Walzer, *The Revolution of the Saints* (New York: Atheneum, 1976).

45 An example of Methodist participation in Chartism can be found in E.P. Thompson, *The Making of the English Working Class* (New York: Vintage Books, 1963). For an example of a Methodist pro-Chartist sermon, see Joseph Rayner Stephens, "The Political Preacher; An Appeal from the Pulpit: On Behalf of the Poor," (1839) 1-45 in *Chartism and Christianity* (New York: Garland Publishing, Inc., 1986).

46 See Paul Christophe, *1789: les prêtres dans la Révolution* (Paris: Éditions Ouvrières, 1986). For more details on Grégoire, see *L'abbé Grégoire: Évêque et démocrate* by Georges Hourdin (Paris: Desclée de Brouwer, 1989).

47 See Louis Le Guillou, *Les Lamennais* (Paris: Éditions Ouvrières, 1990).

48 For a brief overview of the U.S. abolition movement, see Sydney Ahlstrom, *A Religious History of the American People,* II (Garden City, N.Y.: Image Books, 1975), 91-115.

49 The story of John Brown is told in great detail in Stephen B. Oates, *To Purge This Land with Blood* (Amherst: University of Massachusetts Press, 1984 [1970]).

50 Quoted in Zachary Kent, *The Story of John Brown's Raid on Harpers Ferry* (Chicago: Children's Press, 1988), 30.

51 A thorough study on Frederick Douglass is Philip S. Foner, *Frederick Douglass* (New York: Citadel Press, 1964).

52 Rev. George Washington Woodbey, "The Bible and Socialism" in Philip S. Foner, ed., *Black Socialist Preacher* (San Francisco: Synthesis Publications, 1983), 136-37.

53 A powerful and easy-to-read biography of Martin Luther King, Jr. is John A. Williams, *The King God Didn't Save* (New York: Pocket Books, 1971).

54 For material on Malcolm X, see Alex Haley, ed., *The Autobiography of Malcolm X* (New York: Grove Press, 1965).

55 "The Black Manifesto," in Gayraud S. Wilmore and James H. Cone, eds., *Black Theology: A Documentary History, 1966-1979* (Maryknoll, N.Y.: Orbis Books, 1979), 81-82.

56 Albert Cleage, sermon, "Let's Not Waste the Holy Spirit," in Ibid., 338.

57 James H. Cone, *A Black Theology of Liberation* (Philadelphia and New York: J.B. Lippincott Company, 1970), 213-15.

58 Barbara J. MacHaffie, *Her Story: Women in Christian Tradition* (Philadelphia: Fortress Press, 1986), 100-02.

59 Ibid., 136.

60 Martin E. Marty, *Righteous Empire* (New York: Dial Press, 1970), 203.

61 See Dorothee Soelle, *The Strength of the Weak*, and Rosemary Ruether, *To Change the World* (New York: Crossroad, 1985). Also see Jacquelyn Grant, *White Women's Christ and Black Women's Jesus* (Atlanta: Scholars Press, 1989), which provides a glimpse into the unique perspective of black Christian feminism.

62 Elisabeth Schüssler Fiorenza, "Feminist Theology as a Critical Theology of Liberation," in William K. Tabb, ed., *Churches in Struggle* (New York: Monthly Review Press, 1986), 52.

63 Walter Rauschenbusch, *Christianizing the Social Order* (New York: Macmillan Company, 1912), 191-93.

64 Ibid., 321-22.

65 Ibid., 323.

66 Benjamin J. Martin Jr., *Count Albert de Mun* (Chapel Hill: University of North Carolina Press, 1978).
67 For material on Marc Sangnier, see Oscar L. Arnal, *Ambivalent Alliance: The Catholic Church and the Action Française* (Pittsburgh: University Press, 1985). Quotes from Sangnier: his newspaper *L'Eveil Démocratique*: 1) "Un Congrès syndical au Sillon," 21 oct. 1906, 1 and 2) "Les Patrons," 14 oct. 1906, 1.
68 For a description of the JOC, see Oscar L. Arnal, "Toward a Lay Apostolate of the Workers," *Catholic Historical Review* LXXIII, no.2 (April 1987), 211-27.
69 The two following works by Dorothy Day describe her life and the history of the Catholic Worker Movement: *The Long Loneliness* (San Francisco: Harper and Row, 1981 [1952]), and *Loaves and Fishes* (San Francisco: Harper and Row, 1983 [1963]).
70 For details on this New Pentecost epoch, consult Oscar L. Arnal, *Priests in Working-Class Blue* (New York: Paulist Press, 1986), 15-33.
71 See Ibid., 112.

Chapter 3: The Oppressors in Canada

1 William Irvine, *The Farmers in Politics* (Toronto: McClelland & Stewart, 1920), 53.
2 Wallace Clement, *The Canadian Corporate Elite: An Analysis of Economic Power* (Toronto: McClelland & Stewart, 1975), 72-78; Wallace Clement, *Continental Corporate Power: Economic Linkages between Canada and the United States* (Toronto: McClelland & Stewart, 1977), 58-64; Bryan D. Palmer, *Working Class Experience*, 2nd ed.(Toronto: McClelland & Stewart, 1992), 157-61.
3 Clement, *Canadian Corporate Elite*, 80-87; Palmer, *Working Class Experience*, 214-19; Clement, *Continental Corporate Power*, 65-79.
4 Jean Hamelin and Yves Roby, *Histoire économique du Québec, 1851-1896* (Montréal: Fides, 1971), 10-24, 31-33, 35, 41, 51, 66-72, 84-89, 101-19, 121-38, 141-50, 185-200, 207-23, 252-54, 261-82, 347-50, 355-64, 369-75; Paul-André Linteau, René Durocher and Jean-Claude Robert, *Histoire du Québec contemporain: De la Confédération à la Crise, 1867-1929* (Montréal: Boréal, 1979), 75-78, 93-108, 131-37, 142-48, 382-89; Paul-André Linteau, Jean-Claude Robert and François Ricard, *Histoire du Québec contemporain: Le Québec depuis 1930* (Montréal: Boréal, 1980), 207-16, 416-25; John Porter, *The Vertical Mosaic* (Toronto: University of Toronto Press, 1965), 91-92.
5 Clement, *Canadian Corporate Elite*, 89-91.
6 Clement, *Canadian Corporate Elite*, 90-91; Linteau, et al., *Le Québec depuis 1930*, 212.
7 Clement, *Canadian Corporate Elite*, 129. Corporate publications do not deny this vast economic concentration. See *The Financial Post 300: Canada's Largest Industrial, Financial, Merchandising, Property and Resource Companies* (Toronto: Financial Post, 1976), especially 8-9, 15-19.
8 Clement, *Continental Corporate Power*, 91-92, 103-05.
9 James Laxer, *In Search of a New Left* (Toronto: Penguin Books, 1996), 15-22; for "the deal," see Jamie Swift, *Wheel of Fortune: Work and Life in the Age of Falling Expectations* (Toronto: Between the Lines, 1995), 26-29.
10 James Laxer, *False God: How the Globalization Myth Has Impoverished Canada* (Toronto: Lester Publishing, 1993), 13-15. Similar descriptions can be found in Mel Watkins and Duncan Cameron, eds., *Canada under Free Trade* (Toronto: James Lorimer, 1993), 21-22.
11 "Index on Global Corporate Power," *Canadian Forum* (January-February, 1997), 48. See also "Rich World-Poor World: A Map of Global Injustice," *New Internationalist* 287 (January-February, 1997), insert; and "Globalization," *New Internationalist* 296 (November, 1997), 18.
12 "Index on Global Corporate Power," 48; Mel Hurtig, *The Betrayal of Canada*, 2nd ed. (Toronto: Stoddart Publishing Co., 1992), 59, 61-63, 70, 72, 181; *The Third World Guide, 1995-96*, 162; Tony Clarke, *Silent Coup* (Ottawa and Toronto: Canadian Centre for Policy Alternatives and James Lorimer, 1997), 32-33, 54-57, 63-64.
13 John Dillon, "Monopolizing Money: How corporate dictators of the world's money

supply are undermining national economies," *Canadian Forum* (June, 1994), 8-12; "World Bank — The Facts," *New Internationalist* 214 (December, 1990), 16-17; "Squeezing the South," *New Internationalist* 257 (July, 1994), insert; Maude Barlow, "Global Bully," *Canadian Forum* (July-August, 1996), 9.

14 Dillon, *Turning the Tide,* 1-22 (quotes on 1). See also Brahm Eiley, "Fast money," *New Internationalist* 257 (July, 1994), 19-20.

15 Dillon, *Turning the Tide,* 30-31, 34, 63-87. See also Laxer, *In Search of a New Left,* 69-70.

16 Dillon, *Turning the Tide,* 38-49. See McQuaig, *Shooting the Hippo* and Ecumenical Coalition for Economic Justice, *Reweaving Canada's Social Programs* (Toronto: ECEJ, 1993).

17 Laxer, *In Search of a New Left,* 73-74; Dillon, *Turning the Tide,* 1; Tony Clarke, "The Job Killers," *Canadian Perspectives,* Autumn, 1996, 7; Wayne Ellwood, "Seduced by technology," *New Internationalist* 286 (December, 1996), 7-10. For a brief overview of this technological revolution and its impact on workers, see Michael Czerny, S.J., Jamie Swift, and Robert G. Clarke, *Getting Started on Social Analysis in Canada,* 3rd ed. (Toronto: Between the Lines, 1994), 95-106.

18 Jeremy Rifkin, *The End of Work* (New York: G.P. Putnam's Sons, 1995) and Heather Menzies, *Whose Brave New World? The Information Highway and the New Economy* (Toronto: Between the Lines, 1996), see especially 7-14, 29-32, 52-79, 89-102, 117-128. See also the excellent *Progress without People* by the neo-Luddite scholar David F. Noble (Toronto: Between the Lines, 1995).

19 Menzies, *Whose Brave New World?,* 78. The human downside of this technological revolution is described further in the Kingston sections of Swift, *Wheel of Fortune,* and in Julie White, "Automatic Unemployment," *New Internationalist* 286 (December, 1996), 23-24.

20 Stanley B. Ryerson, *Unequal Union* (Toronto: Progress Books, 1968), 342-346; Leo Panitch, "The Role and Nature of the Canadian State," 11-12 in Leo Panitch, ed., *The Canadian State: Political Economy and Political Power* (Toronto: University of Toronto Press, 1979).

21 J.L. Finlay and D.N. Sprague, *The Structure of Canadian History,* 2nd ed. (Scarborough, Ont.: Prentice-Hall, 1984), 255-58; Pierre Berton, *The Promised Land* (Toronto: Penguin Books, 1984), 19, 23, 33-34, 36-53, 308-331.

22 For details, see Gerald Friesen, *The Canadian Prairies* (Toronto: University of Toronto Press, 1984), 331-38, 341-42.

23 For detailed descriptions of the rise and growth of Winnipeg, consult Alan F.J. Artibise, *Winnipeg: A Social History of Urban Growth* (Montreal: McGill-Queen's University Press, 1975) and *Gateway City: Documents on the City of Winnipeg 1873-1913* (Winnipeg: Manitoba Record Society, University of Manitoba Press, 1979).

24 Artibise, *Winnipeg,* 24-33.

25 Alan F.J. Artibise, "Boosterism and the Development of Prairie Cities, 1871-1913," 211-16 in Alan F.J. Artibise, ed., *Town and City: Aspects of Western Canadian Urban Development* (Regina: Canadian Plains Research Centre, University of Regina, 1981).

26 Artibise, *Winnipeg,* 28-29, 77-96.

27 Pierre Berton, *The Great Depression* (Toronto: Penguin Books, 1990), 50-56, 67-76; Barry Broadfoot, *Ten Lost Years, 1929-1939: Memories of Canadians Who Survived the Depression* (Markham, Ont.: Paperjacks, 1977), 309, 311.

28 Berton, *The Great Depression,* 36-45, 56-59, 75-77, 82, 332-37, 355-407, 433-41, 482-97; Lorne Brown, *When Freedom Was Lost* (Montreal: Black Rose Books, 1987), 192-96.

29 Laxer describes this in *In Search of a New Left,* 15-17. See also Swift, *Wheel of Fortune,* 25-27.

30 For detailed overviews of the economic elite's control over Canada's political life in the three decades after the war, consult the relevant material in Panitch, *The Canadian State.* A good summary of the Duplessis years can be found in either Susan Mann Trofimenkoff, *The Dream of Nation* (Toronto: Gage, 1983), 267-74 or Herbert F. Quinn, *The Union Nationale,* 2nd ed. (Toronto: University of Toronto Press, 1979),

76-97. For a brief summary of King's postwar social policy, see Maude Barlow & Bruce Campbell, *Straight through the Heart* (Toronto: HarperCollins, 1995), 20-23.

31 Panitch, *The Canadian State*, 205-09, 212-18.

32 Clement, *Canadian Corporate Elite*, 229-31.

33 For examples, see Ibid., 235-36.

34 Linda McQuaig, *The Quick and the Dead* (Toronto: Penguin, 1991), 91-92; Hurtig, *Betrayal of Canada*, 256-58; Richard Cleroux, "The Party of Corporate Canada," *Canadian Forum*, April, 1996, 16-18.

35 McQuaig, *Quick and the Dead*, 82-92; Barlow & Campbell, *Straight through the Heart*, 91-103; James Winter, *Democracy's Oxygen* (Montréal: Black Rose Books, 1997), 54-68.

36 McQuaig, *Quick and the Dead*, 94-103; Cleroux, "Party of Corporate Canada," 15; David Langille and Asad Ismi, "The Corporate Connection," *Canadian Perspectives*, Autumn, 1996, 11.

37 Cameron and Watkins, eds., *Canada under Free Trade*, 105-24; Hurtig, *Betrayal of Canada*, 24-26, 28-30, 54-57, 130-32.

38 "Seven Years of Free Trade," *Canadian Perspectives*, Summer, 1996, 6-10; "Challenging Free Trade in Canada: The Real Story," *Economic Justice Report* VII, 2 (June, 1996), 1-8, and VII, 4 (Dec., 1996), 2-4, 7-8; Maude Barlow, "Global Bully," *Canadian Forum*, July/August, 1996, p. 9; "Index on Unemployment," *Canadian Forum* (June, 1997), 48; David Barkin, "NAFTA—-no solution to Mexico's problems," *Canadian Dimension* 26, 6 (Sept., 1992), 10-14; Eugenia Martinez, Fernando Herrera, and German Sanchez, "Breaking Mexican Labour," *Canadian Dimension* 26, 8 (Nov.-Dec., 1992), 21-22.

39 Mel Watkins, "The Deficit Scam: From the Folks Who Brought You Free Trade," 159-161 in *Madness and Ruin: Politics and the Economy in the Neoconservative Age* (Toronto: Between the Lines, 1992); McQuaig, *Shooting the Hippo*, 28-37, 52, 117-18, 275; Hurtig, *Betrayal of Canada*, 126, 134-37; McQuaig, *Quick and the Dead*, 15-18; ECEJ, *Reweaving Canada's Social Programs*, 33-35; Barlow & Campbell, *Straight through the Heart*, 49, 51-52, 55-56.

40 Hurtig, *Betrayal of Canada*, 125-29; McQuaig, *Shooting the Hippo*, 51.

41 Hurtig, *Betrayal of Canada*, 130-32; Watkins, "Deficit Scam," 160-64; *Reweaving Canada's Social Programs*, 35-39; McQuaig, *Shooting the Hippo*, 51-52, 56-68, 72-121, 260-62; Barlow & Campbell, *Straight through the Heart*, 79, 84-87, 96-97, 126-31, 133-38.

42 Finlay and Sprague, *Structure of Canadian History*, 302, 334-35, 337-39; Friesen, *Canadian Prairies*, 188; Craig Brown, *The Illustrated History of Canada* (Toronto: Lester & Orpen Dennys, 1987), 339; "The Farmers' Platform, 1918," 257 in J.M. Bliss, ed., *Canadian History in Documents, 1763-1966* (Toronto: McGraw-Hill, 1966).

43 Linda McQuaig, *Behind Closed Doors* (Toronto: Penguin, 1987), 123-53.

44 Ibid., 154-82; Carol Goar, "A big budget for business," *Maclean's* 96, 18 (May 2, 1983), 14-22.

45 Hurtig, *Betrayal of Canada*, 167-77; Linda McQuaig, *The Wealthy Banker's Wife* (Toronto: Penguin Books, 1993), 145-46; ECEJ, *Reweaving Canada's Social Programs*, 39-40; Errol Black, "Tory Taxes Pamper Corporations," *Canadian Dimension*, October, 1990, 6-8; Neil Brooks and Linda McQuaig, "In Tories They Trust," *This Magazine* 26, 5 (December 1992), 13.

46 Black, "Tory Taxes," 7; *Reweaving Canada's Social Programs*, 40; McQuaig, *Behind Closed Doors*, 321; Hurtig, *Betrayal of Canada*, 172.

47 *Reweaving Canada's Social Programs*, 39-40; Hurtig, *Betrayal of Canada*, 173-76; McQuaig, *Behind Closed Doors*, 311, 319-29; Duncan Cameron, "Banks," *Canadian Forum*, March, 1997, 4.

48 Neil Brooks, "The Liberal 'no alternative' tax alternative," *Canadian Dimension*, May-June, 1994, 24-26; Bruce Campbell, "Myths, Manipulation & Liberal Budget Making," *Canadian Perspectives*, Winter, 1994, 6-7; "New tax proposal covers up GST bite," *The Toronto Star*, June 21, 1994, A1, A11; Kathleen O'Hara, "Corporate Wealthfare," *Canadian Forum*, March, 1996, 16-22; Richard Cleroux, "The Party of Corporate

Canada," *Canadian Forum,* April, 1996, 15-18; "Closing the Loopholes," *Canadian Perspectives,* Winter, 1997, 11; and Barlow & Campbell, *Straight through the Heart,* 78, 100, 133, 220. For a thorough examination of global tax injustice, see the issue of *New Internationalist* called "Taxed to Death: The Great Revenue Robbery," 220 (June, 1991).

49 "In Tories They Trust," 16.

50 "Jobs are justice!" *The New Ontario Democrat,* February, 1994, 12-13; "Workers clean up under Bill 40," *The New Ontario Democrat,* May, 1994, 7; Errol Black, "Will Canada's Left support the NDP, this time around?" *Canadian Dimension,* September-October, 1993, 7-9; Buzz Hargrove, "Desperately Seeking the NDP," *Our Times,* March, 1993, 17-18; Leo Gerard, "Changing Economies," *Our Times,* December, 1994, 35-39.

51 Jennifer Stephen, "Progressive Dis-ease," *This Magazine* 26, 3 (September, 1992), 28-30 (quotes from 29); Jamie Swift, "But You Promised," *This Magazine,* 25, 1 (June/July, 1991), 17; George Ehring and Wayne Roberts, *Giving Away a Miracle: Lost Dreams, Broken Promises & the Ontario NDP* (Oakville, Ont.: Mosaic Press, 1993), 277. For other articles providing similar information, see "Ontario's NDP — A year in the life," *Canadian Dimension* 25, 7 (Oct./Nov., 1991), 5-11; Robert Gareau, "Ontario's NDP Government and the Corporate Agenda," *Canadian Dimension* 27, 3 (May/June, 1993), 6-8; Brian O'Keefe, "Bob Rae's Done Deal," *Our Times* 12,4 (Nov./Dec., 1993), 5; and "NDP puts welfare cuts on the table," *The Record* [Kitchener], March 21, 1994, 1; Buzz Hargrove, "Building a Movement," *Our Times,* December, 1994, 30-34; Frank Tough, "Thinking about the NDP's thinking," *Canadian Dimension,* March/April, 1993, 31-32.

52 Berton, *Promised Land,* 23-25, 42-46, 52-54, 394-400. See also "Going Daily," *Horizon Canada* 8, 87 (1986), 2078-83. See Robert A. Hackett and Yuezhi Zhao, *Sustaining Democracy: Journalism and the Politics of Objectivity* (Toronto: Garamond Press, 1997) for a thorough look at the history of the Canadian press and how it works.

53 Sandro Contenta, *Rituals of Failure: What Schools Really Teach* (Toronto: Between the Lines, 1993), 9-30; Alison Prentice, *The School Promoters* (Toronto: McClelland & Stewart, 1982 [1977]), 66-84, 119-64. See also Linteau, *Le Québec,* 94-95, and Terry Copp, *The Anatomy of Poverty* (Toronto: McClelland & Stewart, 1974), 57-69.

54 For some examples of this in Canadian life, see "Picture Palaces," *Horizon Canada* 8, 88 (1986), 2096-101; Linteau, et al., *Le Québec depuis 1930,* pp. 153-165; and Brown, ed., *The Illustrated History of Canada,* 440-42.

55 Contenta, *Rituals of Failure,* 51-58, 71-74, 79-98, 112-20, 126-33, 161-62, 166-69, 192-206.

56 Maude Barlow and Heather-Jane Robertson, *Class Warfare: The Assault on Canada's Schools* (Toronto: Key Porter Books, 1994), 77-137, 146-54, 169-86. For examples, see Wayne Roberts, "The Toronto Board Takes the Pepsi Challenge . . . And Loses," *Our Schools, Our Selves* 5, 3 (July, 1994), 8-15; Gordon W.E. Nore, "pop goes education," *Our Times* 13, 3 (June-July, 1994), 15-17; Michael G. Redfearn, "Dangerous Gifts," *Kitchener-Waterloo Record,* Jan.13, 1994, A7; and Larry Kuehn, "Market Mechanisms plus Education Systems equals Inequality," *Canadian Dimension,* Sept.-Oct., 1996, 21-23.

57 Clement, *Canadian Corporate Elite,* 287-98; Winter, *Democracy's Oxygen,* 91-93.

58 Czerny, et al., *Getting Started,* 123; Winter, *Democracy's Oxygen,* 3, 7-8.

59 Czerny, et al., *Getting Started,* 121-24; James Winter, "The Black Market: Buying Up Democracy's Oxygen Supply," *The Canadian Forum,* July-August, 1996, 25-26; Bill Roberts, "Buying Time," *Our Times* 11, 4 & 5 (September, 1992), 42-43; "Global Digital Highway Super-Babble," *New Internationalist* 256 (June, 1994), 18-19; "Seven things you should know about media ownership," *Canadian Perspectives,* Summer, 1997, 105; and Winter, *Democracy's Oxygen,* xi-xii, 1-7, 12-18, 21-68.

60 McQuaig, *Shooting the Hippo,* 12.

61 Winter, *Democracy's Oxygen,* 116-119; Czerny, et al., *Getting Started,* 125-34. *Manufacturing Consent,* the excellent film about Noam Chomsky, is reviewed by Ron Harpelle in *Canadian Dimension* 26, 6 (September, 1992), 37.

62 Winter, *Democracy's Oxygen*, 127-28, 136. See also Czerny, et al., *Getting Started*, 125-34, and Doug Smith, "The recession is over . . . ," *Canadian Dimension* 27, 2 (March/April, 1993), 47. For a guide to dealing with media distortion, see Eleanor Maclean, *Between the Lines* (Montreal: Black Rose Books, 1981). See also Hackett and Zhao, *Sustaining Democracy*.

63 For two Canadian examples, see Tom Wayman, ed., *Going for Coffee: Poetry on the Job* (Madeira Park, B.C.: Harbour Publishing, 1981) and Dawn Fraser, *Echoes from Labor's Wars*, expanded ed. (Wreck Cove, Cape Breton Island, 1992).

64 For a recent critique on the tyranny and power of pop culture, see "What's Faith Got to Do with It?" *Sojourners* 23, 5 (June, 1994), 14-28. Some more substantive analyses of pop culture and its negative effects include: John F. Kavanaugh, *Following Christ in a Consumer Society*, revised edition (Maryknoll, N.Y.: Orbis, 1991); Alan Durning, *How Much Is Enough? The Consumer Society and the Future of the Earth* (New York: W.W. Norton, 1992); and Neil Postman, *Technopoly: The Surrender of Culture to Technology* (New York: Vintage Books, 1993).

65 The more recent scholarship in church history recognizes the more repressive side of the Christian tradition. For examples, see MacHaffie, *Her Story*, 54-57; Sydney E. Ahlstrom, *A Religious History of the American People*, 2 vol. (Garden City, N.Y.: Image Books, 1975); Martin E. Marty, *Righteous Empire* (New York: Dial Press, 1970); and Norman Ravitch *The Catholic Church and the French Nation, 1589-1989* (London and New York: Routledge, 1990).

66 See John S. Moir, *The Church in the British Era*, vol. II in *A History of the Christian Church in Canada* (Toronto: McGraw-Hill Ryerson, 1972), 113-25, 180-86; John Webster Grant, *The Church in the Canadian Era*, vol. III in *A History of the Christian Church in Canada*, 24-29; Ramsay Cook, *The Regenerators: Social Criticism in Late Victorian English Canada* (Toronto: University of Toronto Press, 1985); and Brian J. Fraser, *The Social Uplifters* (Waterloo: Wilfrid Laurier University Press, 1988).

67 Richard Allen, "Salem Bland and the spirituality of the social gospel: Winnipeg and the West, 1903-1913," 218-21, in Dennis L. Butcher, et. al., *Prairie Spirit: Perspectives on the Heritage of the United Church of Canada in the West* (Winnipeg: University of Manitoba Press, 1985).

68 Allen, "Salem Bland" and Gerald Friesen, "Principal J.H. Riddell: The sane and safe leader of Wesley College," 251-63 in *Prairie Spirit*; Richard Allen, *The Social Passion: Religion and Social Reform in Canada, 1914-28* (Toronto: University of Toronto Press, 1973), 47-60. On the firing of Salem Bland, see also A.G. Bedford, *The University of Winnipeg: A History of the Founding Colleges* (Toronto: University of Toronto Press, 1976), 125-39.

69 Allen, *Social Passion*, 175-96.

70 See the relevant sections in Trofimenkoff, *Dream of Nation*, 186, 195-99, 219-32. Jean Hamelin and Nicole Gagnon, *Histoire du catholicisme québécois, Le XXe siècle*, vol.1: *1898-1940*, and Jean Hamelin, *Histoire du catholicisme québécois, Le XXe siècle*, vol.2: *De 1940 à nos jours* (Montréal: Boréal Express, 1984) are the definitive works in the field.

71 "La Confédération des Travailleurs Catholiques du Canada," *École Sociale Populaire*, no.98, c.1921, 5-6; *Programme-Souvenir du Premier Congrès de la Confédération des Travailleurs Catholiques du Canada*, Montréal, 12-17 août 1922, 6, 8.

72 For a well-researched, though partisan, account of the Asbestos Strike, see Pierre Elliott Trudeau's *La Grève de l'Amiante* (Montréal: Éditions du Jour, 1970), especially 239-62. A study of the Charbonneau case is Renaude Lapointe, *L'Histoire bouleversante de Mgr. Charbonneau* (Montréal: Éditions du Jour, 1962). One example of coverage on the Dominican Tower strike is "le pavillon st-dominique," *Présence Chrétienne*, juin 1974, 4-6.

73 See Reginald Bibby, *Unknown Gods* (Toronto: Stoddart Publishing, 1993). See also Tony Clarke, *Behind the Mitre* (Toronto: HarperCollins, 1995); "A matter of inclusion," *Catholic New Times*, March 9, 1997, 4; and Andrew Cash, "Protecting the face of corporate rule," *This Magazine*, May-June, 1997, 28-33.

74 Brenda Dalglish, "Are they worth it?" *Maclean's*, May 9, 1994, 34-37, and "When

enough becomes enough," *Guelph Mercury*, May 13, 1994, A4; Clarke, *Silent Coup*, 264-66.

75 Ian Delaney, "Rewarding risk: Those executives who create value deserve their pay," *Maclean's*, May 9, 1994, 38.

76 "From Mailman to Millionaire," *Success*, June, 1994, 28-32; table of contents, *Profit*, June, 1994; Wess Roberts, *Victory Secrets of Attila the Hun* (New York: Dell Publishing, 1993). The other books cited in this genre are publications dating from 1991 and are available for examination with the data already provided.

77 Peter C. Newman, *Flame of Power* (Toronto: Longmans, Green & Co., 1959); John DeMont, *Citizens Irving: K.C. Irving and His Legacy* (Toronto: Doubleday Canada, 1991). Newman's most renowned book on the subject is the two volume *The Canadian Establishment* (Toronto: McClelland & Stewart Ltd., 1975, 1981).

78 The Newman portraits provide ample details on both the extravagances and social philanthropy of the elite. For an analysis on food banks, see "Banking on the Food Banks," *The Ram's Horn* 101, January, 1993, 1-5. For an analysis of McDonald's as employer, see Sarah Inglis, "Union Drive-Thru," 19-28 and Randy Robinson, "Big Mac's Counter Attack," 29-30 in *Our Times* 13, 3 (June/July, 1994).

Chapter 4: The Oppressed in Canada

1 Palmer, *Working Class Experience*, 164-66.

2 Irving Abella and David Millar, eds., *The Canadian Worker in the Twentieth Century* (Toronto: Oxford University Press, 1978), 58, 226-27.

3 Kenneth McNaught, *A Prophet in Politics* (Toronto: University of Toronto Press, 1959), 176.

4 From Fraser, *Echoes from Labor's Wars,* 3.

5 Abella & Millar, *Canadian Worker in the Twentieth Century*, 231.

6 Berton, *Great Depression*, 108-18. For statistical data on this worker misery in Quebec, consult: Paul-André Linteau, René Durocher, Jean-Claude Robert, and François Ricard, *Le Québec depuis 1930*, vol. 2 in *Histoire du Québec contemporain*, 14, 21-25, 55-56, 63-64; and Jacques Rouillard, *Histoire du Syndicalisme Québécois* (Montréal: Boréal, 1989).

7 Broadfoot, *Ten Lost Years*, 125-26.

8 Palmer, *Working Class Experience,* 200-04. The basic work on the strike is David Jay Bercuson, *Confrontation at Winnipeg*, revised edition (Montreal & Kingston: McGill-Queen's Press, 1990 [1974]). For a history that includes extensive primary material from the Strike, see Norman Penner, ed., *Winnipeg 1919* (Toronto: James Lewis & Samuel, 1973).

9 Palmer, *Working Class Experience*, 201-05; Penner, *Winnipeg*, pp.xv-xix, xxv-xxvii; Friesen, *Canadian Prairies*, 361-63.

10 Palmer, *Working Class Experience*, 221-24; David Frank, "Coal Wars," *Horizon Canada* 4, 44 (1986), 1046-51.

11 "Away False Teachings of My Youth," 41 in Fraser, *Echoes from Labor's Wars*.

12 Abella & Millar, *Canadian Worker in the Twentieth Century*, 228. See also, Berton, *Great Depression*, 112-31.

13 For details on the Asbestos Strike, see Rouillard, *Histoire*, 278-82; Trudeau, ed., *La Grève de l'Amiante;* and "Déclarations sur la brutalité de la police provinciale à Asbestos," 11 mai 1949, (Montréal: Confédération des Syndicats Nationaux).

14 Two studies demonstrating the massive character of this social service rollback are: ECEJ, *Reweaving Canada's Social Programs,* and McQuaig, *Wealthy Banker's Wife*.

15 "Index on Unemployment," *Canadian Forum* (June, 1997), 48; *Economic Justice Report* VII, 4 (December, 1996), 2-3, 7; Cameron and Watkins, eds., *Canada under Free Trade*, 287-94; Episcopal Commission for Social Affairs of the Canadian Conference of Catholic Bishops, *Widespread Unemployment: A Call to Mobilize the Social Forces of Our Nation*, April, 1993, 5; Czerny et al., *Getting Started*, 84-87; Hurtig, *Betrayal of Canada,* 19; Tony Clarke, "The Job Killers," *Canadian Perspectives*

(Autumn, 1996), 7; "Jobs, jobs, jobs . . . ," *Canadian Perspectives* (Spring, 1997), 7.

16 Mettrick, *Last in Line,* ix. Cyril Dalley, "Sea Change: The Words of a Fisherman," *Our Times* 12, 4 (Nov.-Dec., 1993), 24-27 (quotes on 24 and 27).

17 Bruce Livesey, "Labour's McChallenge in the '90s," *Canadian Dimension* (August-September, 1994), 2; John Lorinc, "Fast Food, Slow Bargaining," *This Magazine,* June, 1994, 25-30; Karen Williams, "Chain Reactions," *Our Times* 13, 3 (June/July, 1994), 31-33; Mary Campbell, "I Was a Harvey's Cashier," *Our Times* 13, 3 (June/July, 1994), 39-41, 43; and Craig Heron and Robert Storey, eds., *On the Job: Confronting the Labour Process in Canada* (Kingston and Montreal: McGill-Queen's University Press, 1986), 309-26.

18 See Heron and Storey, *On the Job.*

19 Rinehart, *Tyranny of Work,* 63-65.

20 Harry Glasbeek and Eric Tucker, "Corporate Crime and the Westray Tragedy," *Canadian Dimension* 28, 1, (Jan.-Feb., 1994), 11, 14; Shaun Comish, *The Westray Tragedy* (Halifax: Fernwood Publishers, 1994); and Les Samuelson, ed., *Power and Resistance: Critical Thinking about Canadian Social Issues* (Halifax: Fernwood Publishing, 1994), 130.

21 Bruce Livesey, "It's Sick: Steve Mantis Diagnoses the wcb," *Our Times* (April-May, 1994), 17.

22 Kealey, "Labour: Boom or Bust?" *Our Times* (May, 1992), 21; Cy Gonick, "The state of the unions," *Canadian Dimension* 26, 4 (June, 1992), 5-8.

23 Winter, *Common Cents,* 67.

24 See Trofimenkoff, *Dream of Nation,* 272-74; Quinn, *Union Nationale,* 95-96; Rouillard, *Histoire,* 259-62, 278-85.

25 Rouillard, *Histoire,* 379-85; Daniel Drache, ed., *Quebec — Only the Beginning* (Toronto: New Press, 1972).

26 Allan Fotheringham, "For this is the law — and the profits," *Maclean's,* April 7, 1980, 64; "Judge slams bid to stop strike," *The Globe and Mail,* November 4, 1997, A1, A7.

27 "Union Drive-thru," 19-28 and Randy Robinson, "Big Mac's Counter Attack," 29-30, *Our Times* 13, 3 (June-July, 1994).

28 For some examples of labour's disunity as well as its efforts to restore solidarity, see Peter Kuitenbrouwer, "Days of Factions," *Canadian Forum* lxxv, 856 (January-February, 1997), 14-18; Jason Ziedenberg, "Labour's dirty secret," *This Magazine,* November-December, 1996, 16-21; Basil "Buzz" Hargrove, "Rebuilding our Collective Vision," *Canadian Dimension,* May-June, 1997, 14-15; and articles in *Our Times,* November-December, 1996 and February, 1997.

29 Friesen, *Canadian Prairies,* 305-09, 329-31.

30 Ibid., 331-33; Seymour M. Lipset, *Agrarian Socialism* (Berkeley: University of California Press, 1971), 57-60.

31 Doris Pennington, *Agnes Macphail: Reformer* (Toronto: Simon & Pierre, 1989), 25.

32 Michael Ryan, *Solidarity* (London, Ont.: Guided Study Programs in the Catholic Faith, 1986), 104-07; Carole Giangrande, *Down to Earth: The Crisis in Canadian Farming* (Toronto: Anansi, 1985), 9-118; Lois L. Ross, *Prairie Lives: The Changing Face of Farming* (Toronto: Between the Lines, 1985), 57-81, 135-53; Brewster Kneen, *From Land to Mouth: Understanding the Food System* (Toronto: NC Press, 1989), 44-68, 77-84.

33 Kneen, *Land to Mouth,* and *Rape of Canola;* Giangrande, *Down to Earth,* 89-134; Ryan, *Solidarity,* 106.

34 Giangrande, *Down to Earth,* 119-34; Brewster Kneen, "Cheap Food," *The Ram's Horn* 110 (Nov., 1993), 1-2.

35 Brewster Kneen, "Value-Added," *The Ram's Horn* 110 (Nov., 1993), 3-4; Brewster Kneen, "Pushing Drugs," 2-3, and Tim King, "As for the Cows," 3-4 in *The Ram's Horn* 113 (March, 1994); Brewster Kneen, "Product or Process," *The Ram's Horn* 95 (June, 1992), 1-3; Brewster Kneen, "Discrediting Biotech," *The Ram's Horn* 116 (June, 1994), 1-4.

36 Brewster Kneen, "nafta — Yet Another Enclosure," *The Ram's Horn* 106 (June, 1993), 1-3; "gatt & the End of European Civilization," *The Ram's Horn* 111 (Dec., 1993),

1-5; Brewster Kneen, "Saskatchewan Wheat Pool Converts . . . to Capitalism," *The Ram's Horn* 117 (July, 1994), 1-2; Brewster Kneen, "Growing Together," *The Ram's Horn* 135 (March, 1996), 1-4.

37 Brewster Kneen, "The Global Marketplace," *The Ram's Horn* 100 (Dec., 1992), 1-4.

38 R.A. Simm, *Land and Community* (Guelph: University of Guelph, 1988), 15-40.

39 Gisele Ireland, *The Farmer Takes a Wife* (Canada Employment and Immigration Commission, Health Promotion Directorate of Health and Welfare Canada, the United Church of Canada, P.L.U.R.A., 1983), 27-29, 44-45, 56-57.

40 Manitoba Farm Wife, "Queen's Bush Rural Ministries . . ." *Eastern Synod Lutheran*, Nov., 1988, 4.

41 For thorough details of this Montreal situation, see Copp, *The Anatomy of Poverty*.

42 Berton, *Great Depression*, 174-79.

43 Quoted by J.S. Woodsworth in the House of Commons. Quote found in Berton, *Great Depression*, 178.

44 Berton, *Great Depression*, 351-407. See also Brown, *When Freedom Was Lost*.

45 J.S. Woodsworth, *Manitoba Free Press*, March 12, 1909, quoted in McNaught, *Prophet*, 56-57.

46 McQuaig, *Wealthy Banker's Wife*, 98-99; Bill Roberts, "Facing Poverty: The New Caste in Canada," *Our Times* 11, 2 (May, 1992), 22; Ken Battle, "Poverty and the Welfare State," *Power and Resistance*; Sheila Baxter, *Still Raising Hell* (Vancouver: Press Gang, 1997), 59; "The other deficits," *Catholic New Times*, May 4, 1997, 5; "We're Out for Justice!," May 3 CLC Day of Protest, Spring, 1997, 2; National Council of Welfare, *Welfare Incomes 1995* (Winter, 1996-97), 26.

47 "Facing Poverty," 24-25.

48 Czerny, et al., *Getting Started*, 33-40 (quote on 35); "Facing Poverty," p. 22; "MPPs pass legislation to gut rent controls," A3, and "Mere survival isn't enough," A24, *The Toronto Star*, Nov. 19, 1997; Carl Mollins, "No Fixed Address," *Maclean's*, Jan. 20, 1992, 20-23; Bruce Livesey, "Staying the Night," *Our Times* 11, 4 & 5 (Sept., 1992), 30-35; and "Home Sweet Home," *This Magazine*, (Nov.-Dec., 1997), 18-23.

49 Terry Copp, *Anatomy of Poverty* (Toronto: McClelland and Stewart, 1974), 32-33, 52-53, 93-100. For other examples, see Friesen, *Canadian Prairies*, 285-89; and Fernand Harvey, "Child Labour," *Horizon Canada* 1, 3 (1984), 68-72.

50 Berton, *Great Depression*, 430-32; Broadfoot, *Ten Lost Years*, 76-77, 79.

51 Broadfoot, *Ten Lost Years*, 89.

52 "Girls — The Facts," 18-19; Kelly Saxberg, "Women and children at the backdoor," *Canadian Dimension*, March-April, 1993, 5-7; Rick Moffat, "Generation Extermination," *This Magazine*, March, 1994, 22-27.

53 Baxter, *Still Raising Hell*, 23-24, 26; Sheila Baxter, *A Child Is Not a Toy* (Vancouver: New Star Books, Ltd., 1993), 41; "Index on Child Poverty," *Canadian Forum*, May, 1997, 48.

54 Ibid., 48.

55 Ibid., 74-75.

56 Moffat, "Generation . . . ," 23-24; McQuaig, *Wealthy Banker's Wife,* 120-37.

57 Baxter, *Still Raising Hell*, 45; Czerny, et al., *Getting Started,* 137-47; Doris Marshall, *Silver Threads* (Toronto: Between the Lines, 1988), 21-23; Mark Kennedy, "Government pits seniors' pensions against job creation," *Ottawa Citizen*, March 9, 1994 and "Critics say government fuelling generational war," *Ottawa Citizen,* March 10, 1994; ECEJ, *Reweaving Canada's Social Programs*, 103-08; "Cutting the Canada Pension Plan," *Canadian Perspectives* (Summer, 1993), 5. See also *New Internationalist*, February, 1995.

58 Alison Prentice, et al., *Canadian Women: A History* (Toronto: Harcourt Brace Jovanovich, 1988), 78-80, 114-20; Sara Brooks Sundberg, "Farm Women on the Canadian Prairie Frontier: The Helpmate Image," 95-106, in Veronica Strong-Boag & Anita Clair Fellman, *Rethinking Canada: The Promise of Women's History* (Toronto: Copp Clark Pitman, Ltd., 1986).

59 Quoted in Pennington, *Agnes Macphail*, 47.

60 Prentice, et al., *Canadian Women*, 121-22, 125-27, 135-41; Trofimenkoff, *Dream of*

Nation, 179-82; Susan Mann Trofimenkoff, "One Hundred and Two Muffled Voices," 82-92 in Strong-Boag & Fellman, *Rethinking Canada;* Gail Cuthbert Brandt, "Weaving It Together," 160-173 in Alison Prentice and Susan Mann Trofimenkoff, eds., *The Neglected Majority*, Vol. 2 (Toronto: McClelland and Stewart, 1987); Mercedes Steedman, *Angels of the Workplace: Women and the Construction of Gender Relations in the Canadian Clothing Industry, 1870-1940* (New York and London: Oxford University Press, 1997). Joan Sangster, "The 1907 Bell Telephone Strike," *Labour/Le Travail* 3 (1978), 109-130; *La Contre-Grève chez Eddy*, Hull, déc., 1934, 1-59 in CSN archives; "Deux soeurs racontent le lock-out chez Eddy," *Nouvelles* CSN, 11-17 sept. 1981; Joan Sangster, "Rewriting the History of Canadian Communism," *Canadian Dimension* 24, 1 (Jan.-Feb., 1990), 13; Joan Sangster, *Dreams of Equality: Women on the Canadian Left* (Toronto: McClelland and Stewart, 1989).

61 "Girls — The Facts," *New Internationalist* 240 (February, 1993), 18-19.

62 Czerny, *Getting Started*, 168; Diana Ralph, André Régimbald and Nérée St-Amand, eds., *Open for Business, Closed to People* (Halifax: Fernwood Publishing, 1997), 104-11.

63 Alexandra Dagg and Judy Fudge, "Sewing Pains," *Our Times* 11, 3 (June, 1992), 22-25; "I was a Cashier at a . . ." *Our Times* 13, 3 (June-July, 1994), 39-43.

64 For examples, see "Double Burden," *Our Times* 11, 3 (June, 1992), 13 and "Justice Denied," *Our Times* 12, 2 (July-August, 1993), 13.

65 "The Boys Just Don't Get It . . ." *Our Times* 13, 5 (Oct.-Nov., 1994), 13-14 (14 quoted).

66 Lesley Hughes, "Add Women and Stir . . ." *Canadian Dimension*, May-June, 1997, 18-20 (quote on 19). For full details, see *If Women Counted* (San Francisco: Harper & Row, 1988).

67 Czerny, et al., *Getting Started*, 175-76; Sheree-Lee Olson, "Lest We Forget," *This Magazine* 26, 4 (Oct.-Nov., 1992), 15; "Women vulnerable to attacks," *Kitchener-Waterloo Record*, Oct. 11, 1989, 1; Megan Williams, "Fighting Back," *This Magazine* 26, 4 (Oct.-Nov., 1992), 16-18; Judy Rebick, "Where Are Women's Voices?" *Canadian Forum*, April, 1997, 24.

68 Ingeborg Marshall, "The Beothuk," *Horizon Canada* 2, 14 (1985), 326-31; John A. Dickinson & Brian Young, *A Short History of Quebec*, 2nd. edition (Toronto: Copp Clark Pitman Ltd., 1993), 16-24; Ken Coates and Carin Holroyd, "The North's Divided Dreams," *Compass*, Nov.-Dec., 1994, 7-10.

69 Ben Smillie, *Beyond the Social Gospel* (Saskatoon and Toronto: Fifth House Publishers and United Church Publishing House, 1991), 49-73; J.E. Rea, "Red River Stand-off," *Horizon Canada* 5, 57 (1986), 1345-51; R.C. Macleod, "Riel's Return," *Horizon Canada* 6, 69 (1986), 1633-39. For more data on Louis Riel, consult *Une Nation, un leader de la naissance au gibet* (Saint-Boniface: Société historique de Saint-Boniface, 1985).

70 Berton, *Promised Land*, 284-95, 332-38.

71 Czerny, et al., *Getting Started*, 149-53; Tony Hall, "The Politics of Aboriginality," *Canadian Dimension* 27, 1 (Jan.-Feb., 1993), 6-10.

72 Czerny, *Getting Started*, 153-66; Marilyn Fontaine-Bright Star, "Breaking the silence," *Canadian Dimension* 26, 2 (March, 1992), 5-8; Ron Bourgeault, "Race, Class, and Gender: Colonial Domination of Indian Women," 129-50 in Ormond McKague, ed., *Racism in Canada* (Saskatoon: Fifth House, 1991); Ron Bourgeault, "The Killing of Leo LaChance," *Canadian Dimension* 28, 2 (March-April, 1994), 21-25; "Aboriginal Rights," *Catholic New Times*, May 4, 1997, 4 of CPJ insert; Mary Macnutt, "Open Season," *This Magazine* 28, 5 (Dec.-Jan., 1995), 19-23; Paul Seeseequasis, "Home and Native Lands," *Our Times* 13, 4 (Aug.-Sept., 1994), 23-26.

73 Marcel Trudel, "Ties that Bind," *Horizon Canada* 2, 18 (1985), 422-27; Donald Clairmont, *Africville: A Spirit That Lives On* (Halifax: Mount Saint Vincent University & Black Cultural Centre for Nova Scotia, 1989); and Julian Sher, "The Hooded Empire," *Horizon Canada* 2, 20 (1985), 471.

74 Smillie, *Beyond the Social Gospel*, 77-79.

75 Randy Enomoto, "Prisoners of Prejudice," *Horizon Canada* 5, 53 (1986), 1262-67 (quote on 1264).

76 Broadfoot, *Ten Lost Years*, 160-61.
77 Clifton Joseph, "On your mark . . ." *This Magazine* 28, 5 (Dec.-Jan., 1995), 24-28; Stan Gray, "Hospitals & Human Rights," *Our Times* 13, 6 (Dec., 1994), 17-20; Barbara Findlay, "Breaking the Colour Code," *Our Times* 11, 4 & 5 (Sept., 1992), 47-48; "Intolerance in Reform — The Exception or the Rule?" *ReformWatch*, April, 1997, 1-4; and the relevant sections in McKague, *Racism in Canada*.
78 Ryan, *Solidarity*, 58-61; Arif Noorani and Cynthia Wright, "They Believed the hype," *This Magazine* 28, 5 (Dec.-Jan., 1995), 29-32. The September, 1991 *New Internationalist*, "The Dispossessed," underscores the global refugee problem.
79 For a detailed examination of this historical reality, read in detail the fine work by Dickinson and Young, *A Short History of Quebec*. The definitive history of Quebec since Confederation is the two-volume work by Linteau, et.al., *Histoire du Québec contemporain*, now available in English. For an excellent analysis of French-English relations in Canada since the Conquest, read John F. Conway, *Debts to Pay* (Toronto: James Lorimer, 1992).
80 David J. Hall, "Room to Spare," *Horizon Canada* 7, 76 (1985), 1801-07 (quote on 1804).
81 Berton, *Great Depression*, 559-64; Richard A. Jones, "Hate for Sale," *Horizon Canada* 5, 60 (1986), 1430-35.
82 Jones, "Hate," 1432.
83 Berton, *Great Depression,* 559-76. See also Alan Davies, ed., *Antisemitism in Canada* (Waterloo: Wilfrid Laurier University Press, 1992) Jacques Langlais & David Rome, *Jews & French Quebecers* (Waterloo, Ont.: Wilfrid Laurier University Press, 1991); and Irving Abella and H. Troper, *None is Too Many: Canada and the Jews of Europe* (Toronto: Lester and Orpen Dennys, 1982).
84 Yaacov Glickman, "Anti-Semitism and Jewish Social Cohesion in Canada," 45-63 in McKague, *Racism*; "Anti-Semitic incidents doubled in Canada last year, study shows," *Kitchener-Waterloo Record*, March 14, 1989, A4.
85 Brian Mossop, "Equal rights for gay families," *Canadian Dimension*, August 1993, 12-16; Pamela Wagner, "Coming Out," *Our Times* 12, 1 (March, 1993), 26-30; Gary Kinsman, "Heterosexual hegemony," *Canadian Dimension* 28, 3 (May-June, 1994), 21-23; and Michael Riordon, *The First Stone: Homosexuality and the United Church* (Toronto: McClelland and Stewart, 1990).
86 Finlay and Sprague, *The Structure of Canadian History*, 295-308, 367-71; Trofimenkoff, *Dream of Nation,* 207-14; John English and Kenneth McLaughlin, *Kitchener: An Illustrated History* (Waterloo: Wilfrid University Press, 1983), 107-34.
87 "The Arms Trade — The Facts," *New Internationalist* 221 (July, 1991), 16-17; "Arms and Conflict — The Facts," *New Internationalist* 261 (Nov., 1994), 18-19; "World at War — 1992," *The Defense Monitor* XXI, 6 (1992), 1.
88 "The Arms Trade — The Facts," 16; Ernie Regehr, *Making a Killing* (Toronto: McClelland and Stewart, 1975); *A Quebec Arms Industry or Jobs for Peace?*, 2nd edition (Montreal: CSN and CEQ, 1984); Stephen Dale, "Guns 'N Poses," *This Magazine* 26, 7 (March-April, 1993), 11-16; and Ken Epps, "Feeding the tigers: Canadian military sales in Asia," *Catholic New Times*, October 6, 1996, 9.
89 For a look at these wasteful industries and their obsession for gain, see the following examples: June Callwood, *Portrait of Canada* (Markham, Ont.: Paperjacks, 1981), 1-16; and Finlay and Sprague, *Structure of Canadian History*, 17-21, 55-56, 81-92, 260.
90 "Canada's Growing Environmental Deficit," *Canadian Perspectives*, Spring, 1997, 10; Heather Breeze, "Canada Welcoming America's Least Wanted," *Canadian Perspectives*, Autumn, 1994, 10-11; Joyce Nelson, "Pulp and Propaganda," *Canadian Forum,* July-Aug., 1994, 14-19; Czerny et al., *Getting Started*, 54.
91 Czerny et al., *Getting Started*, 49-50, 54-55; Dale Stelter, "Saving the Athabaska River," *Canadian Dimension* 24, 7 (Oct., 1990), 21-23.
92 See Stan Gray, "Democracy, jobs & the environment," *Canadian Dimension* 26, 8 (Nov.-Dec., 1992), 17-20; David Orton, "Two environmental tendencies," *Canadian Dimension* 24, 5 (July-August, 1990), 41.

93 Mary Janigan and Anthony Wilson-Smith, "Harris under siege," *Maclean's*, Nov. 10, 1997, 12-20; "Rhetoric, tactics . . . but no talks," *The Record* [Kitchener], Oct. 28, 1997, A1-A2; Daniel Girard, "Teachers' strike: No end in sight," *The Toronto Star*, Nov. 4, 1997, A1-A4; "Classrooms Back in Business," *The Globe and Mail*, Nov. 10, 1997, A1, A6; Steve Cannon, "More Support Teachers," *The Record*, Nov. 1 1997, A1-A2; "Uproar moves to Queen's Park," *The Toronto Star*, Nov. 18, 1997, A1, A6, A27; Oscar Cole-Arnal and 39 other religious leaders, "An open letter to the premier," *Catholic New Times*, Oct. 19, 1997, 9.

94 "The Liberation of the Middle Class," *Catholic New Times*, May 6, 1984. For details on the developments outlined in this paragraph, see Stanley Aronowitz and William DiFazio, *The Jobless Future* (Minneapolis: University of Minnesota Press, 1994); Menzies, *Whose Brave New World?* and Swift, *Wheel of Fortune*; "Ralley leaders thank teachers for struggles," *The Toronto Star*, Nov. 7, 1997, A6.

95 For details on the Bland case, see Allen, *The Social Passion*, 54-60, and Bedford's more thorough *University of Winnipeg*, 124-39. See also Allen, "Salem Bland and the spirituality of the social gospel: Winnipeg and the West, 1903-1913," 217-32 in Butcher, *Prairie Spirit.*.

96 Allen, *Social Passion*, 50-54; Vera Fast, "The Labor Church in Winnipeg," 235-37 in Butcher, *Prairie Spirit* See also Harry Gutwin and Mildred Gutwin, *Profiles in Dissent* (Edmonton: NeWest Publishers, 1997); and, as an alternate opinion, Gauvreau and Christie, "The World of the Common Man is Filled with Religious Fervour," in G.A. Rawlyk, ed., *Aspects of the Canadian Evangelical Experience* (Montreal: McGill-Queen's University Press, 1997).

97 Allen, *Social Passion*, 89-92, 97-102; Fast, "Labor Church," 237-48; J.S. Woodsworth, *The First Story of the Labor Church*, 106-09 in Oscar Cole-Arnal, "Liberation Theology Canadian Style," *Consensus* 19, 2 (1993).

98 See Clarke, *Behind the Mitre* For examples of such statements, see Richard Arès, ed., *Messages des Évêques Canadiens à l'Occasion de la Fête du Travail, 1956-1974* (Montréal: Bellarmin, 1974); E.F. Sheridan, S.J., ed., *Do Justice!* (Sherbrooke and Toronto: Éditions Paulines and the Jesuit Centre for Social Faith and Justice, 1987); and *Violence en héritage?* (Montréal: Comité des affaires sociales de l'Assemblée des évêques du Québec, 1989).

Chapter 5: Liberating the Oppressed

1 From "Sermons and Addresses" in the Woodsworth papers, XV, quoted in Allen Mills, *Fool for Christ: The Political Thought of J.S. Woodsworth* (Toronto: University of Toronto Press, 1991), 26.

2 For a detailed look at these facets of Woodsworth's career, consult the appropriate sections in Mills, *Fool for Christ*; G.N. Emery, "The Methodist Church and the 'European Foreigners' of Winnipeg: The All People's Mission, 1889-1914," *Historical and Scientific Society of Manitoba Transactions*, Series III, 28 (1971-1972), 85-100; and Kenneth McNaught, *A Prophet in Politics* (Toronto: University of Toronto Press, 1959).

3 For further data on these figures, consult the appropriate sections in Allen, *The Social Passion* See also Tom Mitchell, "From the Social Gospel to 'the Plain Bread of Leninism': A.E. Smith's Journey to the Left in the Epoch of Reaction after World War I," *Labour/Le Travail* 33 (Spring, 1994), 125-51; Anthony Mardiros, *William Irvine: The Life of a Prairie Radical* (Toronto: James Lorimer, 1979); Vera Fast, "The Labor Church in Winnipeg," 233-49 in Butcher, *Prairie Spirit*; and Joan Sangster, "The Making of a Socialist-Feminist: The Early Career of Beatrice Brigden, 1888-1941," *Atlantis* 13, 1 (Fall, 1987), 14-28.

4 For details on Salem Bland and his activities, consult the appropriate sections of Allen, *The Social Passion* Also see Allen, "Salem Bland and the spirituality of the social gospel," 217-32 (quote from 232) in Butcher, *Prairie Spirit*.

5 Salem Bland, *The New Christianity* (Toronto: University of Toronto Press, 1973 [1920]), 9.

6 Ibid., 18.
7 Ibid., 28.
8 Ibid., 54-55.
9 Allen, *Social Passion*, 219-30, 305-08.
10 Daniel Phannenhour, "Roots of Liberation Theology in Canadian Campus Ministries (1920-1975), paper submitted for the Waterloo Lutheran Seminary class "Roots of Liberation Theology," 622A-30, December, 1988. See also Newsletter of the Welland SCM Workcamp, Oct., 1945, 14-16, 18-33; *Canada and Christendom* 11, 4 (July, 1958), 1-5; *Welland Little Big Forge* 1, 1 (Sept.-Nov., 1945), 1-4; 1, 2 (Dec., 1945-Feb., 1946), 1-3; and 1, 3 (March-June, 1946), 1-2; Student Christian Movement of Canada, *S.C.M.'s 60th Anniversary Songbook* (S.C.M. of Canada: Muskox Press, 1981).
11 Roger Hutchinson, "The Fellowship for a Christian Social Order: 1934-1945," 17-21 (quote on 20) in Harold Wells and Roger Hutchinson, eds., *A Long and Faithful March* (Toronto: United Church Publishing House, 1989).
12 J. King Gordon, "A Christian Socialist in the 1930s," 137 in Richard Allen, ed., *The Social Gospel in Canada* (Ottawa: National Museums of Canada, 1975).
13 Ibid., 137-38.
14 Gregory Vlastos, "The Ethical Foundations," 55-57 in Scott and Vlastos, eds., *Towards the Christian Revolution* (Chicago and New York: Willett, Clark & Company, 1936).
15 Gordon, "Christian Socialist," 140-50; Hutchinson, "Fellowship," 22-23; and Brian J. Fraser, "From Anathema to Alternative: The Gordons and Socialism," 41-49 in Wells and Hutchinson, *Long and Faithful March*.
16 Robert H. Craig, "Ungodly Capitalism: The Canadian Protestant Left in the 1930s," 53 in Wells and Hutchinson, *Long and Faithful March*.
17 Gregory Baum, *Catholics and Canadian Socialism* (Toronto: James Lorimer, 1980), 202; Gordon, "Christian Socialist," 144.
18 Baum, *Catholics and Canadian Socialism,* 191.
19 Jim Lotz, "The Historical and Social Setting of the Antigonish Movement," *Nova Scotia Historical Quarterly* 5, 2 (June, 1975), 104-10 (quote on 105); Baum, *Catholics and Canadian Socialism,* 191-92.
20 Alexander F. Laidlaw, ed., *The Man from Margaree: Writings and Speeches of M.M. Coady* (Toronto: McClelland and Stewart, 1971), 41-42.
21 Lotz, "Historical," 111-13; Baum, *Catholics and Canadian Socialism*, 192; Rudi Cujes, "Fishermen's Cooperatives in Nova Scotia," in Extension Department Papers, n.d., 16-28; Laidlaw, *Man*, 18-19.
22 See Baum, *Catholics and Canadian Socialism,* 189-203.
23 Laidlaw, *Man from Margaree,* 29.
24 Ibid., 119-22.
25 For more recent descriptions of the Antigonish efforts I have consulted the 1984 annual reports of both the Extension Department and the Coady International Institute. See also Anne Alexander's recent study, *The Antigonish Movement* (Toronto: Thompson Educational Publishing, Inc., 1997).
26 *Global Community Centre News,* January-February, 1995, 2.
27 The Institute publishes a newsletter called *Praxis* For example, the Fall, 1988 issue, vol. 2, no. 2, deals with the farm crisis.
28 For an example, see *Economic Justice Newsletter* 33 (May, 1993). For a description, see Kenneth Westhues, *The Working Centre* (Kitchener: Working Centre Publications, 1995).
29 Two examples of Jesuit Centre' publications are *Naming the Moment: Political Analysis for Action* (1989) and *Getting Started on Social Analysis in Canada,* cited earlier. For descriptions of social justice groups see Christopher Lind and Joe Mihevc, eds., *Coalitions for Justice* (Ottawa: Novalis, 1994).
30 Lind and Mihevc, eds., *Coalitions for Justice*, 99-103 (quote on 99).
31 Ibid., 103-04. GATT-Fly produced a book describing this pedagogy: *Ah-Hah! A New Approach to Popular Education* (Toronto: Between the Lines, 1983).

32 Ibid., 116; "GATT-Fly: What We Do and Who We Are," GATT-*Fly Report* V, 4 (Nov., 1984), 1-2, 4.

33 Lind and Mihevc, eds., *Coalitions for Justice,* 113.

34 One example is *Recolonization or Liberation: The Bonds of Structural Adjustment and Struggles for Emancipation* (Toronto: ECEJ, 1990).

35 Lind and Mihevc, eds., *Coalitions for Justice,* 113.

36 For the work of the right-wing Jesuits, consult Richard Arès, *Le Père Joseph-Papin Archambault, S.J.* (Montréal: Bellarmin, 1983), especially 79-151. Father Lévesque describes his pilgrimage with these efforts in his three-volume *Souvenances* (Ottawa: Éditions la Presse, 1983-1989). For background on these efforts, consult Jean Hamelin and Nicole Gagnon, *Le XXe siècle,* Vol. 1: *1898-1940* in *Histoire du catholicisme québécois* (Montréal: Boréal Express, 1984), 218-29, 417-19; Jean Hamelin, *Le XXe siècle,* Vol. 2: *De 1940 à nos jours* in *Histoire etc.* (1984), 91-96.

37 "Les Politisés Chrétiens," 1, 17-22 in the archives of the *reseau* (PC) found at the Centre Saint-Pierre in Montreal. For a fine study on the *reseau,* see Gregory Baum, "Politisés Chrétiens: A Christian-Marxist Network in Quebec, 1974-1982," 67-89 in Baum, *The Church in Quebec* (Ottawa: Novalis, 1991). All translations in this chapter from French into English are by the author.

38 See appropriate material in Baum piece.

39 Raymond Levac, "Bref Historique du CPMO," 1-9 in CPMO Archives at Centre Saint-Pierre in Montreal; "Brèves notes sur les orientations du CPMO," 1-4.

40 Hamelin and Gagnon, *Histoire du catholicisme québécois,* 359-60; "Colloque des militants chrétiens en monde ouvrier—Cap-Rouge," 22 au 24 novembre 1974, *Dossiers "Vie Ouvrière "* (hereafter referred to as DVO) XXV, 91 (jan., 1975), 4-60. For an example of publications on the *église populaire* by CPMO, see *L'Église Populaire en Amérique Latine et au Québec,* mars, 1981.

41 Carrefour de Pastorale en Monde Ouvrier, "CAPMO," brochure, first four pages at CAPMO headquarters; *Manifeste etc.* (mars, 1980), 36.

42 See Baum's own autobiographical musings in *Faith That Transforms: Essays in Honour of Gregory Baum* (New York: Paulist Press, 1987), 135-51.

43 Benjamin G. Smillie, "An Update on Liberation Theology in the Canadian Context." *Festschrift: A Tribute to Dr. William Hordern* (Saskatoon: University of Saskatchewan, 1985), 54.

44 Ibid., 55.

45 Smillie, *Beyond the Social Gospel,* 16.

46 Interview with Ben Smillie, Saskatoon, August 6, 1992; Ibid., 123-36 (135-136 quoted).

47 Smillie interview.

48 Marilyn J. Legge, *The Grace of Difference* (Atlanta: Scholars Press, 1992), 201-03 (203 quoted).

49 Ibid., 206.

50 For this article, see Mary Jo Leddy, *Say to the Darkness, I Beg to Differ* (Toronto: Lester & Orpen Dennys, 1990). Also see, "'Lady Mary' offers ray of hope," *The Toronto Star,* May 31, 1997, L1-L2, and Mary Jo Leddy, *At the Borders of Hope* (Toronto: HarperCollins, 1997).

51 Bob Haverluck, *Love Your Enemies and Other Neighbours* (Toronto: United Church Publishing House, 1992), 76; Doug Smith, "Haverluck," *Canadian Dimension* 24, 3 (April-May, 1990), 10.

52 Interview with Robert Haverluck, Winnipeg, Aug. 5, 1992.

53 Quoted in Larry Krotz, "Wit writ with wisdom," *United Church Observer,* Jan., 1989), 36.

54 Del Birkey, *The House Church: A Model for Renewing the Church* (Scottdale, Pa.: Herald Press, 1988), 40-62, 87-103.

55 To see details of such communities, consult the following: Jim Wallis, *Revive Us Again: A Sojourner's Story* (Nashville: Abingdon Press, 1983); Jim Wallis, *The Soul of Politics* (Maryknoll, N.Y.: Orbis Books, 1994); Clarence Jordan, with Bill Doulos, *Cotton Patch Parables of Liberation* (Scottdale, Pa.: Herald Press, 1976).

56 Jean Vanier, *From Brokenness to Community* (New York: Paulist Press, 1992), 6-7, 11-14; Jean Vanier, ed., *The Challenge of l'Arche* (Ottawa: Novalis, 1981), 5-15, 269-86. Vanier himself provides in-depth reflections on community in Vanier, *Community & Growth: Our Pilgrimage Together* (Toronto: Griffin House, 1979).

57 Vanier, *Challenge of l'Arche*, 286.

58 Vanier, *From Brokenness to Community*, 7.

59 Ibid., 7, 10.

60 Henri J.M. Nouwen, "Because of Adam," *Reader's Digest*, March, 1990, 51-52.

61 Interviews granted to the author: Goffart, June 2, 1988; Petite Soeur Claude, May 18, 1988; Soeur Marie-Paule Lebrun, May 24, 1988; and Petite Soeur Stephanie, May 25, 1988.

62 Georges Convert, "L'Expérience de COPAM," *Communauté Chrétienne* (*CC*), mai-juin, 1986, 234-44; *La Lettre bleue des équipes de la mission Saints Pierre et Paul*, Montréal, 1987; "Les Équipes missionnaires de la mopp," Montréal, four-page brochure in Georges Convert, private papers; Georges Convert and André Choquette, "L'Évangile . . . ou l'espérance de la fraternité possible!", *Prêtre et Pasteur* 91,2 (fév., 1988), 94-103; and André Choquette, *Viveur de Dieu au quotidien* (Montréal: Éditions Paulines, 1981).

63 "A Hull, 1967-1987," 65-67 in Léon Gahier, *Avec François d'Assise* (Malonne: published by the Capuchins, 1987); Roger Poirier, *Qui a volé la rue principale?* (Montréal: Éditions Départ, 1986), 67-68; Isidore Ostiguy, "Histoire de notre cheminement pastoral," *Prêtres et Laïcs* XIX (*PL*), (déc., 1969), 553-54.

64 "Compte Rendu — Pastorale des milieux populaires," Diocèse de Montréal, 28 jan. 1978, 1-13; "A Pointe Sainte-Charles: éclatement de l'église locale," 1-15; and "Communauté de base de Pointe Sainte-Charles, Se redire notre histoire . . ." six-page brochure, all three from Ugo Benfante, private papers; "La Pastorale des milieux populaires," *Église de Montréal*, 22 déc., 1977, 806-08; Ugo Benfante, "La Residence en quartier du vicaire de paroisse, " *PL* XVII (août-sept., 1967), 319-325; "A Pointe Sainte-Charles," *Maintenant*, mars, 1969, 80-87; Guy Cousin, "Cheminement d'un prêtre-ouvrier," 22 juillet 1977, 1, in Guy Cousin private papers; "Rendre l'église visible dans un quartier," *Prêtres en classe ouvrière*, automne, 1980, 2.

65 Raymond Levac, *L'Église populaire en Amérique Latine et au Québec* (Montréal: CPMO, mars, 1981); "L'Église populaire, église du peuple," *Bulletin de Liaison* (hereafter referred to as *BL*), fév., 1980, 1.

66 "Les Communautés de Base," *Prêtres en classe ouvrière*, printemps, 1982, 1.

67 Interview with Vivian Labrie, Waterloo, March 16, 1989.

68 "Église populaire — solidarité internationale," *BL*, nov., 1980, 1-2; Claude Hardy, "L'Église populaire, une réalité vivante," *BL*, nov., 1981, 1; "L'Église populaire, église du peuple," *BL*, fév., 1980, 1-2. For examples of *Communauté*, see vol. 7, 6 (1977), 8, 3-4 (1978) and 10 (Automne, 1980), 66 quoted.

69 Lois Barrett, *Building the House Church* (Scottdale, Pa.: Herald Press, 1986) is a thorough description of the various facets of house church life.

70 Allen, *Social Passion*, 71-80 (71 quoted); statement quotes from Stewart Crysdale, *The Industrial Struggle and Protestant Ethics in Canada* (Toronto: Ryerson Press, 1961), 29 and Allen, 74.

71 Allen, *Social Passion*, 50-54; Vera Fast, "The Labor Church in Winnipeg," 235-237 in Butcher, *Prairie Spirit*; William Ivens papers in the Manitoba Provincial Archives; and the William Ivens Papers in the DESS Archives found at Emmanuel College in Toronto.

72 Allen, *Social Passion*, 84.

73 For detailed descriptions of this labour church read the appropriate sections in the Fast and Allen publications. See also "Liberation Theology Canadian Style: J.S. Woodsworth's *The First Story of the Labor Church (1920)*" in *Consensus* 19, 2 (1993), 99-120.

74 Quoted from the Manitoba Provincial Archives in Douglas Frederick Pratt, "William Ivens M.A., B.D., and the Winnipeg Labor Church," B. Div. thesis, St. Andrew's College, Saskatoon, 1962.

75 "First Story of the Labor Church," 109. For the church's links to the strike, read Allen, *Social Passion*, 97-102 and Fast, "Labor Church," 242-244.

76 Allen, *Social Passion*, 89-93, 116-17, 159-74; Tom Mitchell, "From the Social Gospel," 125-50; Fast, "Labor Church," 248.

77 Most of this material comes from my personal contact with activists in these ministries. For additional data on the Olive Branch congregation, I have conducted an informal interview with my friend John Chamberlin, who is a principled liberationist in his own right (May 31, 1995).

78 Interview with Nancy Kelly, May 31, 1995. For more background on the Hispanic Ministry, see *Newsletter: Lutheran Refugee Committee* (Spring, 1990) and Nancy Kelly, "Seamos Amigos, Let's Be Friends," *Canada Lutheran* 2, 5 (May, 1987), 14-17.

79 Nancy Vernon Kelly, "The Development of a Diverse Urban Congregation in Canada: The Death of Business-as-Usual at St. John's Evangelical Lutheran Church in Toronto," *Consensus* 22, 1 (1996), 57-80.

80 Comments about this church are based on conversations with former members, especially Dr. Christopher Ross of Wilfrid Laurier University. My wife Bonnie and I also attended a Sunday morning worship service there in 1993.

81 This data is obviously experiential. I make no apologies for that. However, Frank Hamper did give me a number of Sunday bulletins to demonstrate the regular worship practice of the congregation, including, of course, a bulletin for the Sunday described in this paragraph.

82 Group meeting at Trinity-St. Paul's U.C.C., June 4, 1995.

83 "Mandate of the New Ad Hoc Committee," Sept. 25, 1994, Trinity-St. Paul's files. This mandate was reflected in the other material shared with me by Frank Hamper: Trinity-St. Paul's U.C.C., "Annual Report," 1993; TSP *Times* 5, 5 (April, 1995), church newsletter; and the various bulletins I examined (for example, "Sundays may never be the same").

84 "L'Influence de l'église dans les quartiers populaires," *Relations*, nov., 1982, 304-08, and Jean Picher, "Paroissien ou travailler?" *CC* 16, 91 (jan.-fév., 1977), 49-61.

85 Roger Poirier spelled out some of these details in a panel I organized at the Learned Societies Conference in Sainte-Foy, Quebec (June, 1989). See also Paul-Émile Charbonneau, "Nouvelles Orientations de la pastorale," *CC* 2, 11 (sept.-oct., 1963), 354-61; and Paul-Émile Charbonneau, "Présentation: Incarnation de l'Église à Hull," *PL* XIX (déc., 1969), 543-44. See also Poirier, *Qui a volé la rue principale*.

86 Plamandon, Ouellete, Ostiguy, Hardy, Viau, Poirier, and Charbonneau interviews; "A Hull, 1967-1987," 65-67 in Gahier; Roger Poirier, "L'Engagement des chrétiens," *PL* XXIV (oct., 1974), 487-96; "Deux ans d'animation à Hull," *PL* XX (nov., 1970), 521-24; "Dossier: Animation sociale à Hull," *PL* XIX (déc., 1969), 542-74.

87 Mgr. Adolphe Proulx, "La Tâche d'un évêque," 310-13, and Pierre Bergeron, "L'Évêque de Hull prend la défense des travailleurs," 307-09, both in DVO XXVI, 105 (mai, 1976); "Entretien," *Mouvements* 1, 1 (1983), 2-6; Poirier, *Qui*, 21-27, 30-35, 61-92, 128-230; Poirier paper at Learneds; *Une Voix pour les sans-voix: Le Message social de Mgr. Adolphe Proulx* (Ottawa: Novalis, 1987), 33, 35, 37-38, 40-42, 47-50, 69-73, 75-77, 97-98, 103-08, 143-49 (35 and 144 quoted). The diocesan study mentioned is *Bienheureux les pauvres . . . ?* (Hull: Commission d'étude du diocèse de Gatineau-Hull, 1984).

88 Joyce Carlson, ed., "Apology to Native Peoples," *Spirit of Gentleness: Lenten Readings and Prayers* (Toronto: United Church of Canada, 1990), 9.

89 Stan McKay, 15 in Carlson, *Spirit of Gentleness*. For information on the United Church's Saulteaux Centre and other Native training institutions, see *Leadership in the United Church of Canada: Needs and Resources* (Toronto: United Church of Canada, 1993), 15-17.

90 McKay, 73-74, in Carlson, *Spirit of Gentleness*.

91 McKay, 16-17, in Carlson, *Spirit of Gentleness*.

92 Rosemary Radford Ruether, *Women-Church: Theology and Practice* (San Francisco: Harper & Row, 1988) is a vital and practical resource for creating and utilizing

liturgies enriched by feminist spirituality. See also Carol J. Schlueter, *The Forgotten Followers* (Winfield, B.C.: Wood Lake Books, 1992).

93 Bridget Mary Meehan, S.S.C., *Exploring the Feminine Face of God* (Kansas City, Mo.: Sheed & Ward, 1991), xi.

94 Ibid., 12-13.

95 Shirley Jane Endicott, *Facing the Tiger* (Winfield, B.C.: Wood Lake Books, n.d.), 150-57.

96 Leddy, *Say to the Darkness, We Beg to Differ*, 193.

97 Ibid., 246-55 (248 quoted).

98 Interviews with Isidore Ostiguy, May 8, 1988, Claude Hardy, June 22, 1988, and Benoît Fortin, May 13, 1988; Fortin, "Je suis avec vous," jan., 1982, 38-43 (39 quoted).

99 Interviews with Fortin, Hardy, and Ouellete, May 10, 1988.

100 Henri J.M. Nouwen, *The Wounded Healer* (Garden City, N.Y.: Image Books, 1972), 93-94. For a personal journey along this stumbling pilgrimage of imperfection, see Ernest Kurtz and Katherine Ketcham, *The Spirituality of Imperfection* (New York: Bantam Books, 1994 [1992]).

101 Mardiros, *William Irvine*, 214-16 (216 quoted).

102 Bland, *New Christianity*, 20, 22.

103 Brian Mossop, "Equal rights for gay families . . ." *Canadian Dimension* 27, 4 (Aug., 1993), 12-16; Mae Burrows with Victoria Cross, "Breaking the Barriers: Reshaping Environmental Activism — Mae Burrows in Conversation," 77-88 in Steven Langdon and Victoria Cross, *As We Come Marching: People, Power & Progressive Politics* (Ottawa & Windsor: Windsor Works Publications, 1994). For other examples, see Wayne Roberts, "A Green New Deal," *Canadian Dimension* 26, 3 (April-May, 1992), 11-14; Paul Hertel, "Small Town Ontario Environmental Activism," 152-60; and Christopher Genovali, "Alberta's Gold Rush," *Canadian Dimension*, March-April, 1997, 24-26.

104 I am a member of this committee and have participated in the full range of its activities.

105 For details on these activities, see Gary Kenny, "The Inter-Church Coalition on Africa," 37-62, in Lind and Mihevc, eds., *Coalitions for Justice*.

106 For further details, see Joseph Kinsey Howard, *The Strange Empire of Louis Riel* (Toronto: Swan Publishing Co., 1970 [1952]); Janet Rosenstock and Dennis Adair, *Riel* (Markham, Ont.: Paperjacks, 1979); Paul Ogresko, "Reflections on Oka," *Canadian Dimension* 25, 1 (Jan.-Feb., 1991), 9-12; Tony Hall, "The politics of Aboriginality," *Canadian Dimension* 27, 1 (Jan.-Feb., 1993), 6-10; Christian Huot, "Of Mines and Indians," *Canadian Dimension*, March-April, 1997, 21-23; and Peter Hamel, "The Aboriginal Rights Coalition," 16-36 in Lind & Mihevc, eds., *Coalitions for Justice*.

107 My description of the Antigonish Movement portrayed Maritime co-ops, and the Quebec *caisse populaire* movement is well-analyzed in: Yves Roby, *Alphonse Desjardins et les Caisses Populaires, 1854-1920* (Montréal: Fides, 1964); Yves Roby, *Les Caisses populaires, Alphonse Desjardins, 1900-1920* (Lévis, Qué.: Fédération du Québec des Caisses Populaires Desjardins, 1975). For the Ontario farm movement, see Louis Aubrey Wood, *A History of Farmers' Movements in Canada* (Toronto: University of Toronto Press, 1975 [1924]); W.C. Good, *Farmer Citizen* (Toronto: Ryerson Press, 1958); and Charles M. Johnston, *E.C. Drury: Agrarian Idealist* (Toronto: University of Toronto Press, 1986).

108 See S.M. Lipset, *Agrarian Socialism* (Berkeley: University of California Press, 1971) and the relevant sections in Friesen, *Canadian Prairies*.

109 Lipset, *Agrarian Socialism* tells this story in fine detail.

110 Partridge, quoted in Lipset, *Agrarian Socialsim*, 349. For examples of Dr. Bland's columns, see "The Deeper Life," *Grain Growers' Guide*, Dec. 19, 1917, 34; and Jan. 2, 1918, 33. For the GGG's support of Bland in his hour of trial, see June 27, 1917, 22.

111 Good, *Farmer Citizen,* 93-94.

112 See Allen Wilford, *Farm Gate Defense* (Toronto: NC Press, 1984).

113 Kneen, *Land to Mouth* and *Rape of Canola*. For examples of his prophetic outcries, read *The Ram's Horn*: "Saskatchewan Wheat Pool Converts . . . to Capitalism," July, 1994, 1-2; "GATT & the End of European Civilization," Dec., 1993, 1-6; and "NAFTA — Yet Another Enclosure," June, 1993, 1. See also Christopher Lin, *Something's Wrong Here: Globalization, Community and the Moral Economy of the Farm Crisis* (Halifax: Fernwood Publishing, 1995).

114 Alain-G. Gagnon, *Développement régional, état et groupes populaires* (Hull: Éditions Asticou, 1985), 132-39.

115 "Jesuit Farm Project — Statement of Identity," one page, from P.O. Box 1238, Guelph, Ont. N1H 6N6; (519) 824-1250 (x55). Diane Baltaz, a freelance journalist, farm activist, and devout Catholic, has gathered together the testimonies of those who work the land: *Living Off the Land: A Spirituality of Farming* (Ottawa: Novalis, 1991).

116 Wood, *History of Farmers' Movement in Canada*, 296-99; Prentice, et al., *Canadian Women*, 268, 281-82.

117 For examples of her views in this arena, see Pennington, *Agnes Macphail*, 46, 48-50, 58, 77-80, 131-32, 134, 140, 160-63, 197-98. See also Terry Crowley, *Agnes Macphail and the Politics of Equality* (Toronto: James Lorimer, 1990).

118 Crowley, *Agnes Macphail and the Politics of Equality*, 88-94 (quotes on 91 and 94).

119 Ireland, *Farmer Takes a Wife*, 4, 63-66 (quotes on 63).

120 Gail Cuthbert Brandt, "Weaving It Together: Life Cycle and the Industrial Experience of Female Cotton Workers in Quebec, 1910-1950," 160-173 in Prentice and Trofimenkoff, eds., *Neglected Majority*, Vol. 2; Sangster, "The 1907 Bell Telephone Strike," 109-30.

121 Anne B. Woyitka, "A Pioneer Woman in the Labour Movement," 191-99 in Strong-Boag and Fellman, *Rethinking Canada;* Sangster, *Dreams of Equality*, 26-38, 130-39.

122 Susan Walsh, "The Peacock and the Guinea Hen," 144-59 in Prentice and Trofimenkoff, *Neglected Majority*.

123 Sangster, "The Making of a Socialist-Feminist," 14-28 (21 quoted).

124 Sangster, *Dreams of Equality*, 122-23.

125 Prentice, et. al., *Canadian Women*, 169-211.

126 Catherine Carstairs, "The voice of women," *Guelph Mercury*, Aug. 27, 1994, D2; Marta Danylewycz, "Changing Relationships: Nuns and Feminists in Montreal, 1890-1925," 122-43 in Prentice and Trofimenkoff, *Neglected Majority*; Hélène Pelletier-Baillargeon, *Marie Gérin-Lajoie: De mère en fille, la cause des femmes* (Montréal: Boréal Express, 1985); Oscar Cole-Arnal, "Radical Catholic Women in Modern Quebec: The Example of Worker-Nuns," *Consensus* 20, 2 (1994), 57-79.

127 For a popular look at McClung, read Candace Savage, *Our Nell: A Scrapbook Biography of Nellie L. McClung* (Halifax: Formac Publishing, 1979), (81-82 quoted). For a deeper look at McClung's social gospel spirit, see Randi R. Warne, *Literature as Pulpit: The Christian Social Activism of Nellie L. McClung* (Waterloo: Wilfrid Laurier University Press, 1993). The following blunt statement reflects her religious basics: "Christ was a true democrat. He was a believer in women; and never in his life did he discriminate against them" (179 in Savage).

128 Terry Matwichuk, "Charter of Rights Workshop," January, 1985, 7-8.

129 Lois Wilson, *Turning the World Upside Down* (Toronto: Doubleday Canada, 1989), 38.

130 Ibid., 139-40.

131 Judy Rebick, "International Women's Day 1991," *Canadian Dimension* 25, 2 (March, 1991), 6-7 (7 quoted).

132 For two examples, see Marilyn Fontaine-Brightstar, "Breaking the Silence," *Canadian Dimension* 26, 2 (March, 1992), 5-8 and Brian Mossop, "Equal rights for gay families . . ." *Canadian Dimension* 27, 4 (August, 1993), 12-16.

133 Victoria Cross, "Picket Line Power," 14-15 and Mary Rowles, "Solidarity & Diversity," 18-20 (18 quoted) in *Our Times* 14, 1 (March, 1995); Inglis, "McDonald's Union Drive-thru," *Our Times* 13, 3 (June/July, 1994), 19-28; Deborah Prieur and Mary

Rowles, "Violence and Inequality," *Our Times* 11, 3 (June, 1992), 17-18; Prieur and Rowles, *Taking Action: A Union Guide to Ending Violence Against Women* (Vancouver: Women's Research Centre and B.C. Federation of Labour, 1990); Margaret Hosmer Martens and Swasti Mitter, eds., *Women in Trade Unions: Organizing the Unorganized* (Geneva: International Labour Office, 1994); and Julie White, *Sisters & Solidarity: Women and Unions in Canada* (Toronto: Thompson Educational Publishing, Inc., 1993).

134 See Palmer, *Working Class Experience* and Bryan D. Palmer, ed., *The Character of Class Struggle* (Toronto: McClelland and Stewart, 1988).

135 See Trudeau, *La Grève de l'Amiante* and Rouillard, *Histoire de la* CSN, *1921-1981*.

136 For these topics and labour's involvement, see: Youth: *Our Times* 14, 3 (July, 1995); gay and lesbian rights: Pamela Wagner, "Coming Out," cover story in *Our Times* 12, 1 (March, 1993), 26-30; Aboriginal concerns: *Our Times* 13, 4 (Aug.-Sept., 1994); Gender Equality: Linda Briskin, "Women and their new leadership roles," *Canadian Dimension* 24, 1 (Jan.-Feb., 1990), 38-41; and cultural concerns: Clive Robertson, "Artists, Workers and BCTV," *Our Times* 12, 4 (Nov.-Dec., 1993), 38-39, Katheryne Schulz, "Labours of Love," *Our Times* 13, 5 (Oct.-Nov., 1994), 23-29, and Ron Verzuh, "Worker to Worker," *Our Times*, May-June, 1997, 24-28.

137 Joe Flexer, "A Turning Point in the Canadian Class Struggle," 28-30 and Geoff Bickerton, "Alternatives for Airlines," 32 in *Canadian Dimension*, Jan.-Feb., 1997; David Estok, "A fight for rights," *Maclean's*, August 19, 1996, 34-35.

138 See Daniel Tatroff, "Fields of Fear," *Our Times* 13, 6 (Dec., 1994), 22-27; Naomi Klein, "Salesgirl Solidarity," *This Magazine*, Feb., 1995, 12-19; Bruce Livesey, "Taxi Union Drive," *Our Times* 11, 6 (Dec., 1992), 26-31; and the stories cited earlier by Sarah Inglis.

139 Michael Darnell, "Storm Over Erie," 161-75 in Langdon and Cross, *As We Come Marching*.

140 For a glimpse of Quebec's Parti ouvrier, see Rouillard, *Histoire du Syndicalisme Québécois*, 142-47, and sections in Allen's *Social Passion* describing various Prairie' labour candidates.

141 Leo W. Gerard, "Redistributing Power in a Changing Economy," 60-69 in Langdon and Cross, *As We Come Marching*.

142 Buzz Hargrove, "Labour and Politics," 28-41 in ibid.

143 CAW, "Our Kind of Government," *Work,* Fall, 1992, 18-19; Dan Keeton, "On to Ottawa Again," 24-25 and "Reclaiming Our Future . . ." 26-27, in *Our Times* 12, 2 (July-August, 1993).

144 See Gabriel Clément, *Histoire de l'Action Catholique au Canada Français* (Montréal: Fides, 1972).

145 For data describing these events and values, see: Clément, *Histoire*, 285-300; Claude Ryan, "La Crise de l'Action Catholique," *Le Devoir*, 25 oct. 1966; Le Mouvement des Travailleurs Chrétiens . . ." *Prêtres Aujourd'hui* (*PA*) XV (juin-juillet, 1965), 227-43 and *PA* XV (août-sept., 1965), 289-309; Jocelyne Bernier, *Mouvement des Travailleurs Chrétiens,* mai, 1970, 6-15, 49-64; "Colloque des militants chrétiens en monde ouvrier," Cap-Rouge, 22-24 nov. 1974, DVO XXV, 91 (jan., 1975), 17-36; "Quel est le point de départ de la J.O.C. et quelle est sa raison d'être?", 1-11, found in the JOC archives at the Archives Nationales du Québec à Montréal (quote from 26).

146 D.J.M. Heap, "The Church and the Workers," *Canadian Journal of Theology* X, 2 (1964), 132-38 and "René Giroux, prêtre-ouvrier," *Relations*, nov., 1970, 305.

147 "Des prêtres, des religieux, des religieuses . . . ouvriers au Québec: Quelques jalons chronologiques," 1-4 in Guy Boulanger's private papers; in Ugo Benfante's private papers: "Rapport de la 3e reunion 'Recherche d'une Pastorale en Monde Ouvrier,'" 5 mai 1966, 1-3; Commission de pastorale ouvrière," 15 avril 1966, 2; Équipe Sainte Cunegonde, letter to Mgr. Grégoire, 8 sept. 1968, two pages; and official letter from Mgr. Grégoire to Ugo Benfante, 9 mai 1969, two pages.

148 See also: Ugo Benfante, "Après deux ans et demi comme prêtre au travail," *L'Église de Montréal*, 38-41 in Benfante papers; brochure, "Le groupe PRROQ, le monde

ouvrier et l'Église," 1-7 in Boulanger papers; and "Religieux et Religieuses engagés en monde populaire," *Relations* 40, 464 (Nov., 1980), 312-14.

149 Tanguay, Cousin, and Fortin interviews; Jacques Tanguay, *Travailler dans l'frigo, pis manger d'la manne!* (Montréal: CSN, Récit ouvrier, n.d.); Gaston Jodoin and Jacques Tanguay, "De Bélanger à Admiral," *Vie Ouvrière (VO)* XXXI, 154 (mai-juin, 1981), 4-26; "Zellers menace toujours de fermer," *VO* XXXI (mai-juin, 1981), 27-50; "Où en est rendue la lutte des travailleurs de l'hôtellerie?" DVO XXIX, 132 (fév., 1979), 129-32; Paule des Rivières, "La victoire de l'abbé Cousin," *Le Devoir*, 15 fév. 1988, 7; Stephen Cianca, "From Hotel Worker to Capuchin Provincial," *Mustard Seed* 4, 4 (Oct., 1986), 1-2, 6; and Carol Néron, "La glorieuse bataille d'un capuchin en 'blue jeans,'" *La Semaine*, 1 déc. 1985, 52-53.

150 Benoît Fortin, "Quand se lève le soleil de justice," 17 in Fortin private papers.

151 Tony Clarke, *Behind the Mitre*, xvii-xx, 170; Council of Canadians, *Canadian Perspectives*, Autumn, 1994, inside front cover; Keeton, "On to Ottawa Again," 24-25; quote from the back of my 1995 Council of Canadians membership card; *Canadian Perspectives* (Summer, 1997), 6.

152 For examples of these types of Council's publications, see "Jobs or Cuts?" *Canadian Perspectives*, Winter, 1995; "Campaign for Canada—Stop Free Trade," *Canadian Perspectives*, Autumn, 1993; and *Action Link*, January 1995 update; *Canadian Perspectives* (Summer, 1997); and *Canadian Perspectives* (Winter, 1997).

153 Léger, Benfante, Lebrun, Couture, and Fortin interviews; Robert David, "Are we losing Québec . . . to neoliberals?" *Canadian Dimension*, March-April, 1997, 15-17.

154 Cameron Smith, *Love & Solidarity* (Toronto: McClelland & Stewart, 1992), 36-54; Penner, *Canadian Left,* 171-204, 216-17.

155 Ibid., 70.

156 Ibid., 98, 104, 106; Finlay and Sprague, *Structure of Canadian History*, 377-79.

157 Ibid., 99-103; Lewis H. Thomas, ed., *The Making of a Socialist: The Recollections of T.C. Douglas* (Edmonton: University of Alberta Press, 1982), 164-81, 202-03, 219-24; and Thomas H. McLeod and Ian McLeod, *Tommy Douglas: The Road to Jerusalem* (Edmonton: Hurtig Publishers, 1987).

158 McLeod and McLeod, *Tommy Douglas*, 145-55, 198-201; Smith, *Love and Solidarity*, 99-102, 157; Thomas, ed., *Making of a Socialist*, 224-32.

159 Smith, *Love and Solidarity*, 154.

160 John Bullen, "The Ontario Waffle and the Struggle for an Independent Socialist Canada: Conflict within the NDP," *Canadian Historical Review* LXIV (1983), 188-215. See also, Smith, *Love and Solidarity,* 179, 186, 191-92, and Ehring and Roberts, *Giving Away a Miracle,* 52-57.

161 Smith, *Love and Solidarity,* 182-269.

162 For details of betrayals and compromises see Ehring and Roberts, *Giving Away a Miracle* See also Laxer, *In Search of a New Left.*

163 McLeod & McLeod, *Tommy Douglas*, 308.

164 See Trevor Harrison, *Of Passionate Intensity: Right-Wing Populism and the Reform Party of Canada* (Toronto: University of Toronto Press, 1995). The story of Ralph Klein and his Alberta is portrayed in detail in Mark Lisac, *The Klein Revolution* (Edmonton: NeWest Press, 1995). See "Ontarians awaken to Tory blue skies," *The Record* [Kitchener], June 9, 1995, A10.

165 Harrison, *Of Passionate Intensity,* 65-68, 94-96, 103, 106-07, 193-96, 202; Lisac, *Klein Revolution,* 23, 43-56, 82-90, 102-10, 115-29; Murray Dobbin, *Preston Manning and the Reform Party* (Halifax: Goodread Biographies, 1992), 105-23.

166 Dobbin, *Preston Manning and the Reform Party,* 205-07; Harrison, *Of Passionate Intensity,* 120; Guy Marsden, "Protesting for Profit," *Canadian Dimension* 29, 4 (August-September, 1995), 9-11; Ben Cherniavsky and Jack Mintz, "Wealthy would have windfall after Conservative tax cuts," *The Toronto Star,* June 5, 1995, A17.

167 Dobbin, *Preston Manning and the Reform Party,* 123-35, 139-40, 146-56, 177-84, 191-205, 207-10; Harrison, *Of Passionate Intensity,* 120, 208-21.

168 Read Lisac, *Klein Revolution* for full details on Klein's government. See also: Dean Neu, "Klein's Free Market Utopia," *Canadian Dimension*, Feb.-March, 1995, 20-21;

Laurie E. Adkin, "Life in Kleinland," *Canadian Dimension*, April-May, 1995, 31-42; and Gordon Laird, "Cost-Cutting Cowboys," *This Magazine,* July, 1995, 12-18. For some early examples of the Harris team in Ontario, see "A new minister for MET," *Laurier News* 4, 3 (July 18, 1995), 2 and T. Sher Singh, "It takes a pro to do a con job well," *Guelph Mercury*, July 22, 1995, B5.

Chapter 6: Towards Liberation and the Millennium

1 See especially Wink, *Engaging the Powers* (Minneapolis: Fortress Press, 1992), 175-257.

2 For examples of such media and how to subscribe to them, see *Canadian Dimension*, November-December, 1996, 34-35.

3 For examples of these realities, see Laxer, *In Search of a New Left*; Swift, *Wheel of Fortune*; "Facts — The State of Nations," *New Internationalist* 277 (March, 1996), 19; "The Poverty of Aid," *New Internationalist* 285 (November, 1996), 18-22; "The New Globalism," *New Internationalist* 246 (August, 1993) and "Squeezing the South," *New Internationalist* 257 (July, 1994); Tony Clarke, "The Multilateral Agreement on Investments: drafting a corporate rule treaty," *Catholic New Times*, June 15, 1997, 10-11. For details on the MAI, see Barlow and Clarke, *Multilateral Agreement on Investment and the Threat to Canadian Sovereignty*.

4 For recent data portraying the Canadian "corporate agenda" and its media and political allies, see "Canada, Inc.?" *Canadian Perspectives*, Autumn, 1996; Laxer, *In Search of a New Left*; Richard Cleroux, "The Party of Corporate Canada," *Canadian Forum* LXXIV, 847 (March, 1996), 15-18; Jennifer Wells, "The Prince of Papers," *Maclean's*, November 11, 1996, 56-62; Daryl Duke, "The Final Cut?" *Canadian Forum* LXXV, 854 (November, 1996), 14-17; Ian Morrison, "Ontario's Welfare Rate Cuts, An Anniversary Report," pp. 1-33; NAPO, "1996, The International Year for the Eradication of Poverty," October, 1996, 1-12; Tony Clarke, "Ontario under Corporate Rule," Polaris Institute, Fall, 1996, nine pages; and Winter, *Democracy's Oxygen*.

5 Janet Somerville, "If you don't like the corporate security state, you'll love what Tony Clarke is up to," *Catholic New Times*, June 15, 1997, 1, 10. See also, Clarke, *Silent Coup*.

6 Clarke, *Behind the Mitre,* 176-95. For information on the MTC, see chapter 5.

7 The public apologies to First Nations' peoples and a description of the Institute for Christian Ethics can be found in chapter 5. For material on the Interfaith Movement for Social Justice, see stories on the Community Day of Action in the *The Record* [Kitchener], April 20, 1996. For an example of ISARC material, see David Pfrimmer, ed., ISARC *Briefing Book — Issues with Ontario Government*, September, 1996.

8 For ECEJ material, see "Web Networks" and "Faith & Justice Network." "Building a Moral Economy: The Faith and Justice Training Project," one-page, describes the current training program.

9 See chapter 5.

10 In a tragic irony, the financial cost of the OPSEU victory led to divisions within its own ranks. OPSEU's unionized employees found themselves fighting cost-cutting measures being pushed by their own trade union.

11 Materials about the Community Days of Action can be found in the movements that created them, and in the local media. For the Waterloo Region Days of Action, notes and minutes are available from the Labour Council, the Global Community Centre, and the IFMSJ. See also stories in the *The Record* [Kitchener], April 15, 18, 19, and 20, 1996. See also Oscar Cole-Arnal and Robert Kelly, "Waterloo Region Takes to the Streets," *Canadian Dimension*, July-August, 1996, 12-14 and Robert Kelly and Oscar Cole-Arnal, "Taking Heart," *Our Times*, July-August, 1996, 16-17. For further analysis, see James L. Turk, "Days of Action: Challenging the Harris Corporate Agenda," 165-76 in Diana Ralph, André Régimbald, and Nérée St-Amand, eds., *Mike Harris's Ontario: Open for Business, Closed to People*.

12 For the Toronto Days of Action, see *The Toronto Star*, October 26, 27, 1996.

13 Much of what I describe comes from personal involvement. For further details, see Langdon and Cross, eds., *As We Come Marching* and *Economic Justice Report* VII, 3 (September, 1996).

14 For one example of dialogue between the factions, see two articles in Langdon and Cross, eds., *As We Come Marchiing*, by Buzz Hargrove and Leo Gerard. I was deeply impressed by the witness of OFL president Gord Wilson in our local community days of action. He is a firm supporter of the labour-NDP alliance, yet he displayed a dignified solidarity both on a television panel and in his speech at our mass rally. Alexa McDonough's challenge to the corporate agenda is described in Rosemary Speirs, "Liberals silent on investment pact's down side," *The Toronto Star,* June 26, 1997, A27.

15 A good beginning in this direction would be Conway, *Debts to Pay*.

16 "The Present Order Cannot Endure," 63 in *The Heritage of Gene Debs* (New York: International Publishers, 1955 [1928]).

Index

Scripture Index

Old Testament

Exodus 22:20,   115
Leviticus 25:35-38,   23
Deuteronomy 7:7-8,   13
Deuteronomy 10:17-19,   13
Deuteronomy 26:5b-9,   12
Samuel 7:8-16,   17
Psalm 4:2,   75
Psalm 72:1-7, 12-14, 16,   18
Psalm 120:6-7,   122
Isaiah 5:7b-8, 21, 23,   15
Isaiah 9:7,   18
Isaiah 10:1-2a,   104
Isaiah 11:1-9,   18
Isaiah 45:1,4,   163
Isaiah 47:6,   110
Isaiah 55:1-13,   16
Isaiah 66:11-12,   160
Jeremiah 2:30,   127
Jeremiah 4:31,   111
Jeremiah 5:26-29,   15, 57
Jeremiah 6:13,   81
Jeremiah 22:13-16,   15
Jeremiah 23:5-6a,   18
Lamentations 4:4,   108
Ezekiel 34:23,   18
Hosea 2:18-23,   16
Hosea 10:13-14a,   14
Hosea 12:8,   14
Amos 2:6b-7a,   13
Amos 3:1-2,   13
Amos 5:7,   74
Amos 5:12,   15
Amos 6:4-7,   85
Amos 6:4-7a,   15

Micah 2:8-9,   14
Micah 3:1-3,   14
Micah 3:9-11,   14
Micah 5:4-5a,   18
Micah 6:6-8,   14
Micah 7:3,   15, 63
Zechariah 11:2-3,   124
Malachi 3:5,   91

New Testament

Matthew 5:10,   131
Matthew 5:43-48,   26
Matthew 6:24,   27, 87
Matthew 6:25   33
Matthew 8:11-12,   29
Matthew 10:7-14,   29
Matthew 10:16-22   29
Matthew 10:17-18,   131
Matthew 10:34,   26
Matthew 11:4-5,   24
Matthew 11:19,   28
Matthew 15:21-28,   7, 28-29
Matthew 18:23-24,   27
Matthew 20:1-15,   27
Mark 2:15-17,   28
Mark 8:34,   30, 131
Mark 10:17-22,   8, 24
Mark 10:25,   26
Mark 12:13-17,   9
Mark 12:41-44,   27
Luke 1:47-55,   25
Luke 1:52-53,   25
Luke 4:18-19,   25
Luke 4:18,   145
Luke 6:20,   26